SOCIAL WORK ADMINISTRATION

D0171187

SOCIAL WORK ADMINISTRATION

Principles and Practices

HARLEIGH B. TRECKER

University Professor of Social Work
School of Social Work
The University of Connecticut

ASSOCIATION PRESS • NEW YORK

SOCIAL WORK ADMINISTRATION

Copyright © 1971 by Association Press
291 Broadway, New York, N.Y. 10007

Standard Book Number: 8096-1812-5
Library of Congress Catalog Card Number: 77-129440

Printed in the United States of America

4/13/76 ₰₤ 9.95

Contents

The Policy Determination Process
Principles of Policy Determination

The Budget and Its Preparation
Budget Management and Evaluation

The Importance of Evaluation
Criteria and Standards of Evaluation
The Administrator's Role in Facilitating Change
Principles of Institutional Change
Growth of Administrators and Staffs
Staff Development and In-service Training

Principles Defined
The Importance of Principles
Basic Principles of Social Work Administration

Part II: Practices—Resolving Typical Administrative Problems

Figures

Figures

Introduction

Social Work Administration: Principles and Practices is a book for administrators of the nation's social welfare enterprise and for those social workers who aspire to take on the administrative job. Students of social work will find it of value in their professional education. In addition, it may be of value to professional workers in related and allied fields where the goals of human service are reasonably congruent. It is hoped also that it will be read by professionals and volunteers in social work even though they do not carry primary administrative responsibilities. It may be that they will develop a deeper understanding of the importance of the work of the administrator and the complexities of the administrative task.

There seems to be a need for a book of this kind. The field of social welfare is large and is growing each year. New programs under governmental and voluntary auspices call for an ever-increasing number of administrators. Many social workers assume administrative positions each year. While the literature of social work administration is expanding, there is no comprehensive volume which attempts to put together social work administration principles and practices. Perhaps this attempt will result in at least a start toward a viable and growing effort to see administration as an inherent part of social work method. There is general agreement that the way social work services are administered is of great importance to the persons served, to the community, and ultimately to the nation. Agreement is also present that the work of the administrator becomes more and more demanding during times of unprecedented change. His leadership tasks and responsibilities must be accepted as crucial to the well-being of the agency he represents and the people he serves.

In many ways this book is a culmination of many years of administration and the teaching of administration on the part of the author. Readers are perhaps familiar with his earlier works such as Group Process in Administration, New Understandings of Administration, and Citizen

11

BOARDS AT WORK. To a certain extent this volume is an extension and a refinement of the major ideas offered in these books. Yet, it must be admitted that over the years there have been striking and significant changes in the field and there has been a change in the author's comprehension and grasp of all that is involved in administration. While the basic philosophy has not changed, the details of how one proceeds in the administrative situation have changed as a result of the experiences the author has had. Hopefully, the point of view expressed and the methods proposed represent a maturing and even a far-sighted projection as to what will be required in the future. But learning never ceases and new experiences yield new learnings, so it cannot be said that this book is the last word or that any book will be the last word.

The book is written in two parts. Part I—SOCIAL WORK ADMINISTRATION: METHODS AND PRINCIPLES is essentially a presentation of theory. Part II—THE PRACTICE OF SOCIAL WORK ADMINISTRATION is set up to include a selection of cases as illustrative material which can be used for classroom teaching or for agency in-service training efforts. It seemed better to keep Part II separate so that instructors and readers could choose material and adapt it to their own approaches. A bibliography of selected readings and an index are also included.

This is a book to be read and studied. Hopefully, the reader will read Part I in sequence because there is a logic to the way the chapters are offered. Social work administration is discussed and defined in Chapter 1. The role of social work administrators is detailed in Chapter 2. The setting of the social agency is discussed in Chapter 3 and the community is examined in Chapter 4. Chapter 5 concentrates on the role of the administrator with the staff. In Chapter 6 the administrator at work with the board is reviewed. Chapter 7 looks at the administrator and the constituency. Communication is discussed in Chapter 8. Organization, planning, and coordination are considered in Chapter 9. Chapter 10 is devoted to administrators and decision-making. Policy determination is the focus of Chapter 11. Administration and resource utilization is outlined in Chapter 12. Evaluation, growth, and change are considered in Chapter 13. In the final chapter the principles of social work administration are summarized.

While the author takes full responsibility for both the contributions and shortcomings of this book, it must be said that many people have participated directly and indirectly in its preparation. It is almost impossible to name them as individuals because so many have been involved. Faculty members, staff members, and students at the University of Connecticut School of Social Work where the author has worked as Dean and Professor for almost twenty years have given much in the way of ideas, suggestions, and illustrations. Furthermore, and hopefully not to their disadvantage, they have been a testing ground for the author's ideas and usually a source of challenge to the theories and methods he pursues. Over many years in the classroom, students who question sharply have done much to make the author seek constantly to clarify his views and to state them clearly. These students too have put their ideas into this work and much credit is due to them.

When it was first created in 1963, the author had the privilege of serving as Chairman of the Council on Social Work Administration of the National Association of Social Workers. This stimulating experience did much to help him think through the many facets of the administrative role and deepened his conviction that social work administration is a method in social work practice and that it should be so regarded.

Thus, scores of people have had a part in this work and if they see their ideas and expressions recorded herein it is to be hoped that they will be gratified. No way can be thought of to assign to each person his rightful credit because by now the writer himself is a product of all that has influenced him over many years.

There is a special group of people who deserve great appreciation and high commendation. They are my wife, Audrey; sons, Jerrold and James; and daughters-in-law, Janice and Barbara. Their encouragement, support, and confidence has been a source of great strength. Anyone who has this kind of a family is indeed fortunate, and probably he is a better administrator and a better writer because of what he gets from his loved ones.

HARLEIGH B. TRECKER,
University Professor of Social Work
School of Social Work
The University of Connecticut

West Hartford, Connecticut

PART ONE

METHODS AND PRINCIPLES

1 The Meaning of Administration in Social Work

Administrators of the social services are responsible for helping millions of people meet some of their basic needs. These administrators, along with their coworkers, are called upon daily to make decisions of profound importance to the lives of the people they serve. While their tasks are often huge, complex, and arduous, the personal rewards are great. Because of the efforts of social work administrators who man the nation's social agencies, many individuals are given the professional help they need at the time they need it.

Some Assumptions About Social Work Administration

As was stated in the Introduction, this book is based upon the proposition that social work administration is a *method* in social work practice and that social work agencies should be administered by social work administrators. Thus, certain important assumptions have been made. *First,* social work administrators must have an understanding and acceptance of and a deep commitment to basic social work values. *Second,* social work administrators must have substantial knowledge of social work as a professional service to people. *Third,* social work administrators must have a strong identification with the profession of social work and its fundamental purposes. *Fourth,* social work administrators must know and integrate social work practice and administrative theory. *Fifth,* social work administrators are primarily engaged in establishing effective working relationships with and between people. Providing services in line with agency purposes is basically a matter of organizing, coordinating, and motivating the staff to their highest levels of achievement. *Sixth,* social work administrators are responsible for the quality of services rendered. As Fanshel clearly states,

"The manner in which social welfare programs are administered—the efficiency of operation, the clarity of administrative goals, and the degree of rationalization of procedure—has an immediate impact upon the lives of many human beings. Poorly administered services can have as telling an effect as poor diagnosis in casework treatment or inept professional leadership of social groups." [1]

Social work administration is seen, therefore, as a method practiced by social work administrators to enable all people involved in the agency's work to fulfill their responsibilities in accordance with their functions and to make maximum use of resources to the end that the agency provide the best possible social services to the people of the community.

Social work administration is a process of working with people in ways that release and relate their energies so that they use all available resources to accomplish the purpose of providing needed community services and programs. People, resources, and purposes are thus brought together by administration in a continuous, dynamic process. Social work administration is a process of working *with people* to establish and maintain a system of cooperative effort. This way of looking at administration implies a wide distribution of responsibility throughout the whole agency. Many people have administrative responsibilities. Some people, such as agency executives and certain others have primary responsibility for over-all administrative leadership. They must understand that administration as a process has at least three interrelated dimensions. (See Figure 1.) A central dimension is the task or work assignment within the agency structure. Another dimension is the community within which the agency works. A third dimension is the psychosocial one within which people release their feelings and energies. It is the release of energy and feeling, properly channeled and directed by administrators, which enables people to accomplish their tasks in relation to the goals of agency service.

It is further assumed that social work administration has a substantive content and method that makes it different from the administration of other enterprises. The difference arises out of the nature and purpose of social work as well as social work's values and methods. It is assumed that for a person to administer social work he must know both the content of social work and the skills of administration. As Millett points out:

I happen to agree that management or organization, in many different settings and for many different ends, does in fact encounter common problems and make use of common techniques. But, I would agree that these common problems and common techniques are necessarily subordinate to the peculiar substantive problems of any particular enterprise. Professionalism in American society means special competence in special fields of learning and skill. These professional specializations have to do with law, medicine, theology, the scholarly disciplines, public school administration, accounting, business management, national defense, engineering, and many other fields. Every professional field of compe-

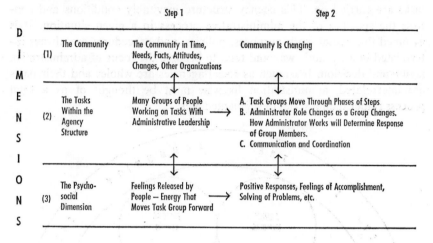

Figure 1
The Administrative Process

tence may involve organizational and management problems; indeed, I would insist that every field in some degree sooner or later does. But what remains pre-eminent in professional experience is the professional competence of the individual. When the professional man or woman becomes involved in management and organization, he or she brings to the background of these particular problems the points of view and understandings of the profession. These points of view and these understandings are important, I believe, in the solution or in the handling of organizational and management problems in any particular enterprise. I do not wish to pursue further the question of professional competence versus management competence. . . . I will record simply my own conclusion that there is a management competence different from or supplementary to professional competence, that in any particular organization both competencies are essential to administrative leadership, and that in order of priority professional competence must take precedence over management competence.[2]

It is assumed that social work administration is work with people. It is a dynamic process based upon an ever-increasing knowledge and understanding of human behavior, human relations, and human organization. The basic concepts and elements from social casework, social group work, and community organization are of fundamental importance in administration, as well. Social work administration is a continuous process in which many persons share. (See Figure 2.) Staff members, board members, clients, and the community must engage in or become involved in the over-all administrative process at points appropriate to their contribution and function. It is assumed that the role of the social work administrator is essentially a dynamic leadership role designed to energize people toward the fulfillment of the objectives of the social work program. It is assumed that the social welfare agency is the structural framework within which administrative tasks are carried on. This agency structure inevitably conditions and controls the specifics of the administrative process in a given situation. It is assumed that social work purposes, policies, and procedures are always interrelated in a dynamic way and tend to become the focus of administrative action and decision. Inasmuch as social agencies are wholes and their parts are interrelated, administration likewise must be thought of as a total process rather than a series of segmented acts.

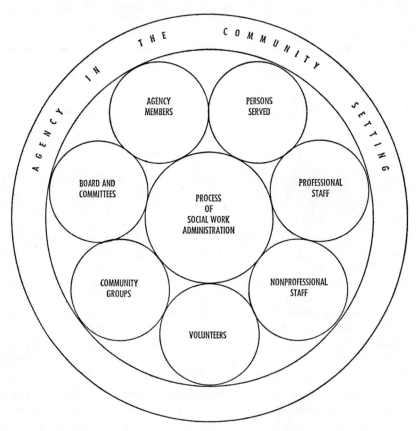

Figure 2
Administration as a Continuous Process

The Importance of Social Work Administration

It is assumed that the quality of services rendered by the social work agency is definitely influenced by the kind of administration the agency has. Because of the inseparable nature of administration and service, the quality of agency program is dependent in a large measure upon the quality of agency administration. The increasing magnitude of the social work task places more and more emphasis upon the necessity of good administration. No matter how one views it, from the standpoint of costs or the standpoint of needs met, social services are large and important in society and must have competence in the administrative realm.

As Vinter puts it, "The American social welfare system has attained a scope and complexity which would strain the credulity of bygone humanitarians. New services constantly emerge, and existing agencies continue to expand. Aid and succor once available from kin, friend, or neighbor are now routinely 'administered' according to 'policies and procedures' as a part of a 'coordinated plan' (with appropriate 'recording and review'). Recognition of today's immensely different modes of service does not imply any nostalgia for the past, with its simpler—and less adequate patterns of help. But acceleration of the trend toward large welfare bureaucracies impels examination of their distinctive features and of the dilemmas they present." [3]

As Clegg points out, "Public welfare affects the lives of millions of Americans, and its programs require the expenditure of billions of tax dollars. While the average citizen has expected public assistance to decrease and disappear, its growth has been spectacular. . . . Public assistance has been a part of society since the dawn of history. In one form or another it will continue to be an increasingly important part of our economic structure. Only as we accept this fact and as we become cognizant of the social and economic phenomena which spawn the need for public assistance will we begin to formulate solutions to the welfare problem." [4]

Society could not function without the social services, for, as Hungate says, "Public welfare programs are tangible evidence of society's concern for the well-being of each individual. The local welfare agency is the instrument of society designed to transform individual work and resources into services for those in need. Public welfare is one of the essential processes of government. Every governmental jurisdiction of any consequence today has as one of its basic functions and prime responsibilities a concern for the rights and dignity of every member of society. There is increasing governmental recognition that every individual must be considered as a person whose basic needs must be provided for in times of stress and also as a potentially effective member of his group and of society as a whole. The individual is the most important resource of modern society, and any enduring governmental system must be concerned with the welfare of every person within its jurisdiction." [5]

The social work ethic fosters responsibility for keeping agency programs and the values of the profession reasonably consonant with the values and needs of the community. Social work knowledge enhances the administrator's ability to integrate program goals, immediate resources, immediate client needs, and community resources. By virtue of the scope, magnitude, and impact of the administrator's job, he needs a systematic approach to organizing the various disciplines and knowledge inherent in good administrative practice.

Fink makes this clear: "Since the administration of a social welfare program is the keystone for maximum efficiency and effectiveness in achievement of agency goals, social work's concern with administrative principles and practices, as with research, has emerged in terms particular to social work. It is social work in an administrative setting and not administration in a social work setting which distinguishes the direction of the social welfare agency from the administration of other kinds of enterprises. The social work administrator is committed to the values and objectives of social work. He is responsible for nurturing the use of social work knowledge and methods for the achievement of acceptable services. Theoretical and technical knowledge applicable to administrative tasks respecting such matters as organizational processes, fiscal operations and control, operational analysis and personnel administration are, of course, essential prerequisites to successful social work administration. The most effective social work administrator, however, is one who uses social work's own rich understanding and experience in human relationships in carrying out the administrative duties necessary to ensure acceptable services for professionally acceptable purposes." [6]

Many Social Workers Engaged in Administration

In 1969 the National Association of Social Workers made a study of its membership. It is interesting to note that a large percentage of social workers are engaged in administration as a primary function. The study reported: "General administration is the primary function most frequently checked by the male respondents, and the percentage is . . . twice as high as that for females—40.0 as compared with 20.1 per cent." The study also reported, "An almost equally large number of women are in general administration as are in supervision, 20.1 and 20.8 per cent respectively." Supervision was cited as their primary function by 15.9 per cent of the male respondents. When asked to check their primary, secondary, and tertiary job functions, the respondents reported that 28.7 per cent of them were engaged in general administration as a primary function. As a secondary function, 7.5 per cent were in general administration, and 9.0 per cent were engaged in general administration as a tertiary function. It is clear that a large number of professional social workers are fulfilling administrative roles in either a primary or secondary sense.[7]

Some Definitions of Social Work Administration

Kidneigh, one of the first authorities to look upon social work administration as an area of social work practice, declared: "Social work administration can be defined as the process of transforming social policy into social services. This definition also includes the process of utilizing the experience gained in transforming social policy into social services to make recommendations that will modify the social policy. It is thus a two-way process: (1) a process of transforming policy into concrete social services, and (2) the use of experience in recommending modification of policy." [8]

Spencer has presented many scholarly discussions of the administration method in social work. She defines administration as follows: "Administration of social agencies is the process of securing and transforming community resources (human and financial) into a program of commmunity service. This process of securing and transforming resources involves the active participation of board (or legislative body), executive, staff and volunteers or constituency in varying degrees. Administration in social work is concerned in a major way with enterprise determination which includes goal formation. It is *not* limited to the management and utilization of resources according to plans provided by an external body." [9]

Stein, a recognized authority, states: "Definitions of administration abound, but central to those most accepted currently is the concept of administration as a process of defining and attaining the objects of an organization through a system of coordinated and cooperative effort. This concept stresses the administrative process, not just the responsibilities of management; defining objectives, which connote the need to modify and reshape them, to be conscious of goals, and not to take them for granted; reaching these objectives, described as the central responsibility of management and the underlying *raison d'être* of administrative process, the latter not then being an end in itself; involvement of people and their contributions in a planned pattern of cooperation, rather than administration being the activities of the executive group only." [10]

According to Johns, "Administration is the process of setting objectives and establishing policies, creating and maintaining an organization, making plans and carrying them out, evaluating the results. It is an inclusive process, shared by everyone in an organization . . . it is a cooperative function, a pervasive function. Everyone participates in it; everyone is affected by it." [11]

Newman defines administration as "the guidance, leadership and control of the efforts of a group of individuals toward some common goal. . . . The work of any administration can be divided into the following basic processes: planning, organizing, assembling, supervising and controlling." [12]

"Administration may be defined as, 'the determination and clarification of function; the formulation of policies and procedures; the delegation of authority; the selection, supervision and training of staff; and the mobilization and organization of all available and appropriate resources to the end that the purposes of the agency may be fulfilled.' " The above definition by Mayo [13] is condensed and summarized by Schwartz in this way: "Administration is the process and the organization of people working toward objectives which entail the production of goods or the provision of services." [14]

Rodney states, "In essence, administration is the process that mobilizes an organization's resources, human and material, to attain predetermined goals." [15]

Hungate calls attention to the fact that "administration is the total functional activity and behavioral influence involved in attaining program goals." [16]

In another definition, environment is stressed. "Successful administration is the creation of an environment—of an appropriate physical setting, of a favorable psychological climate, and of an established pattern for the interpersonal relationships required for the efficient discharge of an organization's function." [17]

From the public health field it is observed that "administration is a process by which the potentials of men and of materials are synthesized and activated for the achievement of defined goals." [18]

In a classic definition Tead says, "Administration is the process and agency which lays down the broad object for which an organization and its management are to strive, which establishes the broad policies under which they are to operate, and which gives general oversight to the continuing effectiveness of the total organization in reaching the objective sought." [19]

In a discussion of the administrative function it is suggested, "The function of administration is to 'carry out' or 'execute' or 'implement' policy decisions, or to coordinate activity in order to accomplish some common purpose, or simply to achieve cooperation in the pursuit of a shared goal." [20]

Blum and Leonard observe: "The word 'administration' encompasses the efforts required to initiate and guide the entire series of agency processes. Included are the determination of the ends or objectives of the agency, procurement and organization of the means or resources necessary to achieve those ends, the conception and effective carrying through of plans that best utilize available resources to achieve the desired objectives, and finally, evaluation of the effectiveness and efficiency of the effort and its impact on the shaping of new or modified objectives." [21]

The common elements that seem to appear in all of these definitions can be summarized as follows:

1. Administration is a continuous, dynamic process.
2. The process is set into motion in order to accomplish a common purpose or goal.
3. The resources of people and material are harnessed so that the common purpose or goal may be achieved.
4. Coordination and cooperation are the means by which the resources of people and material are harnessed.

5. Implicit in the definition are the elements of planning, organization, and leadership.

Major Areas of Administrative Responsibility

If it is agreed that administration has a major leadership role to fulfill in the work of the agency, what are some of the major areas within which administration should assume leadership?

First, administration is responsible for giving leadership to the continuing process of identifying social welfare needs in the community where the agency serves. Naturally, attention will be devoted to those areas of need which are in the general realm of the agency's service mandate. However, administration must be concerned about needs broadly defined even though programs for meeting those needs may ultimately be assigned to some other agency. In the need identification process, administrators are seen as working with the board, the staff, clientele, other agencies, and the community as expert analysts of problems, trends, and possible programs.

Second, administration is responsible for giving leadership to the matter of defining, redefining, interpreting, and utilizing agency purposes as guides for programs and services. Perhaps no task is more demanding or more difficult; however, without clear objectives it is never possible for an agency to operate efficiently nor can it hope to evaluate its work.

Third, administration is responsible for giving leadership to provisioning the agency in terms of financial resources, facilities, staff, and other forms of support. Administration always has the responsibility to inform the community what is needed in the way of resources to do the job. Furthermore, administration has to work diligently through every available channel to see to it that these resources are obtained.

Fourth, administration is responsible for giving leadership to the development of the agency's program of services. To be sure, this task is widely shared with the professional staff and with others but it ultimately is the job of administration to see to it that the program meets the needs of the community.

Fifth, administration is responsible for giving leadership to the development of a form of organization and structure which will provide for the coordination of the efforts of all persons engaged in the work of the agency and which will support the program of services.

Sixth, administration has a major responsibility for giving leadership to the process of policy formation, procedure development, and general operating principles. Without clearly stated policies and procedures it is impossible for any agency to operate soundly and efficiently.

Seventh, administration is responsible for giving leadership to the continuous assessment and evaluation of how well the agency is doing its job.

Here it is assumed that objectives are clear, standards have been set, and criteria of evaluation are understood and followed.

Eighth, administration is responsible for giving leadership to the change process. In a dynamic and changing age with new needs emerging all of the time, most agencies are in a process of change during their entire history. When administration is change-oriented and takes responsibility for helping to bring about needed changes, it can be assumed that the agency will remain viable.

While the eight points given above are by no means all that could be written it does seem that they are the major ones, and if they are followed, one can expect a generally healthy and effective administration. (See Figure 3.)

Hammond and others list three functions of administration: "1.

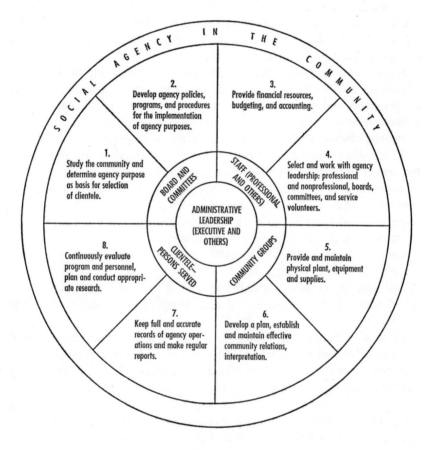

Figure 3
The Unitary Nature of the Administrative Process—
Functions Performed—Groups Involved

Structuring of the organization as an administrative function. If such organizations must exhibit sustained rather than *ad hoc* activity it follows that the actions of their component parts must be patterned and controlled, rather than random. While custom, convention and habit provide a basis for common action, administered organizations must channel and modify such activity in order to meet their specific needs. 2. *Definition of purpose as an administrative function.* If administered organizations have delimited, specialized purposes, it follows that these purposes must be selected and articulated. Organizational goals do not spring automatically out of the performance of non-administrative tasks. In a dynamic context, goals do not remain obvious but mechanisms for their evaluation, reflection, implementation, and periodic revision must be institutionalized. As such activities as bolt-turning, temperature-taking, or rifle-firing do not in themselves define and prescribe collective goals, the definition of purposes is a function of administration. 3. *Management of the organization–environment exchange system as a function of administration.* Some of the necessary exchanges between the organization and the environment occur in the performance of non-administrative activity; but the very essence of organization is task specialization, which calls for coordination. Hence, the management of the system of exchange between an organization and its environment becomes primarly a function of administration. At a minimum this applies to the acquisition and dispersement, from and to the larger system (a) of legitimation or authority; (b) of personnel; (c) of tools, equipment or other facilities; and (d) of a medium of exchange." [22]

Administration as a Social Work Method

The practice of administration as a social work method must encourage wide participation in the decision-making process, rather than centralized decision-making. Within the organization, mutual confidence and consensus rather than imposed authority and coercion must be the major integrative forces. Moreover, responsibility for program decision-making is placed in the hands of the professionally competent and knowledgeable, and is exercised on the basis of rationality.

By the nature of its value commitment, social work administration is practiced within a humanistic frame of reference. It views the organizational setting as a dynamic and complex set of relationships among people to achieve both organizational and individual goals. In order to carry out a relating and releasing function, the consultative or democratic form of administration encourages relevant participation by the principals of the agency (board, staff, and client groups) at all levels. It seeks to give its philosophical framework practical meaning by encouraging full and free communication and by providing an atmosphere that encourages emotional expression and self-realization of human needs within the work situation.

Thus, social work administration implements on an organizational level many of the values which characterize the social worker's relationship to people. It extends the belief in the dignity and worth of the individual and his right to self-determination to the level of the agency's system as a whole. It believes that encouragement of full participation at all levels is not only ethically correct, but that it is the only type of system that will permit human and organizational growth under conditions of change. Thus, it accepts a human rather than a mechanistic view of administration.

The purposes of any agency mirror the underlying value and philosophy of service which the agency represents. Administrative efforts to instill in both staff and community this sense of purpose may be cited as an enabling function. Wise and continuous use of purpose by the administrator may be seen as one of the ways in which individuals and groups are enabled to function more effectively in the production of services and in interpersonal relationships affecting the provision of services. Interpretation of purpose in the community also enables the service population and the sources of political, financial, and community support to have a clearer understanding of agency function. Purpose, therefore, becomes the primary point of reference for the administrator and it should guide all his actions.

The knowledge of the social work administrator differs from that utilized by other social work practitioners on several counts. He must have a deeper understanding of the agency as a whole, of the agency in the community, and of the position of his agency within the network of social welfare institutions. The social work administrator must also be able to perceive systematically the implications of policy formulations and must be able to give rational priority to agency objectives.

Some Issues Before Social Work Administration

The rapid growth of the social services and the increasing responsibilities of administrators have brought into focus a number of issues. A dictionary definition of the word "issue" is: "a point in debate or controversy on which the parties take affirmative and negative positions; a presentation of alternatives between which to choose or decide."

Among the several issues undergoing resolution are first how the administrator is seen and how his responsibilities are defined. Here the range may be wide with some feeling that the administrator's job in social work is primarily that of inside "management" of agency operations. Others feel that the administrator occupies and must exercise a leadership role with his efforts directed not only toward inside operations but increasingly toward the wider community. If one sees the administrator as being primarily concerned with maintaining the institution in terms of the status quo then there will be little expectation that he will carry a leadership role with major responsibility for innovating. If, on the other hand, it is assumed that the administrator is responsible for leading the organization in new directions, he must than have a real desire to seek changes not only in his agency but also in society which must provide adequate standards of community welfare services for all.

The sheer size of the social welfare enterprise gives rise to other issues. With social welfare operations becoming increasingly complex, there are problems inherent in bureaucracy and centralization. The agency may seem to be impersonal and administrative decisions may seem to be made far away from the point of impact of the services. A point at issue, therefore, is how to decentralize operations so that staff providing professional services and persons in need of services will be involved in basic decision-making compatible with their experience and authority.

An issue of increasing magnitude today is the confusion between the policy-making function and the administrative function. Considerable conflict results when there is a lack of clarity between the policy-making task on the one hand and the tasks associated with carrying out policy.

The issue of accountability for results is another important one. Measures of the effectiveness of social work programs are not adequate. Performance criteria for professional staff are also limited. This would seem to indicate that administrators will be giving an increasing amount of time and attention to the whole matter of how they guarantee to the public the efficacy of the programs they direct.

The readily possible conflict between the values of social work and those of the community often comes to a sharp focus in the office of the administrator. Here it is clear that the administrator has a crucial role in reconciling the values of the profession with those of the community always in relation to the needs of and the best interests of the client. Because different communities hold different views at different times and because needs are always changing, the administrator and his board and staff must constantly seek to communicate with and interpret to groups that represent divergent but readily known points of view.

NOTES

1. David Fanshel, "Administrative Research in Social Welfare: A Review of Current Trends," in *Research in Social Welfare Administration* (New York: National Association of Social Workers, 1962), p. 11.
2. John D. Millett, *Organization for the Public Service,* pp. 5–6. Copyright © by Litton Educational Publishing, Inc., by permission of Van Nostrand Reinhold Company.
3. Robert D. Vinter, "The Social Structure of Service" in Alfred J. Kahn, ed., *Issues in American Social Work* (New York: Columbia University Press, 1959), p. 243.
4. Reed K. Clegg, *The Welfare World* (Springfield, Ill.: Charles C. Thomas Publisher, 1968), pp. vii–viii.
5. Joseph I. Hungate, Jr., *A Guide for Training Local Public Welfare Administrators* (Washington, D.C.: U.S. Department of Health, Education and Welfare—Welfare Administration, Bureau of Family Services, Division of Technical Training, 1964), p. 15.

6. Arthur E. Fink, C. Wilson Anderson, and Merrill B. Conover, *The Field of Social Work*, 5th ed., (New York: Holt, Rinehart and Winston, Inc., 1968), pp. 8–9.
7. Alfred M. Stamm, "NASW Membership: Characteristics, Deployment, and Salaries," *Personnel Information* (New York: National Association of Social Workers, May 1969), pp. 39–40.
8. John Kidneigh, "Social Work Administration—An Area of Social Work Practice?" *Social Work Journal,* April 1950, p. 58.
9. Sue Spencer, *The Administration Method in Social Work Education* (New York: Council on Social Work Education, 1959), p. 26.
10. Herman Stein, "Administration," *Encyclopedia of Social Work* (New York: National Association of Social Workers, 1965), p. 58.
11. Ray Johns, *Executive Responsibility* (New York: Association Press, 1954), p. 30.
12. William H. Newman, *Administrative Action—The Technique of Organization and Management,* 2nd ed. © 1963 Prentice Hall, Inc., pp. 4–5.
13. Leonard Mayo, "Administration of Social Agencies," *Social Work Yearbook, 1945* (New York: Russell Sage Foundation, 1945), p. 15.
14. Edward E. Schwartz, "Some Views on the Study of Social Welfare Administration" in David Fanshel, ed., *Research in Social Welfare Administration—Its Contributions and Problems* (New York: National Association of Social Workers, 1962), p. 42.
15. Lynn S. Rodney, *Administration of Public Recreation* (New York: The Ronald Press, © 1964), p. 26.
16. Joseph I. Hungate, Jr., *A Guide for Training Local Public Welfare Administrators* (Washington, D.C.: U.S. Department of Health, Education and Welfare, 1964), p. 5.
17. Group for the Advancement of Psychiatry, *Administration of the Public Psychiatric Hospital* (New York: Group for the Advancement of Psychiatry, 1960), p. 123.
18. Ruth B. Freeman and Edward M. Holmes, Jr., *Administration of Public Health Services* (Philadelphia: W. B. Saunders Company, 1960), p. 21.
19. Ordway Tead, *Democratic Administration* (New York: Association Press, 1954), p. 67.
20. Herbert Kaufman, "The Administrative Function" in David L. Sills, ed., *International Encyclopedia of the Social Sciences* (New York: The Macmillan Company and The Free Press, 1968), Vol. I, p. 61.
21. Henrik L. Blum and Alvin R. Leonard, *Public Administration—A Public Health Viewpoint* (New York: The Macmillan Company, 1963), p. 396.
22. Peter B. Hammond *et al.,* "On the Study of Administration" in James D. Thompson, ed., *Comparative Studies in Administration* (Pittsburgh: University of Pittsburgh Press, 1959), pp. 6–7.

2 Administrators: Roles and Qualifications

It is the point of view of this book that to administer the social services, key administrators must have social work education and experience. The special nature of social work administration results from the complex social welfare system in America and the nature of the social needs this system is designed to deal with. In other words, social work administration has social purposes that it is pledged to fulfill. Furthermore, the social work administrator works with a number of different individuals and groups. Some of the groups are the staff, the board, and the clientele. In addition, the social work administrator has the dual responsibilities of professional leadership and agency management. Social work itself provides a substantive body of knowledge, understandings, principles, skills, and *values* which are the foundation of the work to be done. There is a social work culture which must be understood.

To be sure, there are administrative subpositions in social agencies which do not necessarily require social work education. For example, business management, physical plant and equipment maintenance, and perhaps public relations may not; however, even persons working in these areas must have a deep understanding of social work purposes and a deep commitment to social work goals and values. Such subadministrators should be limited in their work to their areas of competence and should be responsible to the leadership of the social work executive.

It should be pointed out that the social work agency is a nonprofit concern, and it has different measures of efficiency than does the profit-making business. In the case of business, one measure of evaluation is the extent to which profits are made. In the case of the social agency, the measure is the extent to which human needs are met. In addition, business organizations are essentially competitive, and social agencies are essentially cooperative. They are cooperative in that they seek wide sharing of their knowledge and discoveries, and they endeavor to unite their efforts in the services they perform for their clientele.

Another differentiating factor is that in the world of business the customer can "shop around" and make his own choice as to which concern he will patronize. Frequently in the field of social work the client does not have much of a choice, particularly in terms of governmental programs, because they are authorized to meet the needs of special groups. When the network of social services is carefully organized, there should be a minimum of duplication of effort and a concentration upon coverage of particular groups and services to meet particular problems. While the administration of business and industry shares common problems with social work administration and other forms of administration, it seems increasingly clear that to administer the social work enterprise it is necessary that the administrator have both training in and experience in social work.

As Ryan observed "the executive who is a specialist is traditionally an expert in his field, for example, in social work or perhaps in one of its categories such as child welfare or group work. He has been educated quite thoroughly in this field and has been a practitioner for a good part of his professional life. Through the subsequent processes of supervision, consultation, or teaching, and largely on the basis of expert performance in these roles concerning the specialty, he has now arrived at an executive position. His technical knowledge of social work, or a particular portion of that field, and his performance in the specialty has been recognized as excellent by both professionals and laymen alike. In this executive position, he is able to shape his learning into a professional program of high ideals based on the body of knowledge of social work. This expertise is a legitimate basis for authority in the agency and usually disposes workers to obey. The social work staff respond with loyalty to this fellow professional who also is committed to the goals of the agency and the profession. With the combined bases of expertise, legitimate roles, and loyalty of professional staff, any specialist executive has a solid foundation upon which to function as an administrator." [1]

The Professional Social Work Administrator

What do we mean by professional social work administration?

First, the administrator is behaving professionally when he strives for objectivity and seeks and uses factual material in his work. This is another way of saying that the professional person seeks to make use of knowledge and understanding as a basis for his skill, and that knowledge and understanding replace unconsidered judgment and unfounded opinion.

Second, the professional administrator is behaving professionally when he works purposefully and planfully and knows what his role is and what he is endeavoring to accomplish. In other words, his purpose becomes so much a part of him that his every action is governed by the consideration of whether or not the step he takes will lead him toward professional goals.

Third, the administrator is behaving professionally when he exercises conscious self-discipline or control over himself at all times. He keeps his own needs out of the situation insofar as possible. He is sensitive to others. Obviously, this kind of administrator works in the public interest and wants to contribute to man's well-being. In short, his professional integrity is based on the concept that the public interest is always above self-interest.

Fourth, the administrator is behaving professionally when he seeks constantly to make decisions on the basis of the values of the profession. He seeks diligently to formulate for himself the convictions by which he lives and which become the basis for choices or decisions, especially where matters of principle are involved. This may be difficult because sometimes the professional-consensus values run counter to community values, and political realities. When this happens, the mettle of the administrator is indeed tested.

Understandings Needed by the Social Work Administrator

In an earlier publication, the author defined administration as "a process through which staff, board, constituency, and community, individually and collectively in the developing agency setting, are enabled by administrators to fulfill their responsibilities as individuals and groups in accordance with their function, skill, and ability in terms of the whole agency to the end that their agency provides the best possible service to the people of the community." [2] Thus, the administrator's job is seen as that of working with people to establish and maintain a system of cooperative effort. This implies a functional distribution of responsibility widely throughout the whole agency.

The administrative job seems to have two important dimensions. First, there is the dimension of the problem, project, or task on which people are working. Second, there is the psychosocial dimension of feelings released by people as they work on these tasks. It is the release of energy with feelings properly channeled and directed which enables people to accomplish their tasks. An element in this dimension is movement, which means that as people work on problems they grow and change. Thus, the administrative process is dynamic and has the possibility of being analyzed in terms of various steps which occur. In the administrative process it is further assumed that the securing of agreement among people, the making of decisions and the carrying out of decisions are interwoven and interrelated. Of great significance is the assumption that the administrator's job is primarily a matter of establishing effective working relationships with and between people. It is basically a matter of understanding and influencing human motivation.

Although all social work practitioners are expected to have an understanding of community processes and cultural determinants, the social work administrator, as chief planner and coordinator, must have a more sophisticated understanding of these areas. However, this does not mean that the social work administrator is responsible for gathering all of this information by himself, but rather that under a system of consultative relationship, two-way communication between staff members will be encouraged so that other members may be motivated to share in this responsibility.

The social work administrator must also have a knowledge of the agency and its structure and policies, and how these factors relate to the provision of services. Knowledge of the agency includes an awareness of the role responsibilities and tasks attached to each position and the reciprocal interaction between positions.

The knowledge of how to work through the agency and the community may be considered methods knowledge. This level of understanding incorporates the notion that the social work administrator, like other social work practitioners, will know how to work effectively with individuals and with groups in order to achieve value modifications. This approach recognizes that men have needs for status, growth, and self-fulfillment which affect their interaction in their work environment. This means that the administrator must be person-centered as well as task-oriented. The administrator's recognition of motivational factors should enable him to provide an organized work environment in which a system of cooperative effort will release these human feelings and will relate them in a meaningful and coordinated way.

The social work administrator's understanding of people will help him to focus upon the informal group structure that arises within every formal organization. These informal groupings are important to the individual, for his reactions and views provide the basis for his self-image. The informal structures may either compete with or facilitate the formal organizational structure and the social work administrator must have knowledge of their value as "safety valves" as well as of their dysfunctional consequences. By interacting with individuals on a group basis, the social work administrator encourages a more democratic process of decision-making. This is another way of saying that if the administrator is to function as an enabler, he must have knowledge of the agents for both change and stability within his organization.

If the social work administrator is to be able to work effectively in creating a planned and coordinated system of relationships he must have a knowledge of himself, of the quality of his interactions with others, and of the relationship of his own needs and actions to the purposes of the agency.

In working through and with others, the social work administrator must make a responsible and conscious use of himself. This means that the social work administrator must work purposefully and planfully. He must communicate his inner sense of purpose to other relevant goals and must consciously judge all of his actions by their relation to purpose. When the social work administrator judges his actions in terms of the needs of the people he is serving, he is working planfully. When he strives to implement the values of social work, he is working responsibly and professionally. The administrator who practices the social work method must assume responsibility for his decisions, while creating an atmosphere that will enable others to share in this decision-making process. The social work administrator must base his decisions upon sound professional principles and knowledge, and must place the public interest, the interest of the person served, above any self-interest.

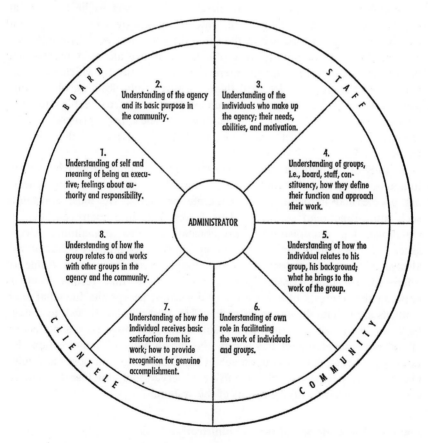

Figure 4
Basic Understandings Needed by the Administrator

As pictured in Figure 4 the administrator must understand himself, the agency, individuals, and groups that make up the agency and how they work together.

The Multiple Role of the Administrator

As Mayo pointed out, "The modern social work administrator finds himself playing a number of different roles within his own organization; i.e., to a certain extent he must identify with the clients and also with the staff because these have to do with his professional responsibilities; by virute of the fact that he is an administrator, he must identify with the board and to some extent he must see things through the eyes of the most conservative elements of the community, and outside of his organization he must identify not only with the agency he administers, be it public or private, but with the community as a whole and its needs. In other words, he must be an expert administrator looking to the interest of his own organization and pushing its program forward; at the same time he must be coordinator and champion of the community as a whole, and above all, as a professional person he has certain political interests and concerns to which he is expected to be responsive. I regard these various responsibilities, obligations, and pressures to be extremely difficult when it comes to keeping them in balance and when it comes to maintaining one's own professional integrity." [3] Figure 5 illustrates the multi-dimensional role of the administrator.

A study of institutional change has stated, "The administrator has to live in a multi-dimensional world with a responsibility for taking action in leading people and in dealing with concrete problems. He must constantly seek multi-functional solutions. This forces him into many paradoxical situations. The administrator must constantly strive to maintain a consistency in his own behavior while accepting the fact that his behavior will always appear inconsistent from any simple, one-dimensional frame of reference. He must constantly seek for solutions that resolve conflicts between the interests of several dimensions, but accept the fact that such conflicts are inevitable and never-ending. He must constantly seek to change behavior in the social system as a viable entity. He must seek a perfection of balanced development but accept the inevitability of imperfection. He must place heavy emphasis upon achieving organization purposes and must maintain the perspective of an outside observer, but not lose his impassioned involvement with the results of the system." [4]

Scope and Importance of the Administrative Task

In recent years it has become increasingly evident that the social work administrator has the ultimate and total responsibility for the work of his

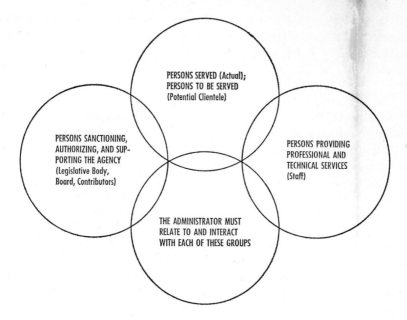

Figure 5
The Multidimensional Role of the Administrator

agency. The impact of services by the agency flows out from the central administration. Much of what the client, the staff, and the board feel or sense about the agency is set by the skill of the administrator. The decisions made by the administrator are far-reaching and seldom can be undone. Decisions made today tend to affect the agency for many years hence. Consequently, the administrator who must make choices among a number of alternatives is always exercising considerable influence. It can also be said that the growth of the agency and to a major extent the growth of the profession of social work is related to the kind of administration it enjoys. Therefore, the leadership role of the administrator cannot be overestimated.

Tead emphasizes this "By an administrator, I shall mean an individual who has the top directive responsibility (or who is an assistant to such an individual) to whom is assigned the initiative in the conduct of an organization for its overall planning, staffing, organizing, or structuring, directing, delegating, overseeing, and evaluating including the use of such objective measures as may be available in the premises. The administrator is the chief facilitator, expediter, and integrator of diversified but necessary functions and labors on the part of a variety of associated individuals and groups." [5]

In discussing the characteristics of the executive's job an institute group noted, "(1) He is responsible for seeing that work is performed by others;

(2) he has to make decisions; (3) he works *through* others; he delegates responsibility; (4) he must use authority; (5) he is the channel between a higher authority and the staff; (6) he is a facilitator; (7) he is a trouble-shooters; (8) he is responsible for keeping the enterprise 'running'; (9) he is responsible for being a 'leader.' " [6]

The executive must have a well-formulated and progressive philosophy of social work. He must project a sound sense of direction for the agency. He must have real capacity to form good working relationships with the staff, the clientele, and the community. He has to be able to keep his poise in the midst of often-conflicting opinions and values.

A community agency describes its administration in the following terms: "C.P.I.'s administration headed by an executive director bears overall re-sponsibility for coordinating and supervising the agency's six divisions and for dealing with the numerous outside agencies with which C.P.I. is allied or on which it is dependent. The executive staff, for example, makes cer-tain that board policies are implemented; conducts negotiations with state, federal and private funding agencies; handles legal affairs through the office of the general counsel and implements directives and special instructions issued by funding agencies. Working closely with C.P.I.'s executive and deputy director is the personnel division, whose functions also include property management and purchasing. This division maintains personnel records and administers employee benefits, interviews potential employees, and is in charge of supplies, equipment, and training materials for C.P.I. programs and projects. It is responsible for leaseholds on such properties as the Skill Center, the young men's and young women's residential centers, and numerous neighborhood employment centers and Community Services offices. Maintenance of financial records; disbursement of grant-in-aid funds; conduct of delegate-agency field audits; preparation of periodic fi-nancial statements for federal, state and private funding sources; processing of invoices and billings, and handling of delegate-agency requisitions are among the functions of the accounting division. Headed by the comptroller, the division also maintains detailed accounts of all funds which support programs." [7]

The Council on Social Work Administration of the National Association of Social Workers has spelled out a detailed list of the administrator's functions. In their words, "The administrator, directing and co-ordinating all operations with the assistance of appropriate staff, is responsible for the quality and effectiveness of the total agency program and for seeing that things get done well and on time. He sets the tone of the agency. In carry-ing out his duties the administrator has a shared responsibility with the official body to whom he is accountable. He is specifically responsible for the following:

1. Giving leadership to policy-making bodies and staff.
2. Identifying, in a continuing process, social needs that can be met by his agency.
3. Taking leadership in defining and redefining agency purposes.
4. Formulating, recommending, and evaluating policy in relation to the agency's mission.
5. Developing and planning short-term and long-range programs with readiness for adaptation to changing conditions and new needs.
6. Maintaining a leadership role in meeting community needs.
7. Developing leadership in appropriate policy-making bodies.
8. Maintaining positive relationships with community leaders and forces, especially in the constellation of social agencies, both voluntary and governmental.
9. Interpreting the agency to the community and developing a proper public image and financial support.
10. Establishing and maintaining positive relationships with current and potential users of the agency's services.
11. Projecting the budget and obtaining financial resources.
12. Recruiting, employing, and developing the staff.
13. Organizing and directing the staff and resources.
14. Providing conditions, resources, and climate conducive to optimum staff utilization and development for productive effectiveness.
15. Administering the financial assets and resources.
16. Maintaining records and reports as a basis for accountability and evaluation.
17. Evaluating program achievements and personnel effectiveness in accordance with goals and standards.
18. Accounting to the appropriate policy-making bodies and to the community for the total agency program and operation." [8a]

Friedlander sums it up in these words: "The main administrative functions of a private or public social agency may be divided into nine activities: 1) fact-finding; 2) analysis of social conditions and of services to meet human needs; 3) decision on the best way of reaching this objective; 4) planning and allocating resources; 5) setting up organizational structure and work assignments; 6) staffing the agency; 7) supervising and controlling personnel and finances; 8) recording and accounting; and 9) supplying financial resources." [9]

Pathways to Administration

There is no accurate information on the educational background of today's social work administrators. There are several pathways to administrative responsibility. For example, many administrators begin their professional social work practice in the area of direct service. They then assume supervisory responsibility, then subadministrative responsibility, and then assume the executive role or the over-all leadership of the agency. Mc-Donald says, "The Family Service movement has been a solid supporter of the view that the chances for success as an administrator are enhanced if he has come up 'through the chairs'—caseworker, supervisor, executive. In small agencies—and a great number of voluntary social agencies of all kinds are not large—this seems especially true. The executive is not purely an administrator—he also functions as practitioner and supervisor. This matter of agency size, then, may be one pertinent spot where there is an administrative issue." [10]

Another route to social work administrative responsibility is the route of transfer from other fields of endeavor. It is not known how many administrators have come into social work from other fields such as education, government service, or the like. It would seem to be true, however, that a certain number of administrators now in practice have come from fields other than social work.

With reference to the field of education, the U.S. Office of Education states, "It would be much easier to recruit people if we knew more about what sort of stuff the successful administrator is made of. Although attributes such as sensitivity, courage, style, and even charisma are as essential to the good administrator as mental ability and scholarship, they are less easily measured, and therefore not often enough considered in recruitment and preparation programs. A true appreciation of the importance of these personal qualities might result in the broadening of the range of people we consider for top jobs in education. In some cases, personal leadership qualities should perhaps even take precedent over particular functional skills, when those skills could be just as easily delegated to another person. Leadership qualities, after all, are relatively rare, while functional skills are not." [11]

Qualifications of the Social Work Administrator

The social work administrator must have a broad background of social work experience and practice. He must have a professional degree in social work and must have a deep commitment to the values of social work. He must be a person who has good health and vitality to cope with the many pressures related to the administrative job. He should be a person who has the capacity to organize his own time and set priorities among the many things he has to do. He should have well-developed communication skills so that he will be able to present his views to the various groups with whom he works. He must have a highly developed sensitivity to the needs of persons and a high sensitivity to the social problems of the community. He must be able to do long-range thinking and planning and must have ability to set goals for himself and for his agency. He must have the ability to listen and hear and learn from many people with whom he has contacts. He must be a growing person, capable of responding to the challenges for change in his agency and in the profession. In his book, Tead underlines the importance of being able to communicate by voice and pen in effective ways. "We are talking about intellectual capacity which is in some considerable measure innate and unlearned," he says, "about high level purposes, about a contagious enthusiasm for goals and methods needed to achieve them, about a total personal drive that catches others up into group loyalty, persistent striving, and gratification simultaneously obtained for personal desires and to those satisfactions realized through one's creative institutional contribution." [12]

The following qualities seem to be necessary if one is to undertake administrative responsibility in social work. Anyone who wants to do administrative work must be willing to assume responsibility. He must be willing to take risks, because inevitably administrators make "chancy" decisions. He must be happy in getting work done through other people and must be willing to forgo the satisfactions that come from rendering direct service to clients. He has to be the kind of person who can live with conflicting interests and can live with the uncertainties of the job. Since the administrative job is never routine and never is it possible to plan the program too far ahead, the administrator must know how to cope with the unknown, the unpredictable, and the inevitable emergency problems. The potential administrator must have a high level of energy and must be able to work long hours. In addition, he should be able to take and handle criticism and must forgo too much need to be liked. He has to be receptive to the communications of other people and must develop thoughtful style in hearing and listening. He must be able to handle the authority component in his role without becoming authoritarian. He must be able to say no without becoming negative. He must have patience and persistence as he gives leadership to the progress of the agency. He must be willing to accept certain inroads into his personal life because the administrative job does not necessarily end at the close of the work day. He must be able and willing to set priorities and make decisions about the use of his own time.

Skills of the Social Work Administrator

The Council on Social Work Administration of the National Association of Social Workers describes the skills needed by administrators in these words: "The skill of the social work administrator refers to his ability to perform well the specified tasks related to his various functions. It is made up of administrative knowledge and experience combined with certain innate characteristics. Administrative skills include the ability to do the following: 1. Think and plan ahead realistically. 2. Assess the feasibility of a particular plan. 3. Consider alternative ways of doing things. 4. Foresee and appraise the likely impact of decisions. 5. Set priorities. 6. Make decisions. 7. Handle multiple roles and tasks simultaneously. 8. Maintain personal equilibrium. 9. Understand the functioning of the bureaucratic system and of organizational theory and utilize this understanding to achieve agency goals. 10. Get others to work productively utilizing specific talents of individuals and groups and offsetting their limitations. 11. Use and delegate authority constructively. 12. Communicate effectively with others. 13. Act decisively. Possession of these skills may be of varying degrees and combinations so that a wide range of performance style may be observed among notably successful social work administrators." [8b]

Another important skill of the administrator is that of communicating feelings and values. The administrator carries a heavy responsibility for the communication of feelings and values between groups and individuals to help them find common ground. In addition, the administrator is responsible for the communication of ideas, orally and in writing, to individuals, committees, groups, and organizations. In addition, he must be skillful in finding and preparing facts in usable form, and he must know how to help individuals and groups do their own fact-finding and properly use relevant facts. Perhaps the most important skill of all is that of helping individuals make responsible decisions. This means help with problem identification, sorting and ranking of problems, seeing interrelationships among problems, problem-solving, and evaluating the consequences of proposed solutions. These are all related to the process of responsible decision-making. Also, the administrator must have skill in policy and program analysis coupled with skill in policy formulation. These twin skills of analysis and formulation are fundamental to the administrator's ability to help individuals and groups analyze problems and make decisions.

In discussing the skills of the effective administrator, Katz describes technical, human, and conceptual skills, which he defines as follows:

"*Technical skill* . . . an understanding of, and proficiency in, a specific kind of activity, particularly one involving methods, processes, procedures or techniques. Technical skill involves specialized knowledge, analytical ability within that specialty, and facility in the use of the tools and techniques of the specific discipline. *Human skill* . . . the executive's ability to work effectively as a group member and to build cooperative effort within the team he leads. *Conceptual skill* . . . the ability to see the enterprise as a whole; it includes recognizing how the various functions of the organization depend on one another, and how changes in any one part affect all the others. Recognizing those relationships and perceiving the significant elements in any situation, the administrator should then be able to act in a way which advances the over-all welfare of the total organization." [13]

Program Directors and Social Service Administrators in Host Settings

In community centers it is customary for program staff members to carry a considerable amount of administrative responsibility. According to Schatz, "Program staff members are deeply involved in daily administration. Just as the executive director administers the total agency, the program director administers the total Center program and the program departments heads administer their respective departments. Although the scope of responsibility of the program director and of the program department directors may be more limited, administrative functions are the same. They have responsibility within their respective jurisdictions for: 1. Defining departmental objectives. 2. Translating objectives into specific programs based on members' needs and interests. 3. Determining what personnel, facilities, materials and budget are required to put the program into operation. 4. Obtaining and coordinating all the necessary factors. 5. Recruiting, training, scheduling and supervising program personnel. 6. Processing intake of members into the program. 7. Maintaining records of programs and participation. 8. Reviewing and evaluating the program in terms of enrollment and participation, quality of leadership, use of facilities, budget. 9. Program planning for the next season based on the evaluation of the current season's experience." [14]

Directors of social service in hospitals, schools, the courts and other host settings are responsible for the administration of the social work program. Referring to medical social work, Moss says, "The director of the social service department should be responsible to the administrator of the medical agency for planning, organizing, assembling resources, directing and controlling the social work activities throughout the agency. This is the proper organizational relationship, regardless of the source of funds which maintain these activities, or the particular part of the medical agency to which the social service department may be related. The methods used and results achieved are also the responsibility of the director. He should be given the authority commensurate with these responsibilities." [15]

In discussing the directorship of a social service department in a hospital setting, Phillips goes into the matter of skills and knowledge required. It is her belief that "social work training and practice experience are essential prerequisites for the job. There are those who believe that 'the generalist,' well-trained in administration, can function successfully as a social service director. Perhaps those who hold this belief conceive of the role in a different way. If the premise that the social work director must set and maintain professional standards for his discipline is valid, then only a professionally trained person can function adequately in this role. However, professional training and practice experience are not the only requisites. Even assuming the presence of these elusive qualities—'leadership ability' and 'organizational ability'—the skilled social worker is not adequately prepared through casework and supervisory roles to become a department director. Administrative knowledge must be acquired. By and large, this is done through accumulated experience 'on the job.' . . . Chief among the things the director must learn as he assumes his role is how to adapt social work knowledge and skill to the administrative task. Knowledge of human behavior, the meaning of interpersonal and group dynamics, skill in working with people or groups, ability to set goals and limits, capacity to observe what is happening, are all necessary and useful to the administrative role. In using them, however, the director must focus on the broad goal of patient care and the concept of multi-discipline responsibilities required to fulfill the goal. He must learn to center on the administrative mechanism through which patient needs are met rather than solely meeting patient needs. He must learn to see his associates as individuals with professional roles rather than as isolated personalities. He must develop an ability to generalize and an acute sense of timing that will permit him to intervene appropriately in behalf of the patient. Usually, the director should not become concerned about an individual patient situation—that is the caseworker's function. Rather, the director must concern himself with the meaning of specific patient problems to the total social service program and its place in medical care. When it is necessary to intervene in behalf of the patient or a group of patients, the director must know when, how, and with whom. If he does not, he stands to jeopardize casework process and/or interdepartmental functional relationships." [16]

The Administrator's Leadership Responsibility

One of the dilemmas faced by many administrators is whether they should be primarily concerned with inspiration or administration. The fact seems to be that they must take responsibility for both. They must spend their time identifying emerging prooblems so that they may deal with them before they become too severe, they must understand the basis for the problems that are emerging, and they must deal with these problems with a clear sense of the purpose of their agency.

Likert declares, "Of all the tasks of management, managing the human component is the central and most important task, because all else depends upon how well it is done." [17]

Leadership can be defined as the ability one has to inspire people to work together in the achievement of a common objective. Zalesnik says, "The crux of leadership is the acceptance of responsibility." [18]

The social work administrator gives, shows, and takes leadership at various times. In what ways does the administrator show, give, or take leadership? It would seem that the social work administrator does so in two broad but interrelated categories. First is the category of giving leadership to the internal operating affairs of the agency. Here would be included such matters as policy formulation, program development, personnel development, evaluation, and long-range planning. Thus, within the agency the administrator should be persistently and consistently giving leadership to these various functions. The second broad category is external. Here the agency within the community setting must be considered. This means that the administrator would be taking initiative to help people know, understand, and hopefully be in support of the important work of the agency because they feel the essential need for it in the lives of the people of the community. In giving leadership in this area the administrator would work with other organizations that share kindred goals, that have a reasonable congruency of values and convictions about the kind of community it should be.

It has been stated that social work must have a broad use of community sanction. This would seem to imply that the administrator would work with the community to create and maintain this sanction. In giving this leadership the administrator must be guided by his philosophy and values. This has been described as social statesmanship and the ability to give guidance to the change process.

As Dimock says, "All large-scale organizations need strong, constructive, imaginative leadership to pull together all the elements of the program which otherwise tend to fly apart, and to focus the organization's attention on the consumer instead of on bureaucracy's inner tensions, moods, and petty concerns. The larger the body, the greater the centrifugal force it develops and the greater is the likelihood that the parts will be separated from the whole; that segmentation will drain the program's energies and halt enterprise. It is integrative leadership that keeps the parts together, and hence leadership is more necessary in large bureaucratic institutions than it is in smaller, more informal, competitive ones. But irrespective of size, organization alone never solves any administrative problem. There must be some one person at the top to watch over the program so as to keep it together, to keep it responsible, to combat self-centeredness, to promote innovation and vitality. And there must be extension of leadership on subordinate levels so as to form a kind of network through which the influence of the top man is carried throughout the organization." [19a]

Green points out that "in large formal organizations, the very size usually means an increase in the need for leadership, co-ordination, and control. Professional social workers, however, take pride in their technical skills and prefer to be able to use initiative and self-direction in employing these skills. The bureaucracy limits the practitioner through its regulations, procedures, and systems of hierarchical supervision." [20]

Knowledge of Self and the Administrative Job

The administrative job places many opportunities and challenges before anyone who would undertake it. Social work administrators, prior to undertaking administrative assignments, have to ask whether or not they have the personality and the temperament to perform satisfactorily in this work. Administrators have *total* responsibility for the work of their agencies. The risks they take are great and the emotional drain upon them is likely to be heavy. The social work administrator is exposed to many forces and most of his work has to be done before the public. The job is fraught with stresses and pressures. The social work administrator thus must reconcile various conflicting points of view and must balance off the many pressures that are put upon him.

The administrator must maintain many relationships simultaneously. (See Figure 6.) He must make decisions—complicated decisions. In addition, the social work administrator must decide how to use his time, what priorities to adopt, what choices to make, and what decisions to make first. The social work administrator receives far less supervision than does the direct service worker. His role changes from that of serving clients directly to the multiple role of helping other people to help clients. Also, the administrator must frequently say no, and in doing so may seem not to be the "giving" person that he would like to be. Nevertheless, setting limits and helping people to work within limits is a very important part of the administrator's responsibility. Along with this is the ever-present necessity to compromise because there are never enough resources to meet all of the needs that should be met. In this light it seems clear that the administrator must have an increasing amount of self-knowledge, self-awareness, and self-insight prior to his entry into administrative work and throughout all of the time that he carries such responsibilities.

The Administrator at Work

When one studies the social work administrator at work seven primary task areas stand out.

1. *Purpose and goal determination*—Skillful administrators make wise and continuous use of purpose. It is their primary point of reference. It influences and guides their every move. Why is it so important that administrators place emphasis upon purpose? As David puts it, "objectives are not merely goals; they are motivating forces for action, and we move toward them or retreat by concerted action. As a practical matter, objectives which have been developed and defined by one group lose some and at times all of their motivating force for action when they are passed on to another group. The success of objectives in stimulating action is proportionate to the spirit of participation in determining the objective. . . . Among

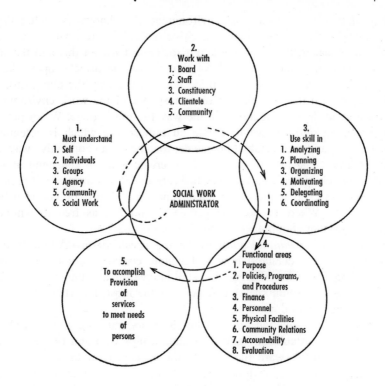

Figure 6
Social Work Administrators
Interrelationship of Understandings, Skills, Functions, Goals

people who are to take action, the process of thinking about objectives is more important than the final words in which they are put on paper. The words of others may be near platitudes, those you forge yourself have life. . . . Objectives, in order to motivate a group into action, must be far enough away and general enough to motivate people with different characteristics to work toward the same goals, perhaps by different means. Action-stimulating objectives, therefore, must be close enough to excite individuals to action far enough away to allow diverse people to work together and not so far away as to induce despair." [21]

2. *Providing an organized work environment*—Administrators are necessarily concerned in a major way with providing an organized work environment. Every social work agency is a community of people, dynamic, evolving, and changing. All of the needs of people including their need for status, recognition, and growth are brought into the agency. It is necessary for the administrator to organize these various people into a system of cooperative work groups so that they will be seen and felt as working together. Administrators are spending more and more time trying to create

healthy humanly organized work environments. It is known that when there is a contagious enthusiasm and a positive outlook on the part of the administrative leader, there is a marked association between this and the success of the staff group. Studies have shown that the pride people take in their work is associated with the pride that is shown by the administrator. It is well known that the climate or atmosphere of the work environment makes a great deal of difference in the way the job is done. When professional administrators strive to create an atmosphere which is essentially free, relaxed, and comfortable, people get together in a cooperative way. As Argyris says, "The task of a leader is to create a warm congenial atmosphere in which individuals feel free to bring out any attitudes and feelings they may have, no matter how unconventional, absurd or contradictory they may be. Wherever possible people should feel as free to withhold expression as they should feel free to give expression." [22]

3. *Facilitating communication within the organization*—Administrators must know and understand how to facilitate communication within their organization. Some would argue that skill in creating and maintaining channels for effective communication is perhaps the most important skill to be had by the administrator.

4. *Establishing relationships*—Administrators must be concerned in a major way with establishing effective relationships with and between many people who carry forward the tasks of the agency. How the administrator behaves, how he works with and relates to people, clearly affects the kinds of behavior responses he gets back from people. The way the administrator behaves in his perception, understanding, and sensitivity toward the behavior of the people in the situation are interrelated. What the administrator sees in the situation, his judgment, his inferences about it tend to control his behavior. Inasmuch as individuals and groups change with experience, the administrator must redefine his role as such changes occur. His primary moves and subsequent directions are determined not in a prearranged sequence but in terms of where the people are and what they need from him and how well he is related to them. The effective administrator is one who knows how to release the energy of people and how to help relate their separate energies so that they may be thought of as a united team.

As Glover and Hower say,

The qualities which, to our way of thinking, distinguish the administrator are his ability to think and act responsibly, to perceive and respond to environmental realities, to work cooperatively with others, and to work effectively and with satisfaction within the group and generally to provide leadership in getting the required work done. . . . Our reason for emphasizing attitude, judgment, and understanding is something like this: We conceive of the administrator as being confronted with, and as being part of, constantly changing situations—situations which are always unique, always related to the past and to the future. What he may usefully do about one particular situation today is unlikely to be exactly ap-

propriate in the situation as it will have evolved tomorrow, or in still another sit
uation (also unique) which has a different past and a still different future. Moreover, we do not think that a human situation, by an action on the part of the
administrator, can be channeled into a simple predeterminable course of evolution in which it will remain—through a sort of kinetic inertia—and in which it
will inevitably unfold just as planned. The administrator may start action as
planned. But what follows thereafter depends upon the successive reactions that
the administrator encounters, the "feedback" that he obtains, and what he himself does in relation to the developing events. He can start a series of interactions, but no one can see very far into the future what the course of events may
be. Accordingly, we think that the very idea of an administrative "solution" or
"answer" to a situation—especially a "solution" or "answer" which can be
applied to other situations—is essentially misleading. The job of the administrator as we see it is to live with his organization from day to day and from
year to year, contributing what he can to the development of the organization
as the circumstances permit and his own qualifications allow. Judgment, attitude,
point of view, way of approaching problems, and such—not "solutions" or "answers"—will help the administrators understand the evolving situation of which
he is a part and will help him to decide what, if anything, he should and can
do at this moment and at the next." [23]

5. *Planning and coordination*—Administrators are naturally concerned
in a major way with the processes of planning and coordination. Effective
work with the staff, the board, and the constituency must be based upon a
carefully conceived plan or design which has been thoughtfully worked out.
Planning is a matter of using considered and thoughtful judgment in place
of haphazard and cluttered thinking or careless judgment. Planning is more
and more appropriate and more needed than it was during simpler times.
Effective planning carries with it the notion that administrators are clear on
what purposes are to be achieved and clear what is being planned for. It
makes good sense to know what we are trying to have happen to people as
a result of our work. Planning also implies that what is to be done will be
done *together* and that people will be involved in deciding what is to be
done. The administrator has the responsibility to bring a sense of wholeness
and a sense of totality to the planning process. When people are engaged
in planning together and in coordinating their efforts under the leadership
of a competent professional administrator, there is reason to believe that
these individuals will experience a sharp sense of discovery and a new
awareness of the many dimensions of the total program.

6. *Dynamics of change*—Administrators are concerned in a major way
with understanding and facilitating change within their organization. Everyone would agree that programs are changing very rapidly today and that
the community is also undergoing considerable change. Thus, administrators have to be skillful in facilitating the change process.

Dimock states, "The administrator who can rise above his daily tasks
and see his institution with a fresh eye is the one capable of providing en-

ergy and drive and of preventing the onset of decline. Unfortunately many administrators are limited to trouble-shooting, to the settling of immediate and often petty crises, and to keeping their noses to the grindstone; as a result, they have no time or energy left over to devote to questions of morale, inspiration, and vitality." [19b]

7. *Dynamic Leadership Role*—Administrators are concerned in a major way with defining their own dynamic leadership role. As Selznick sees it, "Group leadership is far more than the capacity to mobilize personal support. It is more than the maintenance of equilibrium through the routine solutions of everyday problems; it is the function of the leader statesman to define the ends of group existence, to design an enterprise instinctively adapted to these ends, and to see to it that the design becomes a living reality." [24]

It is strikingly clear that the social work administrator must seek to achieve a diagnostic understanding of the total situation with which he is dealing. In addition, he must appreciate, understand, and utilize the dynamic ever-changing forces that operate in all phases of the problem-solving process. Furthermore, the social work administrator must make use of relationships as the force that makes change possible, always respecting the integrity of the people involved and always with a disciplined and professional use of self.

NOTES

1. John J. Ryan, "Social Work Executive: Generalist or Specialist?", *Social Work,* April 1963, pp. 26–27.
2. Harleigh B. Trecker, *Group Process in Administration,* (New York: Association Press, 1950), p. 4.
3. Leonard Mayo, *Excerpts from Letters Received.* Council on Social Work Administration, National Association of Social Workers, New York, February 1965, pp. 2–3.
4. Paul R. Lawrence, *The Changing of Organizational Behavior Patterns* (Cambridge: Harvard University Graduate School of Business Administration, 1958), pp. 225–226.
5. Ordway Tead, "Reflections on the Art of Administration," *Hospital Administration,* Winter 1959, p. 8.
6. *Proceedings of Workshop on Social Agency Administration—Leadership and the Social Welfare Executive,* Richmond Professional Institute, School of Social Work, Richmond, Va., April 12–14, 1967, p. 7.
7. *C.P.I.—The Human Story,* Annual Report of Community Progress, Inc., New Haven, Connecticut, 1968, p. 25.
8. *Social Work Administration* (New York: National Association of Social Workers, March 1968), a pp. 6–7; b 9.
9. Walter A. Friedlander, *Introduction to Social Welfare,* 3rd ed., (Englewood Cliffs, N.J.: Prentice-Hall, Inc., © 1968), p. 202.
10. Joseph McDonald, "The Administrator—Hub of the Social Agency" (New York: Family Service Association of America, June 1965, mimeographed), p. 2.
11. U.S. Office of Education Report, *The People Who Serve Education* (Washington, D.C.: U.S. Department of Health, Education and Welfare, 1969), pp. 7–8.
12. Ordway, Tead, *Administration: Its Purpose and Performance* (New York: Harper, 1959).

13. Robert L. Katz, "Skills of an Effective Administrator," *Harvard Business Review,* January–February 1955, pp. 34–42.
14. Harry Schatz, "Administrative Role and Function of Center Program Staff," *Jewish Community Center Program Aids,* Winter 1962–63, pp. 1–2.
15. Celia R. Moss, *Administering a Hospital Social Service Department* (Washington, D.C.: American Association of Medical Social Workers, 1955), p. 21.
16. Beatrice Phillips, "A Director Examines the Director's Role," *Social Work,* October 1964, pp. 98–99.
17. Rensis Likert, *The Human Organization—Its Management and Values* (New York: McGraw-Hill Book Company, © 1967), p. 1.
18. Abraham Zalesnik, *Human Dilemmas of Leadership* (New York: Harper & Row, 1966), p. 1.
19. Marshall E. Dimock, *Administrative Vitality—The Conflict with Bureaucracy* (New York: Harper, 1959), a p. 175; b 50.
20. A.D. Green, "The Professional Worker in the Bureaucracy," *Social Service Review,* March, 1966, pp. 72–73.
21. Donald K. David, "The Objectives of Professional Education" in *Education for Professional Responsibility* (Pittsburgh, Carnegie Institute of Technology, 1948), pp. 11–12.
22. Chris Argyris, *Executive Leadership—An Appraisal of a Manager in Action* (New York: Harper, 1953), p. 112.
23. John Glover and Ralph Hower, *The Administrator—Cases on Human Relations in Business* (Homewood, Ill.: Richard D. Irwin, 1963), pp. xvii–xix.
24. Philip Selznick, *Leadership in Administration* (Evanston, Ill.: Row, Peterson, 1957), p. 37.

3 Agency as Instrument; Structure; Purpose

Administrators must have a deep and growing understanding of their agency as a human enterprise. In addition, they must help the people who work for or are served by it to understand it as a dynamic, changing entity with a history as well as purposes and ways of getting work done.

The modern social agency is a complex social system involving many people. These may include the board, administrative staff, other staff, volunteers, members, clients, or persons served, and the supporting community. To bind all of these people together into a functioning whole is a major responsibility of administration. When the administrator understands the agency as a social system, he sees it as a whole because each part bears a relation to every other part and all are interdependent.

Social System

Many authorities have made use of the concept of social system in their study of administration.

Kast observes, "Under the systems concept, the business organization is viewed as a series of sub-systems which include the individual, the informal work groups, the formal organization, and finally the environmental system which has a direct impact upon the business organization. Furthermore, under the systems concept, consideration must be given to the means for interrelating and coordinating these various sub-systems. These parts are integrated through various processes, such as the information and communication network, the decision system, and built-in equilibrium mechanisms which exist in every organization." [1a]

Albers says, "A system is commonly defined as consisting of parts that are connected or combined to form a whole. Such a definition is so universal as to include almost any variety of phenomena. Indeed, it would be difficult to find something that cannot be so categorized. The universe, the solar system, a society, an economy, an industry, an automobile, a house, a football game, a coffee pot, a book, a human being, a wolf, a worm, and a dictionary are examples of systems. Some of these systems are aspects of other systems and are themselves composed of subsystems. Scientists are still not sure they have found the basic building block of the universe or whether there is a more comprehensive system than the universe." [2a]

In writing about the mental health field, Brown says, "The systems analysis approach involves looking at any person, institution, or service in the context of all related persons, institutions, and services. A system implies a network of integrated elements. In mental health programs, these elements are the services and facilities that provide prevention, diagnosis, treatment, and rehabilitation. Many separate institutions and many kinds of services are involved in providing these types of care. Accordingly, we are faced with a dual problem. On the one hand we must plan for the individual units or agencies and services themselves, and on the other hand we must plan for their integration into a composite whole of mental health activities." [3]

Frey views the hospital as a social system and illustrates how helpful it is to see it in this manner: "A social system is an entity or whole made up of interacting parts. It contains within it small subsystems that interact with each other and in relationship to the whole. An analogy can be made between the social system and a mobile in which all the parts are interconnected so that even a slight breeze will cause all the parts to shift and move through a series of new positions and relationship patterns before coming to rest at a new and different balance. Viewing the hospital as such an entity of interacting parts and subsystems that operate in relationship to each other is exceedingly helpful to an understanding of particular needs of the patient population. For example, in one hospital poor salaries, a shortage of nurses, geriatrics patients restricted to bed instead of being up and about, a depressive, hopeless institutional atmosphere, and a social work case load with only a few elderly patients in it were all interacting and interdependent aspects of several subsystems within the system. A change in any one of these situations would be expected to bring about shifts at the other points in the system. In this example there is clearly a need for an active rehabilitation program with the elderly patients. How to meet this need depends upon a consideration not just of the case load but of the totality of the system. (This includes the characteristics of the particular system and the essential elements of the social work profession: value, purpose, knowledge, sanction, and methods which determine the social work functions in the setting.)" [4]

As Johnson points out:

The school as a social system has a network of patterned relationships of people, each category of whom has distinctive role-sets or a group of associated roles. The form these relationships have taken in the public school are the outgrowth of its purpose, i.e., the giving and receiving of instruction or the teaching–learning objective. The classroom teacher is, therefore, at the heart of the social system but is surrounded by those above and below him in status. These statuses carry authority inherent in the responsibilities attached to them. They also result in a system of prescribed relations such as social distance, formality in communication, thus giving stability and predictability to behavior and mutual expectations. The structure of the school tends to be hierarchical with power vested in the superintendent and, in turn, in the principal. The larger the school, the more likelihood of autocratic administration; the better the rapport between the members of the system, the less likelihood of autocratic administration.

A number of forces affect the equilibrium of the social system: (1) The internal organization of the school, (2) The external environment of the school, and (3) The social worker as specialist in the school social system. . . . The school as a social system is a complex phenomenon. The social worker in the school must be cognizant of its general outlines, able to accept his place in the system, and well enough oriented to discern what aspects of his experience are characteristic of the social system and what aspects are peculiar and perhaps modifiable. Such knowledge lends consistency and purposiveness to the service he is in the school to render. Of importance also is more definitive agreement among social workers on what comprises the role-set of the school social worker.[5]

Kast points out how useful it is to administrators to understand their organization as a social system: "The systems concept is a useful way of thinking about the function of management. It provides a framework for visualizing internal and external environmental factors as an integrated whole. It allows recognition of the proper place and function of subsystems. The systems within which management operates are necessarily complex. It is important to recognize the integrated nature of specific systems, including the fact that each system has both inputs and outputs and can be viewed as a self-contained unit. But it is also important to recognize that business and industry are a part of larger systems, such as an industry and the total society. General systems theory is concerned with developing a systematic, theoretical framework for describing general relationships of the empirical world." [1b]

Social Work Agencies—Instruments of Society

Social work agencies are instruments of society. They have been established by governmental or voluntary effort to meet the social needs of people. As Figure 7 illustrates, in America there is a dual system of meeting social welfare needs. When the needs of people are properly expressed,

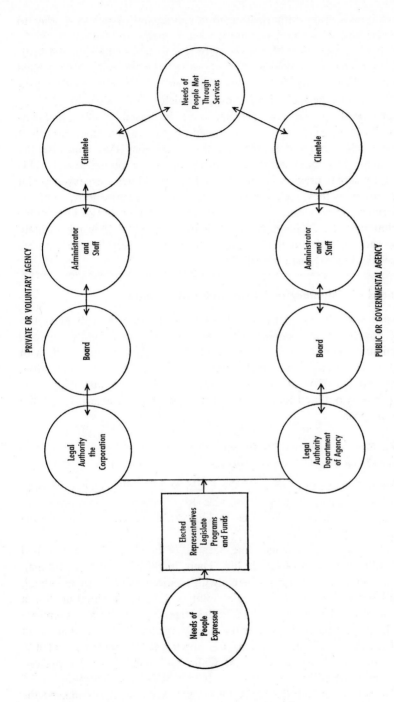

Figure 7
Dual Systems of Meeting Social Welfare Needs

legislative bodies grant authorization to governmental or private bodies to provide services. Many of these authorized agencies are large.

As Coughlin observes, "Modern society is a society of large social institutions. As we have forsaken a laissez-faire social philosophy, so we have moved away from a society that places a premium on individualism to a society that values the social institutions to which individuals belong. These institutions, both public and private, have increased in size and importance. Social role is an important concept; but more and more important for understanding modern society are the institutions that comprise the social system. The main actors in society today are organizations. This means that whereas previously men looked to individuals for certain social verifications, now they seek these verifications in organizations; qualities which formerly were attributes of individuals have taken on an institutionalized character. . . . Therefore, we live in a society that is increasingly based on the principles of the welfare state, and a society in which power largely resides in large institutions." [6]

Descriptions of Voluntary and Governmental Agencies

The case examples of agencies which follow illustrate the role of voluntary and governmental agencies in the fields of child and family services, youth guidance, community centers, residential treatment, and work with the aged. These agencies as social systems with purposes and organization are representative of what many communities offer. The way people receive services is outlined and some of the structural characteristics of the agencies are given.

Child and Family Agency of Belltown—
A District Office of a Voluntary Agency

The Hamilton District Office of the Child and Family Agency of Belltown provides four programs of service to the Greater Belltown area. They are: Family Service, Services to Unmarried Parents, Foster Home Care, and Homemaker Service.

Most of the agency's clients come because of breakdown or threatened breakdown in some area of family life. There might be a marital problem, a financial concern, behavior problems with children at home or at school, or myriad other reasons, at a certain point or in a crisis situation, for a family's no longer being able to handle the stress and strain; and therefore it seeks help. Although the voluntary family agency is designed to meet the needs of the people in Belltown, it is important to remember that it is one of several available agencies. At Child and Family Service persons receive counselling with emphasis on their own self-determination.

Most persons approach the agency first by way of the telephone. At the time of the first telephone call, the person is asked to state generally why he is seeking help and then an appointment is set up for an intake interview. In this interview, the social worker explores with the client his problem as he sees it. The person is asked to tell about the ways he has coped with his problem previously and how he thinks the agency will be able to help him. An effort is made to help the client state what his expectations are. During this intake interview it is explained to him that he may be assigned a different worker later on if the agency and he wish to continue the relationship. Assignments are made on the basis of the presenting problem. Three workers handle the general counseling program, while one staff member heads up services to unmarried parents and another staff member is in charge of foster home care.

Because one person heads up services to unmarried parents all such cases are referred to her. An important part of this service is the concrete help given with living arrangements during pregnancy, prenatal care, hospitalization, financial assistance when needed, and legal aid. Counselling is given to help the mothers plan responsibly for their own future and the future of their babies.

One person is in charge of foster home care. This offers the babies of unmarried mothers responsible care while permanent plans are being made for them. It also serves children who need a substitute home. After careful placement, the social worker consults regularly with the foster parents and the child.

Homemaker service is designed to provide help for a limited period of time in emergency situations. The agency makes an attempt to match the homemaker and the client as compatibly as possible. Specific duties are explained to the homemaker and close touch is kept to ascertain that things are running smoothly. The homemaker's primary job is to keep the family together rather than simply to provide domestic aid.

If someone calls the agency about adoption, an appointment is set up with the representative from Belltown who visits the different districts regularly in order to discuss the needs, desires, and eligibility of applicants in accordance with both their own and the future adoptive child's best interests.

Regardless of the division of services into which the client falls, the social worker in a family agency should be continually aware of the priority of the needs of the individual. There are many who come to a family agency presenting problems that can best be met through other resources in the community. A knowledge of these resources and the ability to make a good referral is perhaps one of the most important services a family agency can render.

Everyone who resides in the district is eligible for service. This is decided during the intake interview when the agency's fee schedule is discussed. The fee schedule is based on a sliding scale and no one is turned away because of inability to pay. Services are made known by auxiliaries in their publicity related to fund raising, in folders distributed by auxiliaries, and by staff participation in community organizations.

Becoming a Client at the Johnson Family Service Agency

The process of becoming a client at the Johnson Family Service Agency begins with a visit or, more commonly, with a telephone call. The prospective client gets in touch with the agency and inquires about help. In the case of the person who walks in, he is met in the hall by the receptionist. At this point, the receptionist asks the client to state his purpose for the visit. He is then asked to wait in an attractive and comfortable waiting room until a social worker can see him. The agency has a rotating system of intake with each worker talking his turn for one half-day. The scheduled intake worker for the day attempts to see the prospective client as soon as possible. If this is not feasible, an intake interview is offered for the earliest possible date.

If the prospective client telephones, he is referred to the intake worker and an initial interview is set for the earliest time that scheduling and convenience for the client allow. The system of intake at the agency is set up so that on each half-day there are two scheduled appointments. This means that the intake worker who sets up an interview by telephone, arranges the appointment for the client to see another social worker. As each period on intake lasts four hours for the individual worker and only two interviews are permitted in this period, the appointment time is set up for the client's convenience.

The next step is for the prospective client to come for his appointment. Usually the client is early and he is asked to wait in the waiting room. The intake worker sees him at this appointed time and begins the interview. The purpose of this interview is to determine whether the still-prospective client has a problem with which the agency can deal. If this is not the case, then an appropriate referral is made. If the difficulty is one that the agency can handle, then the worker inquires into the nature of the problem. The initial phases of study and diagnosis are begun at this time. The decision as to whether or not the client is to be accepted for continuing service is made by the intake worker. If the client is accepted, the fee is established and thereby becomes part of the initial contract. There is no charge for the intake interview; for subsequent interviews, the client has the choice of being billed by mail or paying the receptionist at the time of each visit. At the conclusion of the interview the client is told that the agency will get in touch with him within ten days. Some intake workers keep the cases that they interview initially. Caseload size may prohibit this; if so, the client is told who his permanent worker will be. The client then leaves and awaits a telephone call so that a mutually convenient time can be set up for subsequent interviews.

The intake worker records the interview and includes a tentative diagnosis and treatment plan. This material, along with the fee rate and factual information on the client, is sent to the Business Office for entry in the records of the agency. If assistance from another agency department such as Homemaker Service is necessary, then the intake worker refers this information to that department.

The complete intake process takes from one to three weeks. For a family service agency, intake is very important. The goal is for the client to see as few people as possible during the intake procedure. The client may talk on the telephone with one social worker and he never sees more than two others. Another goal is to provide competent service to the client from the initial contact forward.

The Smith Youth Guidance Center

It is the general policy of the Smith Youth Guidance Center that the parent of the child in question should call the agency to schedule an appointment. If another agency should call regarding this family, a request is made that the parents place the initial call. When the initial call is made by a parent, it is received by an application secretary who makes note of the name, address, and telephone number. The client's call is then returned by a professional staff person who is drawn from a pool of available staff members scheduled to handle initial calls at a designated time during any particular week.

After the call is returned by the staff member the application reflecting a request for service (if it is deemed an appropriate request to the clinic) is referred to a pool which is administered by the chief of the Psychiatry Department. As staff personnel have time available to see new applications, they secure such applications from the pool.

All cases are seen in short-term contact unless there is an administrative designation otherwise. Short-term contact includes up to fifteen interviews with a family. If the person seeing the mother or father in a case desires a diagnostic evaluation of the child, such an evaluation is conducted by the parents' worker or by personnel primarily from the Departments of Psychiatry or Psychology, who maintain a diagnostic pool of personnel available to do such evaluations. All diagnostic evaluations are done within an orientation that attempts to answer questions that are answerable. The decision about the manner of handling the case is not the responsibility of the person in the diagnostic role. Rather, the decisions about the case are made by the worker who has primary contact with the case. Such a worker may call upon his supervisor for consultation regarding the direction a particular case may take, but it is not the responsibility of the person doing the diagnostic evaluation of a child to tell the worker in the case how the case should be managed.

After a case is seen, if it is felt that it will require extended therapy and that this is something that will be useful and profitable to the family, the worker involved in the case brings it to an Extended Therapy Planning Conference which is led by the Director of the Clinic. The decision to bring it to conference can be made after one interview or as many as fifteen. At the time of the conference, the case is considered for extended therapy and, if accepted, assignment of the case is made via referral to the staff person maintaining time schedules of available professional hours. At the time of this conference the worker presenting the case justifies why it should be seen in long-term treatment and spells out what the goals of such treatment would be. All extended treatment cases are evaluated every six months in formal Evaluation Conferences which are headed by designated professional staff members. These conferences are primarily directed toward establishing whether treatment is achieving the goals as set down at the time of the Extended Treatment Planning Conference.

Anderson Community House

The goal of the Anderson Community House is to work with disadvantaged or under-achieving individuals in all of the neighborhoods of the city. The primary focus is on in-school and out-of-school youth. Through group work services the agency hopes that these young people will be able to develop their potential abilities. Agency organization follows agency philosophy. In most instances youth do not come to the agency but are more likely to be approached in a variety of situations by a group work supervisor, an outreach worker, a volunteer, or a part-time worker out in the community. Particular attention is paid to reaching out to young people who live in a housing project, attend an elementary school, and are clients of a multiservice antipoverty agency. In addition to working with youth, the agency is responsible for making its services available to grass roots organizations seeking to bring services into their neighborhoods. The agency also works with the community school team in developing special services for teenagers. The agency functions as a community organization agency in many respects. The detached or outreach workers are constantly seeking out areas of need that would not otherwise be discovered.

Abbott Community Center

When a potential new member comes to the Abbott Community Center his first contact is with the receptionist-secretarial office staff. This initial contact with non-social work staff has important implications for the kind of information that the individual obtains about the agency. Because the office staff members are so important in the initial reception of the new member the social work administrator and the division supervisors work with the office staff to help them be sensitive and accurate.

This initial step gains even further significance when one realizes that the members of the Center are not for the most part referrals from other agencies who have already interpreted the role of the Center to them but instead are people drawn to the Center by word of mouth, by mailings or other circulars, or through some other contact in the community. For these people, then, it is important that the office staff present a pleasant reception and an accurate interpretation of what kinds of services are available to them.

The decision as to particular services offered and which divisions are involved is primarily determined by the age of the person applying and whether the individual is applying for single or family membership. The professional staff of the agency is set up on the basis of services to particular age divisions. These are: the Nursery Division, the Junior Division, the 'Tween Division, the Young Adult Division, and the Senior Division. If the individual is applying for a single membership, the office staff worker will refer him to the professional staff member in charge of the particular Division which encompasses his age group. If the person is applying for a family membership, the office staff worker will refer him to all staff members pertinent to the age groupings of his family. The process of referral to the appropriate staff member is a very informal one. As most new members come in "off the street," they are usually referred to an available staff member as soon as possible and without a formal appointment. An appointment is made only when none of the staff is available for an intake interview and tour of the facilities. The informal nature of this process reflects the goals and purposes of the community center. People who come to the center come because they are interested in the group services which are available to them. It is the task of the social work staff member to further clarify and interpret the goals and purposes of the agency, to explain the structure of the agency, to be sensitive to the needs of the individual, and in this way to establish a contract between the agency and the person involving both agency services and the payment of fees.

The informal nature of the Center's intake procedure provides a major source of problems and administrative concern. Although it is important for the intake process of such a center to be flexible and informal, it is equally important that this process be under constant administrative supervision and total staff discussion in order that the informal process does not succumb to its inherent tendency to become more casual, less sensitive and accurate. A continuing staff discussion and in-service training course on this matter of intake is being developed by the administrator.

A State Child Welfare Agency

The type of service given to a client at Child Welfare Services depends on the nature of the referral and the unit that provides the service. The agency has two intake units: one which handles referrals from the court and other agencies, and one that is exclusively responsible for protective cases. Until fairly recently the only source of referral to Child Welfare Services was the court. The agency now accepts voluntary placements and receives referrals from other agencies and interested citizens. Nevertheless, referrals from the court still make up the greatest number of cases served by the agency.

When a child is referred by the court, the judge requires a social history which includes a psychiatric evaluation, an assessment of the parents' capacity to help the child, and a treatment plan. The Intake Unit is responsible for compiling this information and returning to court with a recommendation. The judge usually accepts the agency's recommendation which may be for commitment, legal supervision, or detention. With any of these recommendations, the case is referred to the area worker who is responsible for providing service to the child and the family. If the child is removed from his home, he is referred to the Direct Care Unit. Because the majority of these children come from highly disorganized families, the goal of direct care is long-term foster care or adoption. If adoption appears to be an appropriate plan, the case is then referred to the Adoption Unit. When a child does return home from a court appearance or from detention or placement in a foster home, legal supervision is usually assigned to the agency to give the family support and to help them improve conditions for the child. A referral is sometimes made to the Home Services Unit if the family appears motivated to accept intensive casework services. The referrals to Home Services, however, are quite selective because of strengths expected from these families. Usually when legal supervision is assigned, the case is referred to an area worker who is responsible for following through on the treatment plan. The main problem with legal supervision is that many of the workers have such high caseloads that their only opportunity to see a family is following a crisis. Obviously, this type of casework is ineffective for achieving long-range goals. Unfortunately, the majority of cases at Child Welfare Services have been assigned legal supervision, and if a crisis does not occur within a year after the referral, the case is closed.

The second intake department is within the Protective Unit. Cases are referred to this unit by the police or interested citizens. The bulk of referrals concern children who have been neglected, abused, or abandoned. These cases remain in this Unit following the intake study, and service is provided to the parents and children. After removal from the home, the children are either detained at the Center or prepared for placement in foster homes. The purpose of this service is to help parents with difficulties that have caused them to neglect or abuse their children. Court studies are often recommended to provide a concurrent evaluation of the family situation. The long-range goal is to return the child to his own home and help him adjust to his family and the community.

Because many of the children referred to Child Welfare Services through either of these intake units come from multiproblem families, the long-range goal of returning the child to his family is often impossible to achieve. For this reason, it is the responsibility of Child Welfare Services and the social work profession to recruit more actively for foster homes. This would enable the agency at least partially to achieve its long-range goals.

A Residential Treatment Center for Emotionally Disturbed Children

The Mountain Road Residential Treatment Center for emotionally disturbed children is an agency of state government. It receives requests for intake from several sources such as the public schools, juvenile courts, child guidance clinics, and the public welfare agency. In addition, many referrals are made by the parents. Whatever the origin of the referral, intake requests are given to the Supervisor of Intake who outlines the general criteria of intake to the referring person. For the most part, initial inquiries are handled by the Intake Supervisor's telephone screening. Occasionally the Intake Supervisor does see the referring person in order to screen applications in more detail. Following this period of initial screening, the case is assigned to a social worker, psychiatrist, or other trained clinic personnel on the basis of the problem presented and the technical and professional skill deemed necessary by the Intake Supervisor and Clinic Director to proceed with the intake study. This intake study determines the type of program most useful to the clients, if in fact any program at Mountain Road can be of service.

Following the assignment of the case to a social worker, the first task is a review of the case material by the social worker and the Intake or Casework Supervisor. If an agency has referred the case, an early step is the notification of the referring agency that the intake phase of the program has begun. Notifying the referring agency also allows the social worker to introduce himself to that agency. Another major step in providing service is the initial contact with the parents. The social worker writes them a letter of introduction. Included in this letter are questions about the parents' idea of the problem, when it began, what they have done about it. A convenient appointment time is also requested of them so they may come to see the worker.

Following the receipt of the parents' letter, a first appointment is made. During the initial interview, the parents' letter is discussed and the agency's program is interpreted. Following determination of the parents' interest at continuing beyond the first interview, the fee schedule is discussed. In conjunction with the fee schedule explanation, an appointment is made with the Director of the agency so that he may discuss with the parents their ability to contribute financially to the diagnostic cost and the cost of treatment if the child is accepted for a treatment program. After the meeting with the Director, the parents and the child are given an appointment with the psychiatrist (if this is considered necessary), the School Principal, and the Assistant Director who is in charge of all treatment programs. Finally, the family is seen by the Director of Group Life, who describes the various types of residential plans of care, such as Day Care, Residence, and Group Homes. If there are noted medical problems with the child, the parents and the child are also seen by the nurse. In conjunction with these interviews that he has arranged, the social worker also sees the family to ascertain background information in order to assess the parents' and the child's ability to utilize the intensive, structured treatment facilities found at Mountain Road.

Following the period of intake evaluation, those individuals who have met with the parents and child meet together at an Intake Conference to determine what program at Mountain Road can be most beneficial to the family. In the event the case is not accepted, a recommendation is made to refer the child elsewhere. This decision is given to the parents; assistance is also given in making a new referral. If the child is accepted, the social worker, as "case control," continues to coordinate treatment programs within and outside the institution. In this contact with the family, the social worker encourages and facilitates their participation in the Mountain Road program as participant observers or more basically, he endeavors to keep the parents in contact with the treatment areas of the institution. By such activity, the parents are kept aware of their child's progress. In addition, the parents, by participating with staff in the treatment program, are able to use this participation as a model of child care or "corrective experience" in interaction with their child. Periodic staff conferences of all treatment staff update and evaluate the parents' and the child's progress and ascertain new ways for them to utilize treatment.

A City Center for the Aged

When a prospective member arrives at the Senior Center, he is usually greeted and helped by a volunteer worker. The volunteer, who is an elderly member, talks to the interested person about the various services rendered by the Center. If there are any unusual questions or circumstances, the potential member is referred to a staff person. Generally, the volunteer, after describing the agency services, helps the new member fill out a simple application form, collects the one dollar membership fee, and provides the new member with a membership card.

The staff workers at the Center become involved with new members by attempting to meet the various requests for services. Part of the membership application consists of a checklist on which agency services and opportunities are listed. The new member chooses his own services by checking his interests. The staff persons then follow up each request by arranging for the new member to be invited into groups in which he is interested. If the member has indicated no interests, the staff person talks with him, either personally or over the telephone, to encourage him and to stimulate his interest in some activity.

This process is generally the pattern; the major exceptions are referrals. If an older person is referred to the Center by another agency or person, the staff discusses with the referring agent the goals for that member's participation, and they select appropriate group activities or arrange for personal counseling with the referred member.

The giving of service to a new member involves not only the volunteers and the program staff, but also the various group leaders. The instructors of classes or interest groups are informed by the staff that a new member would like to join their group and are asked to help the member become a part of the group.

The process of receiving and providing service to new members is flexible and informal. For example, a new member may initially have no desire to join a group, preferring rather to sit in the lounge or to play cards. The staff members are aware of this and always give the new member time to feel comfortable with the agency and its clientele before encouraging him to pursue more involving interests. Often a new member will be recruited by an active center member and will have already been oriented to the agency's functions. These persons usually know what services they want and may make their own arrangements accordingly. The process of rendering services to new Senior Center members, then, involves the volunteers, the program staff, and the group leaders and instructors.

Understanding the Agency Structure

The way the individual or family is received by the social work agency is representative of the care and attention the administrator has given to the matter of structure. Certainly structure is a vital factor in the extent to which the person gets the services needed.

Taylor stresses the fact that the social work administrator must "understand the nature of organizational structure as a factor in service" and must have "awareness of the consequences of such structuring for staff and clients . . . and a willingness to examine his own role in relation to others within the organization." She further emphasizes that the administrator must understand the agency as an organized service in terms of both its formal structure and its informal structure. Under the former she suggests knowledge of personnel allocated by function, formalization of relationships in a constellation of roles—that is, worker-supervisor, worker-client, and supervisor-director. Insofar as informal structure goes, she indicates that it refers to the spontaneous patterns of relationship growing out of shared personal interests that focus on the work situation. She suggests that the informal structure has cohesion and unrecognized but real identity and persists over a period of time. She recognizes that there is a potential conflict between efficiency and economy as organizational goals and professional values. She suggests that service is sometimes limited by function or budgetary restrictions rather than by client needs. She therefore sees a potential conflict between the agency as a means of social control as against professional belief in human worth and dignity.[7]

Social work administrators are necessarily concerned in a major way with providing an organized work environment. Every social work agency is a company of people, dynamic, evolving, and changing. All of the needs of people, including their need for status, recognition, growth, are brought into the agency. It is necessary to organize these various people into a system of cooperative work groups so that they will be seen and felt as working together. Organization is a process of so relating people to each other that they function at their maximum capacity. Organization charts are visual aids for showing the proposed organization, but charts by themselves do not develop an organization. Only when people feel that their needs and goals are being met can it be said that there is an effective human organization.

As Tyler has observed about educational administration, "a college or a university may be viewed as a complex social structure which involves not only individual statuses within the institution, but also relationships without. . . . It is this complex structure involving ambiguous responsibilities and conflicting expectations that breeds misunderstanding and dissension. Studies of effective social institutions indicate certain essential characteristics. Each of the members has a clear perception of his role and of his status in the organization. The perceptions of their several roles by various members of the organization are reasonably congruent when the institution is composed of individuals with different abilities and functions and when their effectiveness depends largely upon their own exercise of initiative, originality, and judgment, the leadership of the institution depends less on rules and directives for achieving some unity and much more on the development among the members of shared values and purposes." [8] Although written in relation to educational institutions, Tyler's observations seem to have considerable relevance for social agencies as well.

According to the Council on Social Work Administration of the National Association of Social Workers, "The effective application of knowledge and the exercise of administrative skills are in large measure affected by the conditions under which the administrator and his agency function. The administrator has major responsibility for creating favorable conditions for optimum productivity of services. At the same time, his own effectiveness is influenced by enabling or limiting conditions. Among the conditions conducive to effective administration are these: (1) Knowledge and skill of the executive equal to the demands of the job. (2) The delineation of the authority of the administrator and of other staff commensurate with their responsibilities. (3) The appropriate definition of the functions of the policy-making body and its relationship to the administrator. (4) The commitment of the policy-making body to the purposes of the agency and a readiness for change including expansion or retrenchment. (5) The relatedness of the agency's purpose and program to the needs of the people and community it strives to serve. (6) Adequate understanding and support of the agency's purposes and program by the various communities and groups it serves or to which it is related. (7) The availability of resources—physical, financial, and personnel—essential to carry out the program. (8) Salary and other benefits sufficient to attract and hold personnel." [9]

In every social agency an organizational life style is apparent. This style or way of doing things sets a pattern for the agency and quite frequently attracts people to join it. In addition, agency style influences the future and creates a distinctive set of possibilities for it. The effective social agency develops an organizational life style which is characterized by real emphasis on cooperation and collaboration. The communication channels are kept open and are well used. There is a mutual understanding on the part of the administration, the staff, the board, and the clientele. All groups understand how decisions are made and at what levels it is appropriate for them to take part. The effective agency encourages broad participation by staff, clients, board members, and the community. The effective agency attempts to make maximum use of informal communication. The agency recognizes and utilizes the specific resources that it has at hand in the way of staff members and working funds. The effective agency utilizes thoughtful procedures for working through matters of conflict and change.

Formal and Informal Relationships in the Social Work Agency

In the social work agency people function and relate their activities to other persons on two levels: the formal level prescribed by the organization and on the informal level created by interpersonal interaction.

Albers discusses the formal hierarchical organization in these terms: "The management hierarchy ranks and relates positions and persons. . . . It represents simultaneously a decentralization and centralization of decision-making. Decisional responsibilities are decentralized in the sense that they are dispersed among whatever number of executives is necessary to do the job. The work division involved in organized endeavor generally is applied to managerial work. But organization requires a coordination of effort if a common purpose is to be achieved. Two people who cooperate in pushing a stalled automobile will accomplish little if they push in opposite directions. Coordination is a necessary consequence of organization; and absence of coordination is disorganization. The ranking of executives in a hierarchy provides a means for coordinating management action. Conflicting and contradictory decisions can be resolved by executives at higher levels. Every executive below the chief executive is subject to planning and control decisions from higher levels. Proceeding from the bottom to the top of the hierarchy, decision-making responsibilities are centralized in fewer and fewer numbers of executives until the apex is reached. All persons in the organization, managerial and non-managerial, are required to respond to decisions from that point. The hierarchy sets the stage for cooperative executive action. Each executive is assigned some part of the total decisional burden. Executives at lower levels function within an area of discretion determined by executives at higher levels. They make decisions on their own initiative, but they are also required to respond to decisions from superiors. The decisional responsibilities at the various levels are differentiated by a process called 'departmentation.' The executives who occupy the basic positions in the hierarchy are generally assisted by staff and service personnel. Committees may also be used to perform decisional responsibilities and serve other purpose." [2b]

Some writers have tended to picture modern organization as comprised of rigid and static structures in which employees operate mechanically. The employees' human needs are modified to conform to the impersonal, static, hierarchical, unyielding nature of the organization. Current research findings refute many of these stereotypes. Students of modern organizations reveal that bureaucratic structures continually create conditions that alter the structure to suit the needs of the human beings in the situation. Modifications come about because human beings ultimately reject formal, rigidly prescribed patterns of behavior and relationships. The forms of patterns that are created represent a new element that is an integral part of the organization as is the formal organization. But because this innovation relates to the network of unofficial, informal, personal, and social interactions of members of the organization, it has an entity apart from the formal structure. People and their relationships are the primary emphasis of the informal organization.

Millett says, "Regardless of the formal structure of organizations in an administrative agency, there tends to develop an informal structure in an agency. These informal relations become an important factor in the internal power structure." [10]

The staff member's concept of the organization as a whole and the meaning it has for him grows largely out of his participation in the informal organization. Here he is a thinking, deciding, relating, acting human being, interacting with other human beings and causing modifications in the formal system which either contribute to or prevent effective unity in the total organization.

Many authorities have pointed out that informal organization is essential to the operation of the formal organization because informality provides a means of communication, of cohesion, and of protecting the integrity of the individual. Thus, the informal organization becomes a valuable aid to the agency's operation if there are well-integrated, cohesive groups to which members belong. In addition, the informal group relationships which grow are characterized by subtle controls in the form of norms and role expectations which are sometimes binding on the members. The more cohesive the group, the stronger the controls. Because the individual finds so many need satisfactions in the informal group, he submits to its controls and attempts to encourage others to cooperate in terms of group norms. Unofficial group norms therefore become an inevitable part of the informal organization. These standards of behavior constitute the subtle pressures of the cohesive group which operate to bring the individual member into conformity with the group. In a sense, a social system is created by people through their thought and action and the system is greater than the sum of its parts.

Barnard says, "One of the indispensable functions of informal organizations in formal organizations is that of communication. Another function is that of the maintenance of cohesiveness in formal organizations through regulating the willingness to serve and the stability of objective authority. A third function is the maintenance of the feeling of personal integrity, of self-respect, of independent choice. Since the interactions of informal organization are not consciously dominated by a given impersonal objective or by authority as the organization expression, the interactions are apparently characterized by choice, and furnish the opportunities often for reinforcement of personal attitudes. Though often this function is deemed destructive of formal organization, it is to be regarded as a means of maintaining the personality of the individual against certain effects of formal organizations which tend to disintegrate the personality." [11a]

In the informal organization are certain factors which contribute to and are essential requisites for the emergence of group norms. There must be effective communication between participants in the informal group. To be effective, the informal group must relate individuals to each other in areas of basic values, ideas, orientations of life, as well as in social, economic, physical contacts. Such informal relationships imply the existence of certain "feelings" of members for each other; in addition, the quality and quantity of these emotional factors are significant in establishing the kinds of communication which will facilitate the development of common norms. Once these are developed, their enforcement requires still stronger networks of communication between members in the group.

Furthermore, the group must have inherent in its totality, sufficient rewards for adhering to these standards of conduct. These rewards are most often intangibles, such as group acceptance and support, feelings of belonging and security. The prevalence of such supportive ties or bonds in what becomes a cohesive group is a worthwhile source of emotional strength for its members. More tangible rewards to the group are often realized in increased productivity, increases in salaries, promotions, special merit awards, and so on.

Baur believes: "Informal systems tend to flourish where large numbers come together and turnover is low, and when the job itself requires communication and cooperation between employees. They are used to show the 'ropes' to new employees, transmit and receive information prior to its official release, amend and amplify information after its official release, aid workers in helping each other in emergencies. Informal groups are essential for organizational stability and can strengthen morale, reduce absenteeism and turnover, promote harmony and increase efficiency." [12]

When enough members in the group have common orientations toward the social conduct of its members, sufficient social pressure is generated to enable members of the group to exert control over individuals within the group. This is possible because the individual, like the group, has internalized the standards of the small society. He, therefore, has feelings of guilt about not living up to his accepted standards. Consequently, pressure that compels conformity comes both from without and from within the individual. The individual's conduct, therefore, is influenced not only by the motivating force of his own internalized value orientations, but also by the pressure resulting from shared group values of the members. This constitutes an external pressure which operates over and above the individual's own thinking, attitudes, and values, and constrains him to act or refrain from acting in a certain way. Blau, in studying twelve supervisory units of caseworkers in a public assistance office, discovered that if pro-client values prevailed in a group, this factor affected the performance of duties of its members independently of the individual's own attitudes toward clients. This difference in attitude was demonstrated in the amount of casework service offered over against the group that was not pro-client-oriented. Members in the former group were motivated to express social approval of those members who were service-oriented and social disapproval of those who were not. In response to those sanctioning patterns, individuals tended to modify their approach to clients. Most members of the agency did not have a callous attitude toward clients; by expressing anti-client sentiments, some were showing acceptance of what were the prevailing norms of their particular group. Blau defines these external influencing factors as "structural constraints" which are exerted on each individual by virtue of his participation in a group which shares common values and norms.[13]

Albers says, "Organizing and reorganizing involves far more than formally defined authorities and responsibilities. Indeed, formal organizing actually disorganizes in that it disrupts and in some instances destroys an informally organized social system. Such a system plays an important part in the process through which people cooperate in pursuing common purposes. The organizer should recognize this fact and retain as much social continuity as possible. Informal groups can cause serious cooperative problems by supporting personal goals that are contrary to organizational needs. In such situations an organizer may deliberately attempt to break up the informal social pattern. Some structural changes may be made specifically for this purpose. Another approach is to change the leadership and membership of informal groups by personnel transfers and forced resignations. This technique represents an attempt to create favorable changes in attitude through different combinations of personality." [2c]

Thus, even though the agency is organized along logical, deliberate lines —the formal organization—informal patterns of staff behavior are of great importance. Vinter underlines this when he says, "Like the human personality, the agency must adapt to its environment, and may develop 'pathologies' in the course of doing so. Unlike the individual person, the agency organization is deliberately created as an instrument to serve designated ends. All features of its structure and action may be evaluated as they contribute to stated goals, and efficiency is the major criterion. Agencies are designed as rational administrative systems; personnel are assigned to positions with specified tasks, each to be performed in accordance with prescribed policies and rules. The totality of positions, tasks, and rules constitute the formal or administrative structure of an agency. Yet these official designs cannot govern all behavior within the agency. Individuals perform somewhat differently in comparable positions, rules can never anticipate every eventuality, and relations of friendship or rivalry develop among staff members. The unplanned patterns of behavior that emerge and persist constitute an organization's informal structure; they may largely complement and reenforce official designs, or they may subvert and conflict with formal norms and requirements. And finally, diverse consequences flow from specific administrative actions, only some of which are either known or intended. Thus, an administrative decision to institute a particular form of intake procedure may have far-reaching implications for clients, for staff members, and for other agency practices. Not all the ramifications of any decision can be anticipated in advance, or observed thereafter." [14]

Defining and Utilizing Purposes

Skillful social work administrators make wise and continuous use of agency purpose. It should be their primary point of reference. It should influence and guide their every move. As Urwick has pointed out, "Unless we have a purpose there is no reason why individuals should try to cooperate together at all or why anyone should try to organize them. This, however, is very easily forgotten. Once an organization is set up, a human group is in being, all the individual and personal motives which have induced persons to join the group, which keep them in the game and playing the game, assume great importance in their minds. Most of us suspect that the main purpose of the undertaking which employs us is to provide us personally with a job. . . . People derive social satisfactions from working together. And they build up, often unconsciously, very elaborate codes of behavior, and loyalties, and affections and antipathies, which may have little or nothing to do with the formal organization of the undertaking, the official relationships which their superiors recognize. . . . Every organization and every part of every organization must be an expression of the purpose of the undertaking concerned or it is meaningless and therefore redundant." [15]

All social work administrators must engage themselves in goal identification and formulation. This point is made by Traxler when he says, "Since the major job of the administrator is the shaping of organizational goals and reconciling these with those of the people involved, it might help to identify goals that are universal to *all* organizations. These are: (1) to maximize the use of all facilities—economic and human, (2) to work toward a common purpose, (3) to sustain a long-range growth potential; and (4) to establish a position for the organization in the community." [16]

Speaking about administration of the public schools, Moore points out: "One of the most difficult but at the same time the most important means of binding an organization together and causing it to work in a given direction is through getting it to agree on and accept common goals. The primary function of the school administrator is developing goals and obtaining their acceptance. In this he functions at the highest leadership level." [17]

One test of the effectiveness of the social work administrator is the extent to which his every action gives support to and helps in the attainment of the basic purposes of the agency. In fact, agency purpose must be a central consideration and a guiding influence in the day-to-day doing of administrative work. Administrators, therefore, must be increasingly clear on the nature and meaning of purposes. They must give attention to the process by which purposes are determined, and they must give thought to the ways by which soundly conceived statements of purpose are utilized by everyone connected with the agency. It is equally important for administrators to give leadership to the process by which purposes are modified to keep abreast of changing conditions.

Barnard states: "The continuance of an organization depends on its ability to carry out its purpose. This clearly depends jointly upon the appropriateness of its action and upon the conditions of its environment. In other words, effectiveness is primarily a matter of technological processes. This is quite obvious in ordinary cases of purpose to accomplish a physical objective, such as building a bridge. When the objective is non-physical, as in the case with religious and social organizations, it is not so obvious. It should be noted that a paradox is involved in this matter. An organization must disintegrate if it cannot accomplish its purpose. It also destroys itself by accomplishing its purpose. A very large number of successful organizations come into being and then disappear for this reason. Hence, most continuous organizations require repeated adoption of new purposes. This is concealed from everyday recognition by the practice of generalizing a complex series of specific purposes under one term, stated to be '*the* purpose' of this organization. This is strikingly true in the case of governmental and public utilities organizations when the purpose is stated to be a particular kind of service through a period of years. It is apparent that their real purposes are not abstractions called 'service' but specific acts of service." [11b]

When purposes are clear, the social work administrator can mobilize, focus, and coordinate individual and group energy in terms of priorities logically stated and soundly developed. There is nothing more important than administrative leadership in the area of formulating and utilizing purposes, but as Selznick says, many administrators default in this area: "One type of default is the failure to set goals. Once an organization becomes a going concern with many forces keeping it alive, the people who run it can readily escape the task of defining its purpose. This evasion stems partly from the hard intellectual labor involved, a labor that often seems to increase the burden of already onerous daily operations." [18]

Statements of Agency Purpose

The following case illustrations of agency statements of purpose are representative of the fields of public welfare on the state and municipal level, the family service agency, a community center, and an agency serving the aged.

The Purpose of a State Department of Welfare

A State Department of Welfare declares that "the goal of the Department, with all of the means available to it—money and medical payments, training programs, casework and specialized services—is to help individuals to use their capacities to maintain or attain self-sufficiency for themselves and their families and to function as useful productive individuals as fully as possible. The Department, as a whole, has responsibility for establishing sound social policy, which has the goal of giving better service to people to enable them to attain the highest degree of independence." In terms of its basic philosophy, the Department declares, "the public assistance program reflects the sense of responsibility of an enlightened public for its members, who for specified reasons, become temporarily or permanently unable to meet their own financial or medical needs. While meeting these needs by medical or money payments, the Department gives services which enable these persons to reach the maximum degree of self-sufficiency with dignity and a sense of their own worth. For some, this means complete independence from public welfare; for others, it means a better future for their children. For the aged, blind or disabled persons, it provides the financial means for being able to stay in their home instead of becoming institutionalized, as in the past when their resources were depleted. Likewise, children deprived of the parental support and care of one parent are maintained in the home of the remaining parent instead of being placed in institutions. In the case of unemployed parents, opportunity is offered for training, rehabilitation or reemployment." [19]

The agency goes on to describe the purpose of their child welfare program as follows: "The child welfare program of the State Welfare Department is two-fold in its purpose. The first purpose is to strengthen family life and to preserve a child's own home whenever possible; and when a child must be cared for away from his own home, to furnish the type of substitute care suited to his individual need, whether in the home of a relative, a foster family home, a group home, or an institution. The second purpose of the child welfare program is to strengthen, extend or establish community services for the protection and care of children. The long-term objective of the child welfare program is to provide for each child under its care: (1) a clean, safe, comfortable place to live, (2) health protection, including medical and dental care, (3) parents or substitute parents to care for him and to provide affection and supervision, (4) normal associations with other children and with adults, (5) leisure time and recreational opportunities, (6) appropriate educational opportunities, including learning experiences for community living, (7) training and experience to foster his spiritual growth." [20]

The Purpose of a City Department of Social Services

A City Department of Social Services states that it "seeks to provide economic security, promote social and economic independence and prevent economic and social breakdown for individuals and families. The Department is geared toward mobilizing the client and the community toward achieving more adequate economic and social functioning through a variety of programs. These include: a screening for employment opportunity, providing referrals or direct job placement and/or training and follow-up services; a screening unit for educational opportunity providing referral and follow-up both during day and evening hours; a housing unit for finding decent apartments; casework services; day care; emergency foster homes; cash grants for all basic needs; and purchase of a variety of services, such as homemaker-teacher, homemaker, psychological, psychiatric, and medical."

The above statement of purpose has numerous implications for the administration of the agency. It would appear that the administrator must be skilled and experienced in social work. He must be capable of recruiting and directing a competent and professionally educated staff whose goals are compatible with those of the agency. Because the agency is concerned with the social as well as the economic functioning of its clientele, a thorough knowledge of the community and its resources would be required of the administrator. He must be aware of the economic trends in the city and should know how these trends may affect the people served by the agency. In addition, he should know about the employment situation in the area. The administrator should use his knowledge of planning to bring about the best possible use of available resources and should take leadership in requesting additional resources from public and private sectors in the community. The administrator must be able to communicate his knowledge, not only to the staff and to the governing body of the city, but to the community at large. His knowledge of community attitudes toward the agency and his involvement of the community in agency activities is especially important because the public provides the resources for accomplishing the goals of the agency.

The Purpose of a Public Child Welfare Agency

In one Eastern state the public child welfare agency has the following mandated functions: "It shall be the duty of the Department of Social Welfare to promote the enforcement of all laws for the protection of defective, dependent, wayward and delinquent children, and children born out-of-wedlock, to cooperate to this end with juvenile and other courts and all reputable child helping and child placing agencies of a public or private character, and to take the initiative in all matters involving the interests of such children where adequate legal provision thereof have not already been made."

As a result of this legal mandate, it would seem that the administrative body of this agency has been instructed to guarantee that the total needs of all of the children in the state are being met. It should be noted that the Department has the duty to promote the *enforcement* of all laws in existence regarding children and that reference is made to *any* child who might be in physical or psychological need. Furthermore, the Department is instructed to take the initiative in matters regarding children where legal provision does not already exist. In addition to carrying forward child welfare service programs the agency also has the responsibility to coordinate all of the services concerning children in need. In this kind of mandated situation, it is clear that administrators must have a broad and comprehensive knowledge of social work and particularly of child welfare services.

The Purpose of a Voluntary Family Service Agency

In an eastern city a voluntary family service agency states its purpose as follows: "The Family Service Society aims to promote the opportunities for families and individuals residing in the area to attain their fullest development in personally satisfying and socially constructive ways. To further these aims, the responsibilities of the Society include the following: (1) to provide social casework for families and individuals in trouble in order that they may cope with their immediate situations and may be better able to meet their problems in the future; (2) to consult with other persons and groups who are assisting families and individuals; (3) to carry on a continuous educational program regarding the nature of personal and family difficulties, the causes of the difficulties and the methods of preventing and treating them; (4) to cooperate with other organizations and agencies in developing adequate social services and health services.

"The agency provides the following services: (1) counseling for people who are troubled with family difficulties; (2) a homemaker service for families with children whose mothers are temporarily unable to care for them; (3) special services for elderly persons, including counseling, homemaker service, and family boarding homes." [21]

There are multidimensional responsibilities in the administration of this agency that extend beyond the primary purpose of offering services to families. The administrator must work with the board of directors, handle public relations, function as a coordinator of professional activities for a staff of full-time and part-time employees, and prepare, organize, and submit the annual budget. There is a vast amount of organizational planning involved in all of these areas, but there is a present wide range of latitude for experimentation. The administrator has the responsibility for taking leadership in the suggesting of new programs to help meet the needs and problems of people in this complex society.

Purposes of Community Centers

A community center says that its primary purpose "is to provide small group services to problem and underachieving residents in the community. The agency also helps the individual participant to achieve personal growth as a member of a family unit, and identifies need where it is the greatest. More specifically, the agency helps people identify positively with their neighborhood, other residents, existing agencies and opportunity programs; involves citizens in handling their own neighborhood affairs, helps to bridge cultural and racial differences; helps serve underachieving and disadvantaged in-school and out-of-school youth; and develops joint public-private services to urban neighborhoods." [22]

Another community center states its purpose as "(1) to work with all ages, regardless of race, creed, nationality, or political beliefs; (2) to provide a program which will meet the demands and needs of the people in the community; (3) to work with individuals and their families to help them to make a good adjustment to their life in the community; (4) to help those who use the facilities to find activities that will result in satisfying their social, physical, and emotional needs; (5) to cooperate with other community institutions, such as churches, schools, public and private social welfare agencies." [23]

Purpose of a Child Guidance Clinic

The constitution of a child guidance clinic states that the clinic seeks to "(1) provide competent full-time psychiatric and psychological diagnostic and treatment services for children with emotional disturbances between the ages of two and eighteen; (2) provide a consultation service to school personnel, social and health agencies, physicians, clergy, juvenile court personnel, and others whose work brings them into close association with children; (3) to participate with others in community education and planning for mental health; (4) to provide, where possible, facilities for training for professional clinic personnel and for research." [24]

This statement of purpose suggests a need for close association between the administrator and the community. The administrator must be aware of the social needs of the community with respect to which groups are in need of service—that is, low-income families, preschool-age children, adolescents, minority groups, and the like—what specific kinds of service are needed, and which kinds of service will be needed in the future. Such knowledge would enable the administrator to deploy the agency resources so as to maximize the achievement of the stated goals and purposes. Accordingly, the administrator has responsibility for understanding the breadth and scope of the agency's resources as well as awareness of how the individual workers can be brought together to function as a team. Because of the necessarily close involvement with the community, the administrator has the task of developing and utilizing good public relations—essential both for the direct revision of service and for the securing of financial resources to allow for continued growth of the clinic. Inasmuch as there is always a limitation in resources, the administrator must take leadership in establishing a list of priorities with respect to services to be offered, programs to be developed or discontinued, and ultimately, the primary goals to be met during a given time.

The Purpose of an Agency Serving the Aging

A social agency designed to provide services to the aging, states its purpose as follows: "The objectives of this program are to provide a multipurpose opportunity center for the aging by: A. relating realistically to the present known needs of the aging such as: (1) effecting referral to appropriate community agencies, (2) stimulating organizations to provide adequate housing, (3) providing social, recreational programs in the present downtown areas and in areas where new housing is to be established. B. to provide an ongoing education program to stimulate self-help by: (1) offering efforts in home economics such as: a. food buying and preparation, b. personal health care, c. housing care; (2) offering constructive leisure time activities and work toward beneficial employment, where possible; C. to provide a training program for volunteers (aging and others), future program assistants, and other paid staff; D. to provide transportation, actual and informational, where necessary to participate in centers; E. to develop a program of pre-retirement counseling in cooperation with local businesses; F. to become an integral part of the present and future plans for the aging of the area." [25]

The implications of this statement of purpose are clear. One of the goals of the administrator must be fact-finding, for the agency aims to relate "realistically to the present known needs of the aging," and must know the facts about these needs. Some of the known needs relate to information and referral, which necessitates finding and working in conjunction with other agencies serving the aging population in the area. There is a great need for housing for the elderly; the administrator must therefore become involved with other community agencies and groups to make this need known and to try to see that it is met. A provision of a social and recreational program for the elderly is the goal that necessitates the coordination and supervision of staff, paid and volunteer.

The Purpose of a Social Service Department in a Hospital

The Social Service Department of a large mental hospital [26] describes its purpose as follows: "Promoting the well-being and morale of patients and families, and providing a link between the hospital and the patients' families." Social service is also responsible "for helping the hospital team in understanding the social, economic, and environmental factors involved in the patient's illness, as they are pertinent to treatment." Therefore, social workers obtain and evaluate psychiatric and social history information. An additional subpurpose is "to help the patient and his family to understand the implications of the patient's illness and to aid them in making appropriate use of psychiatric and hospital resources." Also central to the purpose of hospital social service is "the facilitating of the productive utilization of community resources, and aiding in the development of resources where needed." Also, quite significant is the purpose of "participation in educational programs with other members of the treatment team."

To achieve these purposes, it is the administrator's responsibility to recruit, assign, and develop an adequate number of professionally educated social workers. Furthermore, the Director of Social Service must necessarily form a link between the social work staff and the hospital administrators, if the social workers are going to be productive in their work. The Director of Social Service is a member of the Administrative Council and, therefore, participates in over-all planning for the hospital. He promotes better communication and collaboration between his department and the other departments. To achieve these goals, the administrator must have a rich background in social work practice.

The social work administrator in a host setting must understand the setting as well as professional social work. As Phillips indicates, "The concept of dual identification with hospital and profession is perhaps the core of the role. Unless this is clearly understood and sufficiently integrated to form a basis for decision-making, the director can be caught in the currents of expediency. It is imperative that the director analyze his function, not only in the light of current social work practice, but also in relation to the setting in which he works. In a general hospital, the director must define his department's professional role in terms of the patient population it serves, the medical care goals and practices of the institution, and the hospital administrative pattern. If he fails to do this, the department will become an island, not sufficient unto itself, but limited unto itself, striving for professional excellence to no achievable end." [27]

The Purpose of a School Social Work Department

The purpose of the School Social Service Department in an Eastern city grows out of the basic purpose of the school system itself. It is stated that these schools attempt to meet the educational needs of all children, including those children with individual differences and problems that interfere with their maximum use of the school experience. To achieve this goal, the Board of Education has employed several specialized auxiliary services to assist the educator. The purpose of the School Social Service Department, then, as an auxiliary service, is to offer casework and group work service to those children who are experiencing problems of a social, emotional, or physical nature that may be interfering with their learning experience, school attendance, or social adjustment. These problems may have their basis within the child himself, within his family relationships, or within other relationships; most often within a combination of all three.

It is the purpose of school social workers to work with the individual child, his family, and all other school personnel in a cooperative, intensive, and continuous effort, to help all concerned to understand the child's difficulties—help them to accept his limitations, abilities, and needs—and to help all concerned to understand the need to participate in a child–parent–school relationship which is essential in achieving the goals of education.

The Director of School Social Work must be certain that the purposes, policies, and procedures of the department are made available to all school personnel and parents. He should make certain that they are clearly understood, not only by school personnel, but by his own staff as well. Naturally, the Director of School Social Work must develop satisfactory working relationships with his own staff and must place emphasis upon a cooperative team approach with other professionals in the school. It is necessary to set up a method of referral of children to the school social work department so that there is a clear understanding about which children to refer. The Director of School Social Work must evaluate the effectiveness of his department in cooperation with other school personnel. The School Social Work administrator must organize, coordinate, motivate, and direct his workers so that through their cooperative efforts the purposes of the department are achieved within the framework of the objectives of the school.

To achieve the stated purposes of a social agency, the administrator must carry heavy responsibility. *First,* he must attract and retain professionally qualified staff to insure excellence in the provision of services. *Second,* he must organize the staff to insure defined roles with clarification as to specific responsibilities. *Third,* he must establish and maintain smooth interrelationships with all departments, other disciplines, and other community agencies. *Fourth,* he must maintain a workable system of communication. *Fifth,* he must keep the staff and the community informed of policies, procedures, and limitations of services. *Sixth,* he must serve as a coordinator of the efforts of many people to meet the needs of the clientele being served, and he should constantly review the extent to which services are rendered on a coordinated basis. *Seventh,* he should keep himself informed of the changes within the community and endeavor to see to it that new services are provided to meet new needs. *Eighth,* he must engage himself actively in establishing ties with leaders in the community and in government to further the securing of financial and other forms of support for the agency. *Ninth,* he must have knowledge and skill in the areas of program planning and financial management. *Tenth,* he should encourage new programs as well as research and evaluation.

NOTES

1. Fremont Kast, "Systems Concepts and Organization Theory" in Preston P. Le-Breton, ed., *Comparative Administrative Theory* (Seattle: University of Washington Press, 1968), a pp. 151–152; b 147–148.
2. Henry H. Albers, *Principles of Management,* 3rd ed. (New York: John Wiley & Sons, Inc., 1969), a pp. 74–75; b 102–103; c 296.
3. Bertram S. Brows, M.D., "Concepts Underlying the Development of New Patterns of Community Mental Health Services" in *Proceedings Seminar on Social Welfare and Community Mental Health,* March 1–4, 1966 sponsored by the National Health Council and The National Social Welfare Assembly, p. 24.

4. Louise A. Frey, ed., *Use of Groups in the Health Field* (New York: National Association of Social Workers, 1966), pp. 21–22.
5. Arlien Johnson, *School Social Work—Its Contribution to Professional Education* (New York: National Association of Social Workers, 1962), pp. 60–61.
6. Bernard J. Coughlin, S.J., "Interrelationships of Governmental and Voluntary Welfare Services," *The Social Welfare Forum,* 1966 (Published for the National Conference on Social Welfare by Columbia University Press, New York), pp. 82–83.
7. Eleanor K. Taylor, "The Role of the Administrator in Facilitating Change." *Report of the Cooperative Project on Public Welfare Staff Training, Vol. I, Learning and Teaching in Public Welfare* (Washington, D.C.: Division of Technical Training, Bureau of Family Services, Welfare Administration, U.S. Department of Health, Education and Welfare, 1963), p. 191.
8. Ralph W. Tyler, "Insights from Behavioral Sciences," *Faculty-Administration Relationships,* Report of a Work Conference, May 7–9, 1957, sponsored by the Commission on Instruction and Evaluation of the American Council on Education, pp. 35–36.
9. *Social Work Administration* (New York: National Association of Social Workers, March 1968), pp. 9–10.
10. John D. Millett, *Organization for the Public Service,* p. 105. Copyright © 1966 by Litton Educational Publishing, Inc. by permission of Van Nostrand Reinhold Company.
11. Chester I. Barnard, *The Functions of the Executive.* Thirtieth Anniversary Edition (Cambridge: Harvard University Press, © copyright 1938, 1968 by the President and Fellows of Harvard College, © copyright 1966 by Grace F. Noera Barnard), a p. 122; b 91–92.
12. E.J. Baur, "The Spontaneous Development of Informal Organization," *Hospital Administration,* Summer 1963, pp. 45–58.
13. Peter M. Blau, "Structural Effects," *American Sociological Review,* April 1960, pp. 178–192.
14. Robert D. Vinter, "The Social Structure of Service" in Alfred J. Kahn, ed., *Issues in American Social Work* (New York: Columbia University Press, 1959), p. 244.
15. Lyndall F. Urwick, *Notes on the Theory of Organization* (New York: American Management Association, 1952), pp. 18–19.
16. Ralph N. Traxler, "The Qualities of an Administrator," *Hospital Administration,* Fall 1961, p. 42.
17. Harold E. Moore, *The Administration of Public School Personnel* (New York: The Center for Applied Research in Education, Inc., 1966), p. 33.
18. Philip Selznick, *Leadership in Administration—A Sociological Interpretation* (Evanston, Ill.: Row, Peterson, 1957), p. 23.
19. Connecticut State Welfare Department, *Manual,* Vol. I, Chap. 1, Index 1000, issued July 15, 1968.
20. Connecticut State Welfare Department, *Manual,* Vol. II, Chap. 1, Index 010–011, issued January 1, 1954.
21. Hartford Family Service Society, *Board Members Manual,* 1965, p. 3.
22. Brochure of The Dixwell Community House, 1967, New Haven, Connecticut.
23. *Constitution and By-Laws,* West Haven Community House, West Haven, Connecticut.
24. *Child Guidance Clinic* (mimeographed brochure), The Child Guidance Clinic of Southeastern Connecticut, Inc., 1968.
25. *Services Performed with the Aging,* Hartford, Connecticut, April 1, 1968 (brochure).
26. *Purpose of Social Service Department,* Norwich Hospital, Norwich, Connecticut, 1969.
27. Beatrice Phillips, "A Director Examines the Director's Role," *Social Work,* October 1964, p. 93.

4 Agency-Community Relations

The social work administrator must have effective working relationships with the community. In recent years administrators have found it necessary to devote more time to community affairs because of the many changes that have taken place. Fresh facts about community needs are called for. Deeper understandings of client feelings are required. Developments in social welfare planning are increasingly important to the individual agency. New patterns of citizen participation in policy-making have emerged. Agency public relations, always important, have taken on new significance. Pressure groups of various kinds have brought their weight to bear upon agencies. Programs of interagency cooperation have increased. Board members and agency executives now take more part in community action. The fact that social welfare services are frequently a product of the political process has been more and more recognized. For all of these reasons and many others the social work administrator must be skillful in community relations.

Goldman says, "School-community relations define the mutual understandings of school program and community needs which exist between the professionals who work in the schools and the cititzens who support them. These understandings are necessary if the school is to reflect the values of the community and also be a positive influence on the future directions of it." [1a] Although Goldman is talking about school-community relations his remarks apply to social agency-community relations as well.

As Hardwick and Landuyt say, "Administration as a dynamic social reality cannot escape the influence of the beliefs and philosophies of the environment in which it is practiced." [2]

The Administrator Must Know the Community

The administrator needs to see and know the community in great breadth and depth because the community provides sanction for the service and the necessary financial support. He should be particularly clear about the relationship between his agency and the community. He should have knowledge of the sociocultural factors that exist and he should know about the degree of integration between community groups and the extent to which they hold values in common.

Hungate says, "A knowledge of cultural forms in the community is necessary for the public welfare administrator. A lack of recognition of sociocultural factors and cultural differences may cause the administrator to institute procedures and techniques for achieving program objectives that are culturally unacceptable as goals for the community. The administrator cannot expect community groups to go beyond their cultural limitations; he must know the cultural meaning of what is being done to the social values of those affected. The administrator must be aware that welfare programs operate within several subcultures at the same time; that the public welfare agency does not exist in isolation; nor is the organizational behavior of individuals working as a composite within any agency understandable without a reference to their cultural values. The variable of culture is always interposed between the environment and the welfare agency, which, with its multiple programs, is in the midst of a rapidly changing society. As cultural and social values change, welfare programs must be constantly adapted to solve the problems of human need. However, the administrator is expected to develop welfare programs that consistently conform to the dominant values currently held by the community, even though, with shifting emphasis, these values are constantly changing." [3a]

It is necessary for the administrator to make sure that the agency has up-to-date information and basic social facts about the community for use in policy-making and program planning. In addition, the administrator is responsible for developing a method whereby the agency is constantly studying the emerging social needs brought about by community changes. Furthermore, he must maintain sound communication lines between his agency and other community organizations. He has the responsibility to help see to it that the board members are representatives of the community. It is his responsibility to see to it that new volunteers and staff are given a thorough orientation to the community and are helped to participate in the life of the community. He should make certain that job analyses include specific itemized references to the workers' responsibility for community participation and leadership. Programs of staff development and in-service training should include material on the community. He should work out with the board and the staff a statement of policy on community relationships, and he should represent his agency in total community planning and coordination.

In an earlier publication the author listed ten questions designed to test the extent to which the agency's administrative processes are socially related to the community.

1. To what extent does the agency have up-to-date information and basic social facts about the community for use in policy-making and program planning?

2. To what extent does the agency have a method of arriving at an understanding of emerging social needs brought about by community changes? Consider, for example, the implications of such material as the following, stated by an administrator who is describing the area where a youth-service agency is at work: "It's an area of new homes, vast suburban tracts, many of them very picturesque as they are carved out of the hills. There is much mobility into and within the area and many people travel long distances to employment. The Urban-Redevelopment movement is very strong in the older sections. There are three separate public school systems in the area, as well as many parochial schools. Two Junior Colleges are here. Children are bused long distances to school in some places. Some are on half-day sessions. There is continuous increase in school population with new schools and additions to old ones always under construction. At the present rate, a 55 per cent increase is indicated in school population in the next ten years. A tremendous adult education program is provided. A large Americanization program is conducted both in adult school and high school. Public tranportation is very limited. What there is, is to the metropolitan centers and none between areas."

3. To what extent are sound communication lines maintained between the agency and other community organizations?

4. To what extent are board members representative of the community?

5. To what extent does the orientation of new volunteers and staff include orientation to the community and planned participation in the community?

6. To what extent do job analyses include specific itemized reference to the individual's responsibility for community participation and leadership?

7. To what extent does the agency make a conscious effort to see itself as the community sees it?

8. To what extent do staff development and in-service training programs include material on the community?

9. To what extent does the agency work with other agencies in common service projects?

10. To what extent does the agency participate in total community planning and coordination? [4]

The Administrator and Public Relations

The social work administrator, the staff, and the board find themselves involved with a number of groups that are important in the public relations of the agency. In his writing about school-community relations, Campbell specifies four such groups.[5] These groups include the constituency of the agency, other agencies serving in the same or related area, community planning bodies, state and national organizations, contributors and supporters of the agency, and the community at large.

The U.S. Office of Education observes that "the role of the administrator in relation to the community needs to be clarified, too. While it may be true that the successful administrator does not require the experience of long years of teaching, it is also becoming more important than ever before that he be a 'teacher' in respect to the community at large, that he have an acute awareness of the social structure within which schools operate and be able to communicate the needs of the schools to the community upon which the schools depend and which they serve. Together with this ability, of course, there is a need for the administrator to be knowledgeable about the socio-political environment, so that he may successfully appeal to the proper agencies for support of his programs." [6]

In their recent book on effective public relations for community groups, the Levines present a broad and inclusive definition of public relations. They say, "Public relations is as simple as a thank-you note and as complicated as a four-color brochure. It is as specific as writing a news release and as general as sensing community attitudes. It is as direct as a conversation between two people and as broad as a television panel show reaching thousands of people. It is as inexpensive as a phone call to an editor or as costly as a full-page advertisement. It is as visual as a poster and as literal as a speech." [7a]

They also state, "Public relations is a term often used but seldom defined. In the broadest sense, public relations is good work publicly recognized. There is no secret public relations formula that can be applied to a group to make it respected and successful. Public relations is the group itself saying, 'This is who we are, what we think about ourselves, what we want to do, and why we deserve your support.' Public relations is not an end in itself, nor will it enable a group to gloss over its own deficiencies. If the group is not doing 'good work,' that is, if it is not filling a real need for its members or for the community, if its program is uninteresting, or if its goals are unrealistic, public relations can help, of course, by being sensitive to community opinion and reporting it accurately, by pointing out the areas in which the group is failing, and by suggesting ways to improve. But the group with problems must try to solve them before its public relations will improve. If, however, the program is sound, if the membership agrees on basic values, if the group is performing a necessary function in the community, public relations can be an invaluable aid in achieving specific goals and in winning general community support." [7b]

The Administrator and Social Welfare Planning

A major task of the social work administrator is to relate his agency to the ongoing social welfare planning program of the community. Because social welfare planning is changing rapidly, it becomes necessary for the administrator to see the goals of his agency in relation to the emerging goals of the social welfare field. Although most agencies tend to deal with specific needs and problems there is a trend toward more generalized services.

Gurin and Perlman in discussing social welfare planning and social planning say, "The boundaries of social welfare as a field have always been hard to define, and the ambiguities grow as time goes on. Additionally, social welfare has dealt with specific disabilities of individuals or groups rather than with failures of the basic institutions of society. Social welfare planning has therefore been focused primarily on the more adequate provision of services to meet specific disabilities. The major exception is the field of social insurance where social workers have played a role along with other disciplines but not as the dominant professional group. This focus on disabilities has long been identified as the 'residual' approach to social work or social welfare, and there has been an equally long drive toward moving the field to a more 'institutional' approach that would give it a place within the normal social fabric. One prong of this drive is the attempt to provide social welfare services of a specialized character on a more general basis—to obtain greater coverage of the population—by building them into other institutions, such as the school system and the employment services, and indeed, into the economic system itself. Beyond this lies the still largely unexplored territory of prevention of a more fundamental character, which would involve the revision of patterns of community life in ways that would reduce the incidence of problems requiring services. To state the problems in these terms is to indicate how far away such ultimate goals remain from the reach of existing knowledge. It seems clear that social welfare planning cannot be adequate if it is limited to a narrow range of service programs, if only because planning in broader areas is required both to secure adequate provision of services for current problems and to avoid future ones to the extent that knowledge permits. There is still no clear approach, however, to the specific roles and responsibilities of social welfare within the larger framework." [8]

Administrative Choices, Client Needs, and Pressure Groups

Administrative choices and decisions should always be made in terms of what is best for the client. Often the administrator finds himself at the center or vortex of competing value systems. Value systems may be at variance within the agency and within the community. Here the social work administrator tries to get these variations looked at and understood and sufficiently reconciled to bring about effective service. Even though compromise is needed and even though it may be impossible to secure complete agreement, the administrator keeps working on this matter and tries to create the best possible program of services for clients. How the administrator reacts when faced by failure, frustration, and even defeat is extremely important.

Goldman observes, "A key administrative position in the public schools is that of principal. As the 'man-in-the-middle' posed between central administration and the teaching staff, the principal must put into operation the policies of the school district while at the same time he must meet the personal and professional needs of the teachers. While at times these factors may be congruent, at other times they are in conflict. The position of principal incurs other conflicts as well. While the central administration and the teachers hold certain expectations of the principal, community groups may have other views which further complicate the life of the principal. Moreover, the principal's professional organizations may set expectations which are in conflict with all the groups mentioned above. It is into this cauldron that many 'mere' men are thrust." [1b]

The social work administrator as he strives to meet the needs of his clients may find that pressure groups in the community make it difficult if not impossible for him to provide the programs and services needed. Social welfare and education share a common problem in that they are often subject to the pressures of the community. Melby, writing about education, sees these pressure groups as sources of possible support: "The complex structure of pressure groups in the modern community is seen by many administrators as a body of critics to be appeased, yet different approaches could also convert these groups into resources to be utilized. The pressure groups are most often people who really care about education. Were greater use made of them they would realize more than they do now the complexity of many educational problems. Beyond this their contributions to education would be outstanding. What our school administrators have been taught in their preparation may equip them to deal with those persons and agencies in the community which they control, but increasingly the success of the administrator depends on the way he relates to persons and agencies he does not control. Here compassion, willingness to listen, a cooperative spirit, respect for the feelings of others will be more important than a commanding posture and a cocksure manner. It is also likely that in the years ahead it may be more important to be in communication with labor, the poor, and the minority groups than with the Chamber of Commerce and the exclusive clubs." [9]

Administration and Citizen Participation

A fundamental tenet of social work administration is citizen participation. The skillful administrator involves citizens in policy-making, resource provision, and need determination. However, in large and complex communities it is not easy to develop an effective program of citizen participation.

As Coughlin points out, "In the small societies of the past, citizen participation was relatively easily carried out through the immediate interrelationships between individuals, families, primary and secondary groups. The size and complexity of modern society, however, have removed the individual from his previous strategic position for discovering welfare need, and for the planning, servicing, coordinating, and accounting for welfare programs. In medieval and early colonial times, welfare need was easily discovered by every citizen who strolled into the marketplace; welfare services were so simple that planning and coordinating required little ingenuity; and one could scarcely evade accounting to a public to which one was known on a first-name basis. Today, things are changed. Discovery of real need is not as easy since real causes are remote and buried in a complexity of social values and institutions; planning and coordinating must be of a multiplicity of services, the totality of which is intended to strike at the complexity of the causes of need; and accountability is through impersonal institutions through an impersonal public." [10]

One of the major changes in recent years has been the emergence of a national policy in connection with anti-poverty projects that declares it to be essential that the persons who live in a community have a voice in the project. As Piven points out, "new objectives and strategies are being associated with resident participation in the anti-poverty projects. Three interrelated objectives can be identified: (1) Fostering the participation of low-income people in a variety of local associations. (2) Enhancing the effective influence of low-income people on the policies and practices of institutions that serve the low-income community. (3) Establishing the conditions for effective individual and family life by altering the social context of individual behavior. These objectives for resident participation reflect the concern of the poverty programs with political problems pertaining to democratic participation and influence, as well as concern with the social welfare problems to which the programs are principally addressed." [11]

Related to the matter of resident participation is the fact that more and more agency executives, staff members, and board members are themselves becoming active in programs designed to improve the lot of the disadvantaged.

Brodsky reports: "The professional staffs of thirty-five Centers in thirty cities were described as being 'very active' in community planning and action groups concerned with the problems of the disadvantaged. The staff of twenty-eight additional Centers in as many cities were described as 'active' in such community groups. Only nine Centers reported no staff involvement.

"Generally, staff involvement has meant active participation by the Center's executive director. Center professionals have been appointed to serve on mayors' committees concerned with disadvantaged youth, or serve in an advisory capacity to local anti-poverty agencies. There are numerous instances of outstanding professional leadership given by Center staffs to local anti-poverty agencies.

"Forty-eight Centers in forty-five cities reported that some of their board members were 'active' or 'very active' in community planning and action agencies. Many board members tended to serve as individuals rather than as formal representatives of the Center." [12]

Mogulof asks, "What is a competent community?" He continues, "For one, it is a place where the leaders are of the people and are a power in effecting the decision of all those agencies that provide resources to that community. In low-income communities, it is the place where the neighborhood representatives know how to deal with the police and courts, how to make their public schools aware that the price of the continued failure of their youth will be high, and where the welfare department, housing agencies, and so on know they are not dealing with a supine mass. Do such communities exist? Probably not, but that they must is clear, especially while the United States has a large 'underclass' dependent for most of its resources and opportunities on the decisions of public agencies." [13]

Administrators and the Political Process

Although actual records of the amount of time spent are not available it is evident that the administrator devotes considerable energy to the matter of interpreting his agency to political and governmental bodies. He does this to create an understanding of his agency and to get financial support for its programs. As Hungate says, "Administration of public welfare is one of the political processes of government. Although there is some flexibility within the programs, administration of welfare activities is thoroughly dependent upon and must interact with all other political processes. Therefore, provision of welfare services at an optimum level is contingent upon the attitudes of public welfare administrators toward public affairs and, in turn, the attitudes of public officials toward welfare. Because the legislative authority for welfare services is derived from political activity, it is in relationship to public affairs that public welfare administration tends to differ most decisively from administration of a voluntary agency." [3b]

Millett remarks, "Every administrator is a participant to some degree in the political process. As an administrator he is expected to give advice to the chief executive and to the legislature about desirable policy and program, about desirable scope of activities, and about the desirable authority (organizational and otherwise) needed to accomplish assigned purposes." [14]

NOTES

1. Samuel Goldman, *The School Principal* (New York: The Center for Applied Research in Education, Inc., 1966), a p. 63; b vii.
2. C.T. Hardwick and G.F. Landuyt, *Administrative Strategy* (New York: Simmons-Boardman Publishing Corporation, 1961), p. 324.
3. Joseph I. Hungate, Jr., *A Guide for Training Local Public Welfare Administrators* (Washington: U.S. Department of Health, Education and Welfare—Administration, Bureau of Family Services, Division of Technical Training, 1964), a p. 109; b 45.
4. Harleigh B. Trecker, *New Understandings of Administration* (New York: Association Press, 1961), pp. 92–94.
5. Roald F. Campbell and John A. Ramseyer, *The Dynamics of School-Community Relationships* (Boston: Allyn and Bacon, Inc., 1958).
6. U.S. Office of Education Report, *The People Who Serve Education* (Washington, D.C.: U.S. Department of Health, Education and Welfare, 1969), p. 8.
7. Howard and Carol Levine, *Effective Public Relations for Community Groups* (New York: Asosciation Press, 1969), a p. 15; b 17–18.
8. Arnold Gurin and Robert Perlman, "Current Conceptions of Planning and Their Implications for Public Welfare" in David G. French, ed., *Planning Responsibilities of State Departments of Public Welfare* (Chicago: American Public Welfare Association, 1967), p. 17.
9. Ernest O. Melby, "Needed: A New Concept of Educational Administration," *The Community School and Its Administration,* July 1965, p. 3.
10. Bernard J. Coughlin, S.J., "Interrelationships of Governmental and Voluntary Welfare Services," *The Social Welfare Forum,* (Published for the National Conference on Social Welfare by Columbia University Press, New York, 1966), pp. 83–84.
11. Frances Piven, "Participation of Residents in Neighborhood Community Action Programs," *Social Work,* January 1966, pp. 74–75.
12. Irving Brodsky, *The Jewish Community Center and the Urban Crisis.* (New York: National Jewish Welfare Board, 1968), p. 13.
13. Melvin B. Mogulof, "Involving Low-Income Neighborhoods in Antidelinquency Programs," *Social Work,* October, 1965, p. 56.
14. John D. Millett, *Organization for the Public Service,* p. 135. Copyright © 1966 by Litton Educational Publications, Inc., by permission of Van Nostrand Reinhold Company.

5 Staff Roles and Responsibilities

Most social work administrators agree that they carry major responsibility for seeing to it that their agencies are well staffed. As Friedlander says, "Competent, reliable, conscientious personnel is the most important factor in social agency administration as it is in other professional services, medicine, nursing, law and teaching. Only a well-trained staff of adequate size can perform social services as required for the welfare of the people. In this sense adequate staff means economy, because too few or untrained workers cannot perform qualified social work which is necessary to achieve the social agency's objectives. Personnel policy of the social agency demands three basic elements: 1) clearly formulated written standards of employment for specific positions, based upon competence; 2) provisions for fair-dealing on grievances; and 3) delegation of final authority to the executive in dealing with matters of competence and discipline." [1]

With reference to the public schools, Moore observes, "The strength and effectiveness of a school system is largely determined by the adequacy and quality of its staff. Recognizing this fact has led the total administrative process to be greatly concerned with personnel policies and practices." [2]

Pomeroy points out, "It is through the worker that the client typically relates to the agency. Thus, the worker not only can be viewed as a participant in a two-way relationship (between him and the client), but also as a link (albeit a mediating one) in the relationship of the client to the agency." [3]

Administrative Responsibility Shared with Staff

Many people carry administrative responsibility in the social agency. The chief executive is one, the department heads and supervisors are others, then there are special staff people such as heads of business, finance,

91

and buildings. The chief administrator is responsible for the entire work of the agency and he is responsible for all of the people on his staff. Therefore, he has more complex relationships and he has a much greater degree of authority. He must delegate work assignments to other people and must serve as a supervisor and a coordinator. He is closer to the policy-making realm than are his subadministrators.

As a workshop group pointed out, "Every social welfare agency exists to give one or more services; but in order to produce those services, many facilitative or supporting activities must be carried on. These include the activities of the executive and supervisors, board and staff meetings, financial operations, record keeping, and a host of other activities. Administration may be regarded as the sum of the facilitating and supportive activities which are not themselves service activities but which are necessary and incidental to the production of the service. Administration is the 'effectuation' of service. And, from this point of view, not only the executive but every member of the board, every member of the staff, every volunteer has a relation to and is a participant in administration. There is no such thing as a 'pure service' job. Every staff member carries on administrative as well as service activities—dictation, keeping records, attending staff conferences, conferring with supervisors, etc." [4a]

As Hungate says, "Within the organization, the administrative process is performed in some way by every individual. The director may be the one 'executive' for the program, but he's not the only one engaged in the practice of administration. . . . Within the sphere of their activity, all staff members perform administrative tasks; thus all program activity involves administration. Many persons who have the responsibility to direct and manage some phase of agency activities are not aware that they are engaged in administration. The administrative aspect of each job may not be readily distinguishable: (1) The typist must organize, plan, and direct the typing of records, and set schedules for getting out letters and for a variety of other clerical functions. (2) The supervisor of casework must direct the activity of the assigned workers, and many administrative considerations are evident in assignment of cases to specific workers. (3) A portion of the worker's time is spent in administration of the case load. Many case workers have been heard to exclaim that they do not want to be placed in administrative positions, but want only to see clients and 'do casework.' Analysis will show that the caseworker in many agencies is one of the most facile of administrators. No one would deny that managing a case load of 50–150 clients requires abundant administrative skills. Thus, administration permeates the whole structure. Everyone using personal judgment and skill to perform an assigned duty effectively is constantly solving individual problems of administration." [5]

The Administrator's Attitude Toward and Relationship with the Staff

The social work administrator is the professional leader of the staff. He carries major responsibility for helping the staff to set goals, achieve high standards of work productivity, and provide high quality services to clients. His attitudes toward the staff should express faith in their ability to do the job. As Clapp says, "Given two agencies with reasonable similarity in respect to the competence of its individual members, what makes one lethargic, apathetic, and erratic in its course and performance and the other purposive, energetic, and reasonably creative in its performance? I suspect that at the root of the causes may be found a fundamental difference in at least two respects—the presence or absence of a deep faith within the key administrators in the latent intellectual and emotional reasonableness of human beings and rejection or acceptance of the desire to reform people as contrasted with the willingness to let them reform themselves. I believe that one's beliefs and convictions about these two variables lie close to the heart of whatever may be the administrative art. A more limited and suggestive hypothesis might be something like this: the key to the performance of an organization is the positive willingness of individuals to spend and apply their energies, singly and in groups, to the tasks committed to their hands. How to elicit within and among the farthest reaches of an organization the positive self-induced desire, intent, and energy to decide to act is the central problem of administrative leadership." [6a]

As a goal-setter for the staff the administrator has much to do with determining work output or productivity. As Argyris says, "The leader seems to exhibit realistic goal-setting ability. He tends to set his goals just high enough so that effort is required to achieve them, but not so high they are unattainable." [7]

Likert says, "To achieve and maintain high performance, it is necessary that the subordinates, as well as the superiors of an organization, have high performance goals and have their work well-organized. Subordinates are unlikely to set high performance goals for themselves and organize their work well if their superiors do not have such aspirations for each salesman and for the whole office. A superior with high performance goals and excellent job organization is much more likely to have subordinates who set high goals for themselves and organize their work well when he uses group methods of supervision and applies the principle of supportive relationships effectively than when he does not." [8a]

The administrator is thus a key person in work productivity. Increased productivity and job satisfaction of all members of the work group appear to be related to the administrator's activity in developing in the employees a feeling of self-confidence and security in the way the agency is managed. The administrator must be able to demonstrate adequate control over the formal organization, in order to win the allegiance of his staff. He must command the respect of his workers in order to contribute to the development of cohesive ties which bring about unity. The absence of such bonds produces strains and tensions which find expression in more critical attitudes toward the administrator.

A workshop group reported: "Basically, administration is a process that involves working with other people. Wherever there is administration, there are people; the administrative process involves primarily working relationships with others. Thus, (a) equipment, procedures, records are important only as they relate to human beings; they exist and have significance only insofar as they are used by people to facilitate the achievement of the goal of giving services; (b) the fabric of administration is woven from the multi-colored threads of *human relationships*. The executive, the sub-executive, the supervisor, the social worker, the office manager, the typist, the janitor, the maid—these are people, each with a job to be accomplished within an overall agency program, and as each works at his job, he does so in relation to the work being done by every other member of the staff within the total program. The relations are 'there' because the people are 'there'; wherever there are people associated in an enterprise, there are relationships." [4b]

Likert says, "The principle of supportive relationship is a general principle which the members of an organization can use to guide their relationships with one another. The more fully this principle is applied throughout the organization, the greater will be the extent to which (1) the motivational forces arising from the non-economic motives of members and from their economic needs will be harmonious and compatible and (2) the motivational forces within each individual will result in cooperative behavior focused on achieving organizational goals. The principle is stated as follows: The leadership and other processes of the organization must be such as to ensure a maximum probability that in all interactions and in all relationships within the organization, each member, in the light of his background, values, desires, and expectations, will view the experience as supportive and one which builds and maintains his sense of personal worth and importance." [8b]

The social work administrator seeks to promote the growth of his staff, for, as Clapp says, "The highest purpose of administration is to build processes which encourage and promote the growth of human talents, especially the talent to select progressively richer ends or goals and more effective means to achieve them." [6b]

Tead elaborates on this theme when he says, "My considered judgment is that for long-time success, the best administrative leaders are those who have socially justifiable purposes and who enlist loyalty to them by provocative creative appeals to those groups involved. This is the essence of *democratic* leadership in that the effort is consciously being made to achieve the institutional goals while trying simultaneously to assure that those implicated are realizing and actualizing themselves *as* they labor and *through* their labor for the corporate good. The development or realization of the personalities of the followers has always to be one-half of the dual goal of the leader, the other half being to assure that the institution's purpose is well served by the integrated labors of all." [9]

The social work administrator has a role to play in helping the staff to understand the heritage of the agency. In writing about the job of the school principal, Goldman makes a point which is pertinent for social agency administrators as well. He says, "In his role as administrator, the principal works with his staff to preserve and transmit to present and future generations the accumulated heritage of the past. This tends to provide a certain stability to the on-going activities of the school. By lending stability to the program, the principal can instill a feeling of security and trust in those who work with him. By resisting impulsive action or hastily conceived 'instant change' the principal can contribute to diminishing the feelings of insecurity among staff members and in this way obviate a major cause of entrenched resistance to change." [10]

The social work administrator tends to become a model for the staff. The way he carries on his task activities has a considerable influence on those around him. Task behavior as discussed by Moment and Zaleznik has an element of leadership in it which is of great importance. They say, "Task behavior involves the individual in an aggressive mode of action. By thinking and weighing ideas, his own and others, he becomes committed to the points of view that he must formulate and assert, both forcefully and confidently, if he is to work with conviction. He seeks to influence other persons, to change and modify their points of view, which involves him in competitive activity. To assert and to compete opens the individual to aggressive behavior from others. If he is functioning in task activity, the individual has to be able to take competitive behavior from others; this includes criticism, evaluation, and attack. One of the main characteristics of task-oriented behavior is the release of energy and its direction on to a problem-solving situation and at the same time the absorption of energy display resulting from the direction of energy by other persons." [11]

The Staff Member as a Part of the Agency

The social work administrator must strive to understand the staff member as an individual *and* as a part of the agency.

Bennis calls attention to the fact that "individuals who come to work for the organization bring into the system some needs which they desire to have satisfied on the job and certain expectations about the job they are to perform. On the other hand, the organization has certain needs to be fulfilled and a set of expectations to be fulfilled by the people who work for it." [12]

It is the task of the administrator to help staff members become integrated with the agency even though their loyalties may be in conflict at the outset.

As Green observes, "when the problem of conflicting loyalties is considered in its broad perspective, it is essentially one of reconciling the professional worker's need for autonomy and the organization's need for employees to be integrated within the complex of its activities. For the social worker, autonomy means maintaining professional standards, developing a creative and resourceful approach to practice, and finding opportunities for professional development and research activities. For the organization, integration involves maintaining administrative standards and the rational coordination of activities, together with the development of responsibility and loyalty in the employee. As the professional social worker needs the resources of the organization, and as the latter needs the skill of the professional worker, there is considerable motivation to find some accommodation to the interests of both." [13]

What the Professional Social Worker Wants from Administration

The number of professionally educated social workers is in chronic short supply. Consequently, qualified professionals have their choice of jobs. A prominent factor in this choice is the kind of administration provided by the agency. What kind of administration do professional social workers want? *First,* they want an administration which makes it possible for them to practice their profession, that is, to make use of their knowledge and skill in professional service to people. *Second,* they want an administration which allows them to make decisions about client needs based on their professional judgments. *Third,* they want to be accepted as responsible professional persons who can be depended upon to carry out their work assignments with competence and commitment. *Fourth,* they want opportunities for growth plus new responsibilities and challenges as their experience warrants. *Fifth,* they want an administration which both permits and encourages them to contribute their practice knowledge and experience to the process of problem-solving and policy-determination. Utz says, *"The administrative staff should share fully and frankly with the casework staff the problems and issues confronting the agency as soon as they are identified and their dimensions are assessed.* Sharing such knowledge clears the air, removes a shroud of secrecy, and releases staff energy that might otherwise be consumed in speculation and anxiety. Furthermore, it provides a challenge to staff members who are capable of assuming some of the responsibility for seeking solutions to the problems and dealing with the issues." [14] *Sixth,* they want an administration that is constantly striving for high standards of professional service. *Seventh,* they want an administration that provides strong and sound leadership.

"A major function of the executive," says Taylor, "is the provision of sound leadership to his staff. There are many problems in this area that can give rise to stress. There is the matter of individual as opposed to group decisions and the thorny problems surrounding the manipulation and engineering of consent." [15]

Eighth, social workers want an administration that respects and seeks to implement the nationally agreed-upon personnel standards and practices.

According to the National Association of Social Workers, "As a member of the profession, an administrator has the responsibility to acquaint the governing body of the agency with NASW standards for personnel policies and salaries. These include providing opportunity for employees to bargain collectively with management, if they so choose. Job descriptions should state clearly which positions are considered managerial and are therefore excluded from the collective bargaining unit.

"If the majority of employees in an agency determine that a union is their preferred method of carrying out their program for recognition and ultimately their collective bargaining activities, the first consideration should be whether the union should be a craft or an industrial union. In making this choice, the employees should explore, among other factors, what kind of a union would best facilitate conditions for good professional practice and which would be most effective in improving working conditions and salaries in social agencies.

"Useful methods in achieving recognition and in collective bargaining include exploration, education, persuasion, negotiation, enlistment of influential allies, representation by council, presentation through news media, use of professional mediators, and arbitration." [16]

The Staff Member's Responsibility to Administration

Social workers are responsible to administration in many ways. Their professional ideals and ethics are the foundation for responsible behavior on their part. The National Association of Social Workers declares: "Social work is based on humanitarian, democratic ideals. Professional social workers are dedicated to service for the welfare of mankind, to the disciplined use of a recognized body of knowledge about human beings and their interactions, and to the marshaling of community resources to promote the well-being of all without discrimination.

"Social work practice is a public trust that requires of its practitioners integrity, compassion, belief in the dignity and worth of human beings, respect for individual differences, a commitment to service, and a dedication to truth. It requires mastery of a body of knowledge and skill gained through professional education and experience. It requires also recognition of the limitations of present knowledge and skill and of the services we are now equipped to give. The end sought is the performance of a service with integrity and competence.

"Each member of the profession carries responsibility to maintain an improved social work service; constantly to examine, use, and increase the knowledge on which practice and social policy are based; and to develop further the philosophy and skills of the profession." [17a]

The code of ethics of the social worker must govern his behavior in all of his relationships. As the National Association of Social Workers states:

This code of ethics embodies certain standards of behavior for the social worker in his professional relationships with those he serves, with his colleagues, with his employing agency, with other professions, and with the community. In abiding by it, the social worker views his obligations in as wide a context as the situation requires, takes all the principles into consideration, and chooses a course of action consistent with the code's spirit and intent. The code of ethics includes the following:

I regard as my primary obligation the welfare of the individual or group served, which includes action for improving social conditions.

I will not discriminate because of race, color, religion, age, sex, or national ancestry, and in my job capacity will work to prevent and eliminate such discrimination in rendering service, in work assignments, and in employment practices.

I give precedence to my professional responsibility over my personal interests.

I hold myself responsible for the quality and extent of the service I perform.

I respect the privacy of the people I serve.

I use in a responsible manner information gained in professional relationships.

I treat with respect the findings, views, and actions of colleagues and use appropriate channels to express judgment on these matters.

I practice social work within the recognized knowledge and competence of the profession.

I recognize my professional responsibility to add my ideas and findings to the body of social work knowledge and practice.

I accept my responsibility to help protect the community against unethical practice by any individuals or organizations engaged in social welfare activities.

I stand ready to give appropriate professional service in public emergencies.

I distinguish clearly, in public, between my statements and actions as an individual and as a representative of an organization.

I support the principle that professional practice requires professional education.

I accept responsibility for working toward the creation and maintenance of conditions within agencies that enable social workers to conduct themselves in keeping with this code.

I contribute my knowledge, skills, and support to programs of human welfare.[17b]

In discussing the methods by which the school social worker discharges his responsibility to administration, Nebo lists:

1. Demonstration of the value of the service by his work and changes in children. 2. Initiation and participation in case conferences involving both school

and community personnel; 3. Planned conferences with both principals and superintendents or their delegated representative; 4. Participation in curriculum-planning committees and other committees; 5. Participation in orientation meetings, PTA functions, faculty meetings, and meetings of groups outside the school to interpret his function, and also to further a general understanding of children; 6. Submission of monthly and annual statistical and narrative reports to the superintendent and other key administrators; 7. Preparation and distribution of specially prepared written material. In summary, the school social worker can be of value to administration by: 1. Understanding the role of social work as it operates within an institution whose primary function is to educate children, and focusing his goals on this educational function; 2. Understanding the over-all educational philosophy, practices, and policies of his school district and of the individual buildings he serves; 3. Understanding, respecting, and using lines of authority, responsibility, and communication as they operate within the school district and within individual buildings; 4. Working closely with teachers, principals, and other school personnel on individual cases, sharing appropriate information with them, and utilizing their knowledge and skills; 5. Maintaining cooperative relationships with representatives of other special services within the school, and, with administrative leadership, participating with these representatives in a mutual delineation of each person's responsibilities and in a recognition of overlapping elements in their roles; 6. Understanding the functions, policies, and procedures of community agencies and interpreting them to the school; and interpreting the school's functions, policies, and procedures to the community; 7. Attending faculty meetings, serving on committees, and assuming other appropriate responsibilities which will promote his integration with the faculty.[18]

Authority and Administration

It is widely recognized that authority is inherent in every social work job. Authority goes with the function, the task, and the position. It is also agreed that the amount of, or degree of, authority varies with the position held and is specific to the given position. In every case authority implies knowledge, experience, and a degree of competence. It also implies trust, responsibility, and acceptance by people. Thus, in social work, authority is widely distributed throughout the enterprise. It is shared by a large number of people. Insofar as the social work administrator is concerned, it is necessary for him to make substantial use of his authority of competence. He uses it to design and set limits on individual and group responsibility. He uses it to establish methods, procedures, and policies. He uses it to foster coordination and to create agency unity and wholeness.

Albers says, "Organized executive action is impossible without authority. . . . Power and authority are closely related concepts. Power may be defined as the capacity to change individual or group behavior. . . . Power is present when an individual or group is able to affect the activity of another individual or group. It gives rise to behavior that differs from the behavior that would have occurred otherwise. The power that evolves from a managerial position is usually categorized as authority. People with authority have power, but power does not always denote authority. A subordinate may have no authority, but he can have a great deal of power. The 'authority of position' is the power (or authority) that a person has by virtue of his superior position. Subordinates normally accord authority to those who occupy higher hierarchical positions. This authority is to a great extent unrelated to the particular person who occupies the position. Authority would arise even though the occupant does not have the personal capacity to create power." [19a]

Walton says, "By authority we mean simply the power and the recognized right of the administrator, enforced by whatever sanctions he may employ, to make decisions necessary for the coordination of the activities of persons working within the organization. The authority of the administrator to coordinate is similar to the teacher's authority to teach." [20]

Administrators may have certain feelings about authority and may have difficulty in accepting the fact that they must use the authority vested in them and in their position. Problems may arise from misunderstandings, and from the failure on the part of administrators to spell out precisely the degree of authority involved in the various positions in the agency.

To summarize: 1) authority is inherent in every job; it goes with the function, the task, the position held. 2) The amount of or degree of authority, its specific nature, varies with the particular job. 3) Authority implies knowledge and experience, and is both earned and conferred. 4) Authority is distributed and shared, and is best regarded as authority *with* people rather than authority over people. 5) Authority implies trust, responsibility, and acceptance by people. 6) Authority is essentially positive; in fact, it is very useful, even essential. 7) All of us need the help of authority, few people can function long without it. Therefore, the administrator uses authority to define and set limits on individual and group responsibility. He uses it to establish methods and procedures and policies for performing work, and he uses it to foster coordination and agency wholeness.

A Survey of Staff Attitudes

Frequently social work administrators are lacking in information as to how staff members really feel about their jobs and their agency. Although the administrators try to keep the lines of communication open, staff members may be reluctant to reveal their feelings.

In a hospital an employee attitude survey was conducted by a university research agency. The findings as reported in the following newspaper account indicate that social agencies as well as hospitals can learn much from such a formal study.

Hartford Hospital is the first medical institution in New England to use an attitude survey program to keep up with its employees.

A year and a half ago, the 2,800 employees each spent an hour filling out questionnaires of the Industrial Relations Department of the University of Chicago.

Hospital personnel director Robert C. Gronbach reports the reason behind the program is to have truly "participative management." Workers are asked to make suggestions and take part in the constant realignment of duties.

Gronbach said Hartford Hospital started with generally good morale and has improved it. Nurses are asked to answer 93 questions, "agree," "don't know," or "disagree." Other workers answered 78 items. The unsigned sheets were then sent to Chicago for tabulating.

The hospital's mean score was 61 per cent favorable replies—the exact mean the Chicago quiz found after testing 100,000 industrial firms, and well above the mean among hospitals using the survey.

Key to making the survey work, Gronbach said, is follow-up and feedback. The University of Chicago supplies a management development program to teach supervisors to make use of the survey results. A "workbook" comes with the test scores and each department head goes over the questions and answers with his personnel.

What did Hartford find besides a few personal gripes and attacks on individuals?

It found that communications were poor–within and especially between departments. It also found that coordination was often absent so that time and money was wasted.

It found that pay was generally good—much better than other hospitals surveyed. But the nurses said that scheduling of shifts was unsatisfactory.

Employees had a page on which to write criticisms and ideas—responses that were sent unread to Chicago and then typed up and returned to the Hospital. Many of the ideas, reports Gronbach, have been put to good use.

Employees now have a formal Employees Council that meets once a month. It is made up of 35 representatives from the more than 40 departments within Hartford Hospital. This group discusses specific issues and files reports with management. Management has agreed to discuss any personnel proposals with the Council, first.

A year from now, another attitude survey will be made. In the meantime, department supervisors are attending conferences to improve their techniques, antiquated equipment has been replaced, coordination has been improved and 140 other suggested changes have been implemented.[21]

Delegation of Responsibility to Staff Members

The skillful social work administrator learns how to delegate responsibility and authority to members of his staff. In fact, delegation is a necessity, as Albers points out: "Delegation becomes necessary when the work load of an executive position exceeds the physical and psychological capacity of the executive. The delegation process reduces the executive work load, but it also adds to the work load by increasing the number of subordinates or span of management. This process can continue until the work load that evolves from an increasing span of management exceeds the executive's capacity to carry the burden. Additional levels of management become necessary when this limit is reached. The superior's responsibility is not absolved by the act of delegation. Delegation involves taking a risk on the capability of subordinates. This risk cannot be entirely avoided, but it can be mitigated by exercising some degree of supervision over the activities of the subordinate. Decentralization is greater or less to the extent that executives are willing to delegate important decision-making responsibilities and exercise a minimum of supervision and control." [19b]

Clegg, in analyzing his experience in public welfare administration, places much importance on delegation: "The successful executive does not do anything himself which can be done as well or better by some member of his staff. The Welfare Administrator who is to follow this admonition needs to examine critically his daily activities to ascertain if he is performing unnecessary and useless tasks. The proper delegation of authority is one of the keys to successful administration. Its accomplishment requires constant study and reconsideration. The wise executive attempts to surround himself with staff who are the most competent available. He may be successful in employing assistants who are his equal or superior in management phases. This is a promising situation, for it permits the executive or administrator to operate the organization at a high level of performance and to bask in the light of the talents of those who surround him. It is quite obvious that it will be of no avail to acquire competent staff unless they are permitted sufficient delegated power to perform at maximum and to develop their personal talents." [22]

Differential Use of Staff

Increasingly, social work administrators are making differential use of staff defined by Barker and Briggs as "a social work organization's allocation of its functions to the organization members who are considered most capable of fulfilling them efficiently." [23a]

As Epstein points out, "making maximum use of professional staff time in productive direct work with clients occupies high priority in the administration of social services. Need for improved methods in use of staff is intensified by the shortage of trained caseworkers, the increasing demand for social services, and their increasing cost. Advances in diagnostic and treatment knowledge and in administrative techniques are making some older methods obsolete and in need of revision and up-dating." [24]

In an interesting report on how one agency made differential use of staff, Epstein cites the administrative assumptions which were made at the start of the project. They are: "(1) Structure was considered a prerequisite for the full use of technological knowledge in social work, as in other disciplines. (2) Job specialization was viewed as a way to produce expertise in a particular segment of agency function, permitting some use of less-trained staff, thus lowering some costs. (3) Job specialization in a closely structured administrative design was believed to require disciplined staff performance and a system of job coordination which must be built into the work process and is not achievable by supervision alone. (4) It was considered to be primarily an administrative responsibility to design, install, and control the systems used, rather than depend on independent staff initiative for improvisation in implementation. It is this element of sole administrative responsibility, which, when combined with consistent teaching in supervision, builds the work process both into the system and individual workers' performances. (5) It was considered professionally valid to construct empirical classifications of the caseload so as to obtain a practical working base for differentiating case assignments among different categories of staff." [24b]

In describing one differential work assignment system, Epstein says, "The characteristics of this staff-use plan may be stated as follows: (1) Professionally trained, fully qualified casework staff to be used as exclusively as possible at their highest level of skill. (2) Adjunctive personnel to be used maximally to enable the casework personnel to attend fully to their particular role. A full array of essential services will thus be made available, raising the level of all services. (3) Job descriptions that accurately portray existing duties and differences between categories to be made explicit in writing. (4) Casework assistant personnel to be developed. It was found expedient to change the job title of 'case aide' to 'casework assistant' because deprecating connotations seem to have grown up around the former title. Casework assistants are never to be made to assume full professional responsibility for diagnosis or outcome, but to be offered readily accessible professional supervision at all times. Conversely, caseworkers are expected to assume professional responsibility, using supervision to develop knowledge and technique for diagnostic clarity and treatment efficiency. (5) Volunteer personnel to be used maximally on assignments tailored to be within the limits of their knowledge and skill, their duties also to be defined explicitly, and never to be assigned without immediate access to professional supervision. (6) Work-simplification devices to be developed to reduce time spent on clerical duties and to standardize and economize on repetitive professional procedures." [24c]

Epstein summarizes the results of this special project on differential use of staff in the following words: "In conclusion, the project reported here has demonstrated that a structured, differential use of staff can be developed and can increase staff productivity and impact on the social problems for which the agency assumes responsibility. The basic elements of the administrative design described here are explicit role clarification among the different types of personnel; built-in safeguards against demands in excess of defined areas of staff competence; assumption of administrative responsibility for classifying and making decisions on key areas of caseload characteristics, focus, and content of services to be offered." [24d]

In developing patterns of staff usage in differential terms, social work administrators must take into account not only their agencies but the profession as well. Barker and Briggs accent this point: "Differential use of staff to meet the needs of clients better is a joint responsibility involving agencies, which must be clear regarding job specifications and delineation based on agency role and client needs; the profession, whose obligation is to establish and/or redefine the legitimate status positions for various levels of personnel; and education, which must retool and design educational programs along the whole continuum based on new designations and roles." [23b]

NOTES

1. Walter A. Friedlander, *Introduction to Social Welfare,* 3rd ed., (Englewood Cliffs, N.J.: Prentice-Hall, Inc., © 1968), pp. 205–206.
2. Harold E. Moore, *The Administration of Public School Personnel* (New York: The Center for Applied Research in Education, Inc., 1966), p. 1.
3. Richard Pomeroy, *Studies in Public Welfare: Reactions of Welfare Clients to Social Service* (The Center for the Study of Urban Problems, Graduate Division, Bernard M. Baruch College, the City University of New York, undated), p. 69.
4. *Proceedings of Workshop on Social Agency Administration, Leadership and the Social Welfare Executive.* Richmond Professional Institute—School of Social Work, Richmond, Va., April 12–14, 1967, a p. 2; b 3.
5. Joseph I. Hungate, Jr., *A Guide for Training Local Public Welfare Administrators* (Washington: U.S. Department of Health, Education and Welfare—Welfare Administration, Bureau of Family Services, Division of Technical Training, 1964), pp. 10–11.
6. Gordon R. Clapp, "The Social Scientist and the Administrative Art" in Leonard D. White, ed., *The State of the Social Sciences* (Chicago: University of Chicago Press, 1956), a pp. 395–396; b 397.
7. Chris Argyris, *Executive Leadership—An Appraisal of a Manager in Action* (New York: Harper and Brothers, 1953), p. 23.
8. Rensis Likert, *The Human Organization—Its Management and Value* (New York: McGraw-Hill Book Company, © 1967), a p. 63; b 47.
9. Ordway Tead, "Reflections on the Art of Administration," *Hospital Administration,* Winter 1959, pp. 10–11.
10. Samuel Goldman, *The School Principal* (New York: The Center for Applied Research in Education, Inc., 1966), p. 92.
11. David Moment and Abraham Zaleznik, *Role Development and Interpersonal Competence* (Boston: Harvard University, Graduate School of Business Administration, Division of Research, 1963), p. 158.
12. Warren G. Bennis, "Problem-Oriented Administration," *Hospital Administration,* Winter 1960, p. 53.
13. A.D. Green, "The Professional Worker in the Bureaucracy," *Social Service Review,* March 1966, pp. 82–83.
14. Cornelius Utz, "The Responsibility of Administration for Maximizing the Contribution of the Casework Staff," *Social Casework,* March 1964, pp. 138–139.
15. Graham C. Taylor, "Executive Stress" in Alan McLean, ed., *To Work Is Human*

—*Mental Health and the Business Community* (New York: The Macmillan Company, 1967), p. 158.

16. *Guidelines in Labor-Management Relations* (New York: National Association of Social Workers, March 7, 1968), p. 3.

17. *Standards for Social Work Personnel Practices* (New York: National Association of Social Workers, 1968), a p. 7; b 7–8.

18. John C. Nebo, *Administration of School Social Work* (New York: National Association of Social Workers, 1958), pp. 34–35.

19. Henry H. Albers, *Principles of Management,* 3rd ed., (New York: John Wiley & Sons, Inc., 1969), a pp. 255–256; b 188–189.

20. John Walton, *Administration and Policy-Making in Education* (Baltimore: The Johns Hopkins Press, 1959), p. 104.

21. David H. Rhinelander, "Hartford Hospital Notes First in Attitude Survey Program," *The Hartford Courant,* Sunday, February 26, 1967, p. 24.

22. Reed K. Clegg, *The Administrator in Public Welfare* (Springfield, Illinois: Charles C. Thomas, Publisher, 1966), pp. 71–72.

23. Robert L. Barker and Thomas L. Briggs, *Differential Use of Social Work Manpower* (New York: National Asosciation of Social Workers, 1968), a p. 53; b 270.

24. Laura Epstein, "Differential Use of Staff: A Method to Expand Social Services," *Social Work,* October 1962, a p. 66; b 66–67; c 68; d 72.

6 Board Functions and Relationships *

The social work administrator is responsible for working with and giving leadership to the board of his agency. The board may be either policy-making or advisory.

In this country, from its very beginning, there has been a great tradition of citizen participation and volunteer service in community affairs. Cohen calls citizen participation "the backbone of democracy." [1] Service on boards is a part of this system of personal responsibility for meeting social welfare needs. Seider sets it in a broad framework: "Volunteers are a traditional and integral part of the American social welfare system. . . . The specific duties assigned differ from agency to agency. . . . These may be classified as: (1) identifiers of human conditions or problems requiring social welfare services; (2) initiators and makers of policy in agencies created to prevent, control, or treat the social condition; (3) contributors of service based on knowledge, skill, and interest; (4) solicitors of public and voluntary support; (5) spokesmen and interpreters of agency program and problems to which they are directed; (6) reporters of community reaction, critical or positive, to the agency's program; and (7) collaborators in community planning activities for the purpose of modifying or designing services to meet changing social conditions." [2]

As was reported in a national survey, "volunteer work, in general, can be divided into three types: executive and policy-making, administrative, and direct service. The job of the board volunteer is essentially advisory or policy-making, as it has been traditionally. Such volunteers are found not

* Most of the material in this chapter appeared in Harleigh B. Trecker, *Citizen Boards at Work: New Challenges to Effective Action* (New York: Association Press, 1970).

only on the boards of voluntary and non-profit agencies but also participating in such community services as school boards, planning, and other local government operations. Administrative volunteers may be engaged primarily in fund raising, but their functions may also include assisting in management or supervising other volunteers. In some private agencies, volunteer members control personnel policy, set salary standards, and negotiate union contracts. Service volunteers give direct assistance to the agency client." [3]

Administrative Philosophy and the Board

As Millett puts it, "Administration is not and cannot be a one-man show. No enterprise can be performed by one person, unless it is the most simple of endeavors. Administration usually involves the cooperative efforts of many persons. Indeed, administration is a system of people working together, it is a pattern of cooperative activity in which the specialized talents of various individuals are brought together to achieve a common purpose. By definition, I am disposed to say that administration is a team operation." [4]

As has been stated previously, the social work administrator must have a philosophy which is basic to the carrying forward of the work of his agency. The following concepts are offered as a summary of that philosophy:

1. *The concept of the work group:* Social welfare services are carried on by groups of people working together to solve problems, to make decisions, to establish legislation, to create policy, to determine needs, to develop programs and procedures. These *work groups* include the board, the staff, various committees, community groups, and others. Some of these groups are established by the legal instruments of the agency, namely, the articles of incorporation, the constitution, or the by-laws. Some of the groups are special ones set up to deal with special problems. Each group, whether it be regular or special, has authority, responsibility, and limits as granted by the legal articles or the appointing authority. While each group is similar to every other group, each group is also different. Some groups are made up of direct service participants, and some are made up of representatives who are a number of steps removed from the services being rendered. Boards usually fall into this category, but increasingly, service participants and recipients of service are being included on boards.

2. *The concept of leadership:* The various work groups mentioned above require leadership if they are to accomplish their assigned tasks. None of these groups is leaderless. All of them require the efforts of people, particularly prepared and particularly competent to enable them to understand their jobs and get them done. These leaders are both professional workers and volunteers. The methods they use should be essentially democratic.

3. *The concept of the leadership team:* In most community agencies

leadership is given to these work groups by teams of persons. The usual team consists of the professional worker and the lay or volunteer worker. By this is meant the chairman of the Board of Education and the superintendent of schools; the chairman of the board and the social agency administrator; the library board and the professional librarian. This team pattern proceeds across the agency structure with committee chairmen frequently teaming up with related staff members and so on. Teamwork is the heart of democratic administrative leadership. In fact, the way the social work administrator and the volunteer board president work together does much to set the tone of the entire organization.

4. *The concept of structure:* In every community agency there are many work groups going about their affairs, simultaneously. Thus, it is necessary to arrange these groups into a form of organization or structure which will show people as being interconnected and in communication with each other. Out of the continuous relatedness and communication of these work groups comes the totality of the agency or organization.

5. *The concept of time and timing:* As the professional and volunteer team provide leadership for the work group, the work group goes through a cycle which can be plotted on a time continuum. Each session of the work group requires different leadership as the group becomes more able to fulfill its task role. Each session of the work group produces a product, and subsequent sessions grow out of what has been accomplished before. The leadership needs of the work group change, making it necessary for the leadership team to redefine the ways in which they will work. Leadership roles are dynamic and changing just as work groups are dynamic and changing.

6. *The concept of coordination:* Since the many work groups are engaged in a variety of tasks and are usually at different stages in their progress, they must coordinate their several separate efforts if maximum output is to occur. The task of providing the impetus for this coordination and the mechanisms for its occurrence is a primary one in the portfolio of the social work administrator and the board president. Coordination skills are also paramount in key leaders such as board presidents and social work administrators.

7. *The concept of reporting, decision-making, and implementation of decisions:* As the many work groups carry forward their endeavors, it is necessary to prepare reports for transmittal to the parent authority. Then decisions must be made and plans prepared for the implementation of the decisions. In all agencies, especially in large ones that have scores of work groups, the question of when to report, what to report, and to whom to assign followup is of great importance. Once this has been done, a new cycle of activity gets underway.

Functions of the Administrative Board

The functions of the administrative board can be summed up in this fashion. 1) To establish the legal or corporate existence of the agency, whether it be under the auspices of government or voluntary efforts; 2) To take responsibility for formulating general objectives, policies, and programs; 3) To inspire community confidence in the program because of the competence and dedication of the board members as active trustees of the agency; 4) To assume responsibility for the provision of adequate finances and to be accountable for the expenditure of funds; 5) To provide conditions of work, personnel policies, and staff. The board is particularly responsible for the selection and evaluation of the administrator; 6) To understand and interpret the work of the agency to the community; 7) To study, know, and interpret general community needs to the agency staff; 8) To relate the services of the agency to the work of other agencies and to concentrate upon the improvement of community conditions; 9) To conduct periodic evaluations of agency operations with a view toward improving and strengthening the amount and quality of work that is done; 10) To provide the continuity of experienced leadership so that major staff changes will not weaken the agency.

Writing from his perspective as a social work administrator, Schmidt lists nine responsibilities of the board: "1) Attaining the goals or purposes of the agency . . . making certain that the established goals are being pursued and advising when the goals need changing because of changed conditions. . . . 2) Creating the structure . . . the board has the responsibility of seeing to it that the agency's legal structure is proper and that it continues to remain so under all state and federal laws. . . . 3) Providing the necessary facilities . . . needed by an agency to conduct its activities. . . . 4) Employing the executive . . . select, fix compensation, establish duties, delegate to him the necessary authority to administer the work of the agency, evaluate his work, relieve him of his duties if necessary. . . . 5) Fixing the policies . . . It is the duty of the board to prescribe the services to be provided as well as the basic policies for the administration of these services. . . . 6) Setting the budget and providing the finances . . . The obligation rests upon the governing board to set the budget and thereby establish services. . . . 7) Checking the operation . . . The board must check the operations periodically and see to it that all is going well. . . . The trustees of an agency are accountable to the public for their stewardship of the agency. . . . They must know that the services are provided as they have directed. 8) Interpreting the services . . . is a special concern of the members of the governing board. . . . 9) Participating in community planning . . . The board has a clear duty to participate in community efforts to plan and raise funds for health and welfare operations." [5]

The Minnesota Department of Public Welfare has an excellent handbook for county welfare board members. In it they state: "In reviewing the role of the county welfare board it is necessary for the board as a group and as individual members to understand the legal basis for the composition and organization of welfare boards in the state of Minnesota . . . the law clearly states that it is the welfare board that has the responsibility for administering the public welfare program in Minnesota. Consequently, welfare board members must have an understanding of public welfare programs and services even though the board hires professional staff to carry out these responsibilities. First of all, it is incumbent upon the welfare board member to have some knowledge of public welfare and the social problems which exist on a state and nation-wide basis, as well as doing everything possible to increase his understanding of the needs of his own community and the social services which are required to alleviate or correct the social problems existing therein. Board members need to learn about the way in which their board is organized. They should learn about its chief functions and the way these functions should be performed so that an effective welfare program will be carried on in their community." [6]

The Administrator and His Work with the Board

The way the agency board and the administrator work together is of tremendous importance. This fact holds true in all fields of community service and in all types of agencies, governmental and voluntary. In thousands of social welfare agencies work is done by two groups of people. There are the hundreds of thousands of volunteer board members who enter into or offer themselves for service by their own free will and without remuneration. Working along with these volunteers are professional staff who have acquired special knowledge as a result of professional education and experience. They are engaged in social work as a means of livelihood. They have been hired to guide, advise, and work with the boards. There is a general agreement that both groups of workers are needed and have important tasks to do. Certain assumptions underlie the way they must work together if the goals of the enterprises are to be achieved.

A first assumption is that the volunteer board members and the professional workers of the agency constitute a leadership team. They are partners in a common task. In discussing the concept of partnership and shared responsibility one agency states, "Leadership in the Y.W.C.A. is both volunteer and employee. Volunteers bring to the Association not only their own individual skills, abilities, and often accumulated Y.W.C.A. experience but a broad knowledge of the community as well—its resources and organizations, its patterns of life, its feelings, its tensions, its values, its sources of pride. The contributions of the employed leaders include individual skills and experience, knowledge of specialized resources for program and administration, an objective way of looking at the community and the Y.W.C.A. with understanding and insight, and concentrated time for the work." [7]

Second, it is assumed that professionals and volunteers have specific responsibilities as well as common and shared responsibilities. Both groups are fundamentally motivated by a common interest in and a wish to serve people. As for the professional workers, their primary role is that of carrying on or providing the program of professional services which the agency is set up to offer. For the volunteer workers, their chief responsibility is generally thought of as that of providing the conditions under which the agency may render the best quality of service. To a great extent there is an overlapping of responsibilities between professionals and board members. This will be elaborated upon later in the discussion of policy-making.

Third, it can be assumed that communication is of the utmost importance as board, staff, and administrator work together. They must be in continuous communication about the major concerns of the agency if they are to define, understand, and carry their separate and combined responsibilities.

Fourth, it is assumed that volunteer board members and professional workers have much to learn from each other. In fact, their learnings are continuous as board members glean insights from the problems faced by staff and as staff develop a grasp of the feedback from the community by the board.

If the above assumptions are correct, what is meant by the term "role" when used in connection with either the professional or the board member? In this context, role means a set of tasks which the individual is expected to perform in the defined agency situation. In other words, it is a work role. A work role is a function allocated to a particular person. In the social agency, role has the dimension of the task or what is expected of the person, and it has the further dimension of responsibility as to how the task will be done and in what time span. The concept further assumes that persons so entrusted with tasks will have the competence necessary to fulfill those tasks. Furthermore, to define the role of the professional worker it is necessary to define the role of the volunteer because what they do is so *interrelated*.

Admitting the fact that there are many variables of agency size, situation, community conditions, purposes, and so on, it is likely that the professional staff member will frame his role by selecting items from the task needs of the organization. Since the professional social worker is prepared by education and experience to bring professional knowledge and skill to the job, it is rightfully assumed that he is there to exercise his professional skills in providing service to people. The employing agency has hired him precisely for this reason. Consequently, his major role would seem to be that of doing the work of the agency. Since the board is the policy-making group which decides what work is to be done, it can be assumed that policy making is their primary role. Every board member, thus, commits himself to a partially predetermined role. But, because the agency is dynamic and changing, purposes, policies, and programs are also in a constant state of flux. This means that the professional worker has the further task of bringing to the policy-making board, information needed to arrive at sound policy judgments either in terms of formulation or revision. Thus, the professional worker cannot be removed from the policy-making process because he must carry the role of helping the policy-making group to arrive at the best possible decisions. The way in which the worker fulfills this policy participation role varies with the position in which he finds himself. Obviously, the agency administrator has a great responsibility in this realm, which would not hold true for the beginning junior staff member.

So the role of the volunteer board is policy determination. The board must determine policies regarding purpose, program, personnel, finance, public relations, and the like. But board members bring to the agency general life experience rather than specific professional education. Out of their general experience they have the responsibility to study and understand and interpret community needs for service. They must know the history, purpose, programs, policies, and prevailing procedures of the agency. They must seek constantly to evaluate the work of the agency to assure that policies are not only being carried out but that they are achieving the agency goals. But they cannot do this alone. They must do so in cooperation with the executive and staff. There must be a coming together of insight, experience, wisdom, and professional expertise. Policies, of course, are voted by the board, but no board can make wise judgments without the contribution of the staff members who have the firsthand experience with the services being rendered and the clientele being served.

A review of literature on the role of the social work administrator in his work with the board shows that the following points are frequently discussed. 1) The administrator instruments the policies of the board. 2) The administrator prepares reports, budgets, personnel recommendations, program plans, and other information to keep the board well informed. The administrator reports needs in the agency and the community which indicate that changes in services may be required. 3) The administrator is the liaison person between the board and the staff and other agencies. 4) The administrator is responsible for a program of in-service training to improve services. He helps board members to develop their skills both within agency service and externally in community relations. 5) The administrator is a key person in helping the board to understand its job and perform its tasks. However, he does not seek to dominate or control the board. 6) The administrator interprets policies and actions of the board in the agency and in the community. 7) The executive helps in the selection of board members but, of course, does not make the final selection.

In an interview study a number of social work administrators were asked to describe their role with the boards as they saw it and tried to carry it out. All of them stated that it was their responsibility to carry out the decisions of the board and to translate the board's policies into action. The majority felt that they were suppliers of information to the board as aides to the making of policy decisions. They felt that data such as reports of operating experience, service statistics, and the like were essential to effective board decision-making. Approximately three-fourths of the administrators interviewed saw the supplying of information as only a subsidiary part of their major role, namely that of supplying leadership for the board to help it develop policies, provide resources, and make the agency more valuable and useful to the community. They agreed that it was their continuing task to stimulate the board to devote time and attention to the major problems of the agency. They assumed that it was their job to encourage the board to develop its powers of judgment and discrimination in the always vital area of policy-determination. Recognizing the inevitable gap between the board and persons served, these administrators stressed the fact that they had a key job in helping the board to understand the program of services being offered. They saw themselves as interpreters of changing conditions in the community and as the initiators of program changes based upon revised policies.

The same administrators reported that they carried an important liaison role between the board and the staff. Frequently this role had dual aspects, helping the board members become aware of problems encountered by the staff in providing services (and staff problems in general) as well as interpreting staff attitudes and thinking; helping the staff to understand board thinking and attitudes. Other administrators reported that one of their major responsibilities was to work with individual board members to help them to develop their capabilities and to enable them to make the maximum possible contribution to the agency. Some administrators stated or implied that it was their role to bring and interpret the values, standards, and principles underlying good practice in their field of service.

As the interviewed administrators described their roles, certain words appeared again and again. The most frequently used words were to stimulate, to interpret, to guide, to motivate, to integrate, to initiate, to direct, to advise, and to suggest. Two-thirds of these administrators used several of these words denoting a philosophy of active leadership insofar as their work with the board was concerned.[8]

In another study [9] the author discovered that social work administrators saw their role with the board growing out of ten major areas of executive leadership responsibility that they felt had to be exercised in the total work of the agency. They stressed that they took responsibility for: planning and co-ordination, helping to formulate clear plans and then coordinating the work of various individuals and groups within the structure of the total agency; facilitating communication, keeping the channels open within the organization; presenting knowledge of the total agency so that various groups would develop understanding; providing an organized work environment in which group and individual tasks are defined, carried forward, and coordinated; helping to develop clear assignments of responsibilities for board and staff members; analyzing tasks in terms of their relevance to specific aspects of program; studying, understanding, and interpreting the community situation in which the work of the agency takes place; establishing and maintaining effective working relationships with the groups to which defined tasks have been assigned; making continuous and creative use of the purpose of the agency with the board, the staff, and the community; providing opportunities for individuals to experience creative growth in their jobs.

The Administrator and the Chairman of the Board

The way the board chairman and the agency administrator work together is a major factor in agency operation. If their relationship is a good one they can be fairly sure they will set a pattern for other relationships throughout the agency. If it is a poor one, this also will be influential.

The administrator and the board chairman are the persons who make up the primary leadership team. To lead effectively they must have: 1) An understanding and acceptance of and a deep commitment to the basic values of the agency; 2) Substantial knowledge of the professional services that the agency is rendering to people; 3) A strong identification with the fundamental purposes of the agency. Administrators and chairmen are continuously engaged in establishing effective working relationships with the people. Getting work done to accomplish agency purposes is primarily a matter of motivating people to their finest and highest levels of achievement.

As one observes effective board chairmen at work, they seem to have certain basic characteristics. *First,* they are well informed about the work of the agency; they have the facts; they know what they are talking about because they have spent long hours studying the work of the agency they represent. *Second,* they care deeply about the work of the agency; they couple competence and concern with commitment. *Third,* they see the connection between conditions which exist in the community and the need for the agency to provide services. *Fourth,* they know how to work within and through their organization and in cooperation with other organizations that have similar goals. *Fifth,* they have a sense of history and a grasp of the processes of orderly, democratic change. *Sixth,* the effective chairman is generally aware of what is happening in the field and strives to keep up with new developments and new trends.

What are some of the major responsibilities carried by the leadership team of the administrator and the board chairman? A partial list would include: 1) They are responsible for giving leadership to the continuous process of identfying community needs. 2) They are responsible for giving leadership to, defining, and realizing agency purposes. 3) They are responsible for giving leadership to provisioning the agency in terms of financial resources and other forms of support. 4) They are responsible for giving leadership to the development of program and services. 5) They are responsible for giving leadership to the development of a form of organization and structure which will support the program. 6) They are responsible for giving leadership to the continuing process of policy formulation and reformulation. 7) They are responsible for giving leadership to the evaluation of the agency. 8) They are responsible for giving leadership to the change process.

However, in carrying these responsibilities the chairman and the administrator clearly cannot do everything themselves. They must work with and through many persons in creative and productive ways. The work of the administrator and the board chairman is thus seen as a process of working with people in ways that release and relate their energies so that they use all available resources to accomplish the purpose of providing needed social welfare services and programs. People, resources, and purposes are thus brought together by the administrator and the board chairman in a continuous dynamic process. The administrator and the chairman, as the primary leadership team, are seen as working with people to establish and maintain a system of cooperative effort with the total agency as the point of focus. Because many people must carry separate and specific tasks if the agency is to do its work, and because they inevitably see only a part of the picture, the job of seeing the whole agency and providing over-all leadership falls to the administrator and the board chairman.

The board chairman and the administrator are also responsible for community leadership. This means the taking of initiative in helping people know about, understand, and hopefully be in support of the important work that the agency is doing. It also means sharing leadership with other agencies that have like goals and that have a reasonable similarity of values and convictions as to what kind of a community it should be.

Of great importance in assessing the relationship between the executive and the board chairman is the extent to which they truly trust one another and have confidence in one another. When trust and confidence prevail, it is apt to permeate the institution and be reflected in the other essential team relationships among staff members and committee chairmen and the like. Here it is basic that board chairmen and administrators see their leadership as being essentially helping, enabling, and supporting, so that an increasing number of new leaders will be developed year after year. Thus, board chairmen and administrators must maintain many relationships simultaneously. They must make more decisions and more complicated decisions.

While the administrator is in no sense "supervised" by the board chairman, the chairman and the board do have the responsibility to evaluate the work of the executive at periodic intervals. Regular evaluation rather than crisis evaluation is of great importance. The executive has a right to know how the board views his work, and the board has the responsibility to share its views with him.

The Administrator, the Board, and Policy-making

One of the crucial responsibilities of the board and the administrator is that of policy-making. While there is widespread agreement that it is the job of the board to make policy and the job of the administrator to carry it out, there is ample evidence to support the thesis that it is not so simplistic as this sounds. In fact, the process of policy-making is so involved and so complicated today that it often looms as an area of conflict and confusion. As Stein pointed out, "We have been told in no uncertain terms that policy determination is the responsibility of the board alone, that policy execution is the responsibility of the executive and staff, that the executive is ultimately responsible for the results of agency programs. Nearly everyone understands these points, and yet boards and executives have had trouble ever since there were boards and executives. It is not, of course, only in social work that problems arise. Every field has its own version of the same *concerns*." [10]

Perhaps a part of the problem is caused by the fact that persons are not clear on the meaning of the term "policy." A look at a number of definitions reveals a variety of meanings. One national youth agency declares: "A policy is an established course of action to be followed in recurring situations. . . . Policies serve many purposes. They point the way for developing plans, solving problems, and attaining objectives. They provide the framework for carrying out the work and the means by which the board can delegate authority and still maintain control. They permit uniformity and consistency of action throughout the council. For example, in dealing with a question covered by a policy affecting troops, all personnel concerned are able to handle the question in the same way. They bring about quick and effective decisions. Without a governing policy it would be necessary to refer each case as it occurs to the board for decision. When there is a policy, the detection can be made at the point of occurrence without delay." [11]

In the field of education, one writer defines the role of the board as "legislative, that is, the establishing of policies and the role of the superintendent as administrative, or the carrying out of policies. By definition, policies are principles adopted by the board . . . to chart a course of action for its administrator and to define the limits within which he shall exercise judgment and directions. Essentially, policies are a guide to the what, why, and the how much of desired educational operations." The same authority states further that "rules and regulations, as distinguished from policies, are the detailed directions necessary to put policies into effect. They are more likely to be formulated by the administrator with the informal approval of the board than to be initiated or formally acted upon by the board itself. Essentially, rules and regulations provide a blueprint as to the how, the who, the when, and the where of actual educational practice. Procedures are working rules, or bylaws for the board itself as it regards its organization, meetings, . . . order of business, minutes and the like." [12]

With brevity and focus, Faatz said agency policies are written statements which "express the purpose, intentions, conditions under which the agency effectuates the service for which it was created." [13]

Reid says, "The board's responsibility includes establishing the basic policies of the agency and constantly reexamining and modifying those policies." [14] Sher agrees that "the board has a profound responsibility, in partnership with administration, to establish policies dealing with such matters as determining priority in offering service. Equally important, it should join with other enlightened people in the community to determine ways and means of making such service available to the total community on a broader community and governmental level." In addition, Sher observes, "If policies are to be wisely fashioned, they must stem from a basic grasp of the agency's purpose within the community and of the extent to which that purpose is met by the agency." [15]

Sorenson declares, "Policy formulation and planning are the responsibility of both board and committee members and of professional staff. . . . Policy determination is the responsibility of the board alone. . . . Policy execution is the responsibility of the executive and his staff." [16]

There is increasing evidence to support the notion that while the board must determine what the policy is to be, a great many people should be involved in working with the board to help it understand how to make wise policy decisions. Surely the administrator and the staff have a great deal to contribute. But what about the persons being served by the program? Some would say that clients should have no part in the policy process. Yet how can the policy be in tune with the views of the constituency unless they too are involved? There is a rising tide of feeling that policies should not be made by remote boards and then simply imposed upon persons on a "take it or leave it" basis. As Jennrich declared, "All persons affected by policy should have some part in creating it, and any social agency that operates under the hoary concept that the board alone makes policies and the staff alone carries them out, should be well on the road to extinction. Ideally, on major policies, neither the executive nor his board nor staff should make final decisions, since the community that picks up the check for these costly services should be involved. Only as we work toward responsible participation and integration of policy-making and operations can we have a dynamic agency." [17]

In his study of voluntary social welfare agencies, Kramer isolated four variables that influence the extent to which the will of the board or the executive will predominate in the policy process: "1) The organizational structure of the agency; its size, complexity, and degree of bureaucracy. 2) The character of the agency's services or program, whether they are technical or highly professionalized in content or conceived as residual or institutional in character. 3) The type of policy issues, e.g., programmatic, housekeeping, professional, ideological, or fiscal. 4) Aspects of the board member's status and relationship to the agency, such as the duration of his membership, degree of financial responsibility and contributions, role as a consumer of agency services or participant in its program, number of his other organizational affiliations, and his social status in the community. 5) The executive's professional status and duration of employment . . . the executive exerts a greater influence than the board member in the policy process to the extent that these variables are maximized." [18]

What are the sources of data, information, opinion, thinking and feeling that must be considered in the important task of policy-making? Beyond the defined purpose of the agency it seems necessary to recognize that other things enter into policy-making. *First,* there is the matter of specific community characteristics and conditions that will influence what services should be provided, to whom they are to be given, and how they should be conducted. *Second,* there is a major source of policy material in the operating experience of the agency critically reviewed and evaluated. *Third,* suggestions from persons served, clientele, and general constituency represent a vital source of data and expression both regarding need for policies and how they should be stated. *Fourth,* current best practice as revealed by study and research in the field should be considered. *Fifth,* interagency cooperative projects often provide useful material for policy determination. *Sixth,* special committees such as professional advisory groups may offer experience particularly pertinent to a given policy problem. *Seventh,* agencies that are a part of a national organization may receive much help from communicating with their parent body.

The process of policy determination consists of a series of steps or phases in which many persons play a part. The board, the administrator, the staff, the constituency, and the community must all become involved. Any one of these groups or individuals within them may feel, recognize, and express the need for a stated policy to guide some phase of the work of the agency. The policy process thus can begin at any point. When the need is recognized and accepted by the board, responsibility for fact-gathering and preliminary formulation of tentative policy must be assigned. The assignment can be made to the administrator and the staff, or it can be made through a board committee, or it can be made to a joint committee of board, staff, and constituency. In any event, as a matter of principle, those persons to be affected by the policy should participate in the presentation of facts, suggestions, and ideas prior to the first formulation. Although they may not be legally responsible for the ultimate decision, their views are important if the final policy is to be understood and followed.

Ordinarily, it is wise and helpful to prepare a trial formulation of a new policy and give consideration to the implications of it before it is enacted. Thought must be given to the effect of the policy on persons served, program, budget, staff workload, and community relations. It is time well spent to check up on the impact of the policy in advance of adoption. In some situations a new policy may be tried out on a time-limited basis before it is enacted as a permanent one. When a policy has been adopted it is vital that a timetable be established for its review and a decision made as to who will be responsible for the review. When major policy changes are to be made, time must be devoted to advance interpretation of them as a way of preparing the persons affected by them. As a general rule, policy-making should proceed in an atmosphere of openness and sharing with maximum participation on the part of the people involved. Good policies grow out of a process of participation on the part of many individuals and groups. They are evolutionary and flow out of operations to a great extent. Policies are tools for the board, the administrator, and the staff, and the constituency to use. Policies should be positive statements clearly offered as helpful tools for those who follow and implement them.

In summary, good policies should be based upon and develop out of the agency purpose. Adequately evaluated facts are the essential ingredients in policy formulation and reformulation. Persons affected by policy should share in the creation of it. There must be an organic unity and consistency among the various policies of the agency, and the relationships between policies and purposes should be apparent. Although the board has the legal responsibility for the final determination of policy, the entire agency should participate in the process leading up to the final decision. Policy-making, planning, and operations are integrally related and cannot be disassociated. New policies should grow out of the evaluation of the effectiveness of old policies. The carrying out of policies in the spirit of their intent is an integral part of the administrative responsibility of the administrator and the staff.

Problems of Administrators and Boards

In some agencies the administrator and the board seem to have difficulty in working together. There seem to be problems which must be dealt with. *First,* there is the problem of confusion between board and administrator as to respective roles and responsibilities. In some situations the board and the administrator seem to be working at cross-purposes and getting in one another's way. The most serious problem seems to center around the difference between policy determination which is the primary legal responsibility of the board and administration of policy which is the job of the administrator and the staff. When clarity is lacking with reference to these functions, there are bound to be many situations where major difficulties can arise. *Second,* in far too many agencies, particularly the large ones, there is inadequate communication, slow communication, or even breakdown in communication between the administrator and the board. Under these circumstances the board is not fully informed as to what is going on and, as a result, it is out of touch with current policies, programs, and procedures. Consequently, it may work at cross-purposes and with a considerable waste of energy. *Third,* sometimes administrators feel that board members are not doing a good job of interpretation in the community. They feel that they are not utilizing their normal and natural community contacts to tell the story of the agency effectively and to build growing public understanding. This same charge is sometimes stated by board members who feel that the administrator as the first-line representative in the community fails to capitalize on opportunities for good public relations. *Fourth,* in some cases the board fails in its responsibility to do a regular, comprehensive evaluation of the work of the administrator. The administrator does not know where he stands. In some instances the failure to evaluate periodically has resulted in very serious problems. *Fifth,* in some cases the administrator does not really want the help of the board and prefers to operate as a one-man agency.

Problems of the kind listed above are in no way new, unusual, or universal. Every situation is different and no one situation will have all of these problems, but most situations have a chance of occasionally having some of them. When these problems exist they result from reasons which can be enumerated. For example, agencies have not given enough thought and study to the matter of board-administrator relationships. They have tended to assume that good relationships develop automatically without any particular planned effort. Some agencies have not been careful enough in choosing the administrator, and they have not been careful enough in choosing board members. Consequently, incompatibility results.

When the administrator and the board are working in harmony the agency can be seen and felt as united. The responsibility for achieving this unity is shared by both parties.

NOTES

1. Nathan Cohen, *The Citizen Volunteer* (New York: Harper, 1960), Chap. 3.
2. Violet Seider, "Volunteers," *Encyclopedia of Social Work* (New York: National Association of Social Workers, 1965), pp. 830–836.
3. *American Volunteer,* Manpower/Automation Research Monograph No. 10, April 1969, p. 7. U.S. Department of Labor, Manpower Administration.
4. John D. Millett, "National Conference of Professors of Educational Administration," *The Community School and Its Administration,* Vol. IV, No. 1, September 1965, p. 2.

5. William D. Schmidt, *The Executive and the Board in Social Welfare*. (Cleveland: Howard Allen, Inc., 1959), pp. 39–50.
6. *Handbook for County Welfare Board Members* (St. Paul, Minnesota, Division of Field Services, Minnesota Department of Public Welfare, n.d., p. 23.
7. *The Board and the Executive Director*. (New York: National Board, Y.W.C.A., 1953), p. 6.
8. Harleigh B. Trecker, *Social Agency Boards—An Exploratory Study* (School of Social Work, University of Connecticut, 1958.
9. Harleigh B. Trecker, "Understandings of Administration," *Y.W.C.A. Magazine,* (June 1960).
10. Herman D. Stein, "Board, Executive, and Staff," *Social Welfare Forum 1962*. (Published for the National Conference on Social Welfare by Columbia University Press, 1962), p. 217.
11. *The Council Manual,* Copyright © 1960, 1969 by Girl Scouts of the U.S.A., p. 23. Used by permission.
12. Edward M. Tuttle, *School Board Leadership in America,* rev. ed., (Danville, Ill.: The Interstate Printers, 1963), p. 107. Reproduced by special permission of the author and copyright owner, Edward Mowbray Tuttle.
13. Anita J. Faatz, *The Nature of Policy in the Administration of Public Assistance* (Pennsylvania School of Social Work, University of Pennsylvania, Philadelphia, 1943).
14. Joseph H. Reid, "The Board's Responsibility" in *The Board Member of a Social Agency* (New York: Child Welfare League of America, Inc., 1957), p. 26.
15. David Sher, "Boards Must Do More Than Manage," in *Making Yours a Better Board* (New York: Family Service Association of America, 1954), pp. 36–38.
16. Roy Sorenson, *The Art of Board Membership* (New York: Association Press, 1950), p. 30.
17. Lorraine H. Jennrich, "Social Policy Comes from Knowing Families" in *Making Yours a Better Board* (New York: Family Service Association, 1954), p. 35.
18. Ralph M. Kramer, "Ideology, Status, and Power in Board-Executive Relationships," *Social Work,* October 1965, p. 114.

7 Constituency Participation and Cooperation

One of the newest developments in social work administration is the extent to which agencies are seeking to involve the persons they serve in the administration of the agency. While it is true that social agencies have always had some kind of a relationship with clientele or constituency, the trend in recent years has been to make this relationship more meaningful and truly dynamic.

Many of the institutions of society are undergoing a similar surge of interest in, even demand for, relevant participation on the part of persons served. Colleges and universities, public schools, churches, government agencies are all engaged in one way or another in restructuring their services so that a greater share in governance is allocated to the clientele. The power to make decisions once reserved exclusively for the board has now shifted to include staff and constituency in appropriate ways. Thus, the social work administrator must develop his skill in working effectively with the persons the agency serves.

The Importance of Participation

In field after field the importance of broad participation has been accented. In community organization and planning the matter of citizen participation has received extended treatment. Gurin and Perlman offer a brilliant discussion of the theory of participation and raise a number of fundamental questions. They state:

In the social welfare field, planning and community organization have been closely linked, particularly at the local community level. The common element is citizen participation, a concept that holds a firm place, historically, in all types of social welfare activities. In theory, the responsibility for setting goals and developing plans lies with the responsible policy-making bodies of the community and the professional role is one of serving these groups and enabling them to achieve their objectives. So much has been written on this subject in recent years, that we feel no need to review the different concepts of planning roles that have been put forward. Let us assume it has been demonstrated that the so–called enabling role is never pure, and that it is intermixed with elements of expertness and leadership. There remain the issues of *what* citizen? Participation in *what*? These questions need further discussion. Citizens' participation involves both the development of plans, including setting goals, and the implementation of plans. There has always been interest in developing citizen participation in both areas. Each presents its own problems. On the level of formulating goals and policies, it is not always clear where the responsibilities should lie. Even in areas where the responsibility is fixed by legislation, as in the case of boards of education or departments of public welfare, there is room for discretion in the extent to which this responsibility will be shared by others, at least in an advisory capacity. Since there is no such single entity as a "community," it becomes necessary to locate and choose the people who are to engage in these roles, and to develop a rationale that will provide the criteria for such selection. The engineering of participation, hopefully democratic, therefore becomes a major planning function in itself. The tendency to stress direct participation by citizens in formulating the policy of operating agencies obscures the fact that the basic structure for participation in a democratic society is the governmental system, whereby citizens participate in formulating policy, not directly, but through their representatives. In major issues of social welfare, such as taxation, income maintenance, and provision of general services for the entire population, the crucial decisions are legislative. For policy to be established, the will of the people must be transmitted through the actions of those who make the laws. The function of community organization and social action is in large part to influence the lawmakers. That function is widely distributed through society. Administrators in charge of executing programs are a major element in policy formulation, and much of their planning is inevitably directed toward influencing the lawmakers to enhance and improve the programs for which they carry responsibility.[1]

Since it is evident that the agency constituency has a function within the agency beyond that of merely accepting services, the administrator must understand the place of constituents in the total administrative process of the agency. Among the many contributions of the constituency are: *first,* they can be helpful in pointing out the needs which must be met; *second,* constituency can give expression regarding the kinds of programs or services that are most likely to meet these needs; *third,* constituency can participate helpfully in the process of policy formulation and reformulation; *fourth,* constituency can become a vital resource for agency interpretation and support; *fifth,* constituency can assist the agency in evaluating the quality of its work and can suggest ways of improving the services.

Carlton says: "It seems to me that every voluntary social service agency today should seek the participation of those who use its services, its consumers, in formulating policy and judging program. . . . The reality is that no matter what the service may consist of, even though it involves the most highly technical, professional care, such as surgery in a hospital, the voice of the recipient of the services, patient, client, neighbor, local resident, consumer—whatever he's called—must be piped to management loud and clear. I state this categorically because the evidence of functional breakdown is so clear when his voice is not heard." [2]

It is interesting to note that one study revealed little real participation on the part of welfare clients. In 1962 Schwartz and Chernin made a study of the participation of recipients in public welfare planning and administration. They found "that public welfare agencies had had little experience with client participation other than at the level of the caseworker-client relationships." They felt "that experimentation in recipient participation in welfare agency programming could profitably be initiated at local levels by group discussions with recipients and subsequent appointments of recipients to advisory committees. The results of this study further indicate that the incorporation of welfare recipient opinion into welfare agency planning might have a beneficial effect on the operation of these agencies and could stimulate new responses in welfare recipients by making them more aware of themselves as contributing members of society." [3]

The Poor as a Constituent Group

The passage of the federal Economic Opportunity Act of 1964 in Section 202 (a) (3) dealing with community action programs states that the program must be "developed, conducted, and administered with the maximum feasible participation of residents of the areas and members of the groups served." [4] This mandate from the Congress has had a profound influence not only on the anti-poverty projects but on many different kinds of community services.

A number of authorities have begun to do evaluative research on the "maximum feasible participation" concept.[5] Studies have been made of the types of participation, the extent to which the poor are really involved in policy-making as board members, and the relative impact of their involvement. While findings vary, there is general agreement that the poor have much to contribute to the process of understanding community needs.

Sylvester offers a penetrating discussion of the reasons why the poor must become more involved in all social welfare programs and he suggests several important roles for the poor as constituent groups:

The demands upon the bureaucracies are consistent, varied and competing. All too often that pressure group which is most vocal or best organized sees its demands gratified, despite contrary national priorities. Therefore, the poor must press their interests constantly, not just at the top of the bureaucracies, but up and down the line at every level of decision. Almost every interest in this country has, within the Federal establishment and most State and Local governments, people who in addition to their regular duties, understand and represent its specific point of view. In the Labor Department many officials are from the unions and the labor movement. Similarly, the Office of Education is inhabited by educators from the establishment. They are present in the daily dialogue that takes place while policies are developed, decisions are made and procedures promulgated. But there are no poor anywhere and very few blacks where it really counts.

Now, partially as a result of OEO and the Poor People's Campaign, some correction is taking place. Commitments to include representatives of the poor on a wide range of governmental advisory committees are being implemented. This is no easy task, considering the fact that HEW alone has nearly 500 of them.

Representation of the poor on committees is not the answer in itself. I should like to propose at least three other devices. These proposals are based on the notions that our institutions, in their present form, have some, but not all, of the ability to serve the poor; that these institutions are not going to adjust rapidly to the current need; and that it is more feasible to supplement their current capability than to try major overhauls and restructuring. I believe that all the foregoing supports these premises.

First, cohesive constituencies, capable of bringing about change within the framework of the service institutions themselves must be created. These constituents would serve to balance off the well-entrenched interests which do not represent the ultimate client population. Such creation will be slow—perhaps almost evolutionary. . . . Secondly, these same constituencies must operate to bring about changes in the constraints and parameters within which the institutions function. This too will be slow developing. The real rules of institutional practices are highly sophisticated, more often than not hidden, and almost always quite different from those on the books. An excellent example, at least at the national level, concerns the relation between the executive branch and the legislative branch, the latter being a particularly complex and almost unfathomable bureaucracy. It is, however, very effective in its own way. This relationship is carried on in such a way as to make it almost impossible for the citizens of this country, rich or poor, to determine with any certainty exactly where the root of a problem lies. And yet, this knowledge is absolutely essential if the democratic process is to have real meaning. The poor and black, of course, are doubly handicapped. The shell game of who did what to whom and when and why leaves the unsophisticated little idea of where the pressure points are and no idea of when to apply the pressure. . . . all of this compounds the difficulty for any concerned constituency which attempts to change the external framework and to gain helpful allies in the effort. . . . Third, is the need to develop a series of new public and private institutions to span the gap between the poor and the black and the large existing institutions. These new institutions should operate at the local level and should serve to shortstop and resolve many problems at that level. They should serve as conveyances into the existing institutions and they should train their clients in how to operate successfully with the existing institutions. This is not proposing anything really new—insofar as the total institution scene is concerned. What is suggested in large part is an adaptation of techniques tried in other areas, to the problems of the poor and the black. Nor is any great increase in bureaucracy meant. These new institutions ought to be accommodated out of the continuing expansion of existing institutions—particularly state and local governments." [6]

As Piven points out, "The anti-poverty project itself is a potential arena for resident participation. This has lately become something of a public issue and several different organizational forms of participation are being recommended: (1) Residents should participate on policy-making structures—ordinarily the board—either on the city-wide or local level. These residents are regarded as representatives of the resident population in the areas served. It is this kind of participation that has usually been associated with the legislative mandate for 'maximum feasible participation of residents.' A certain proportion of the seats on these structures are allocated to residents, with different schemes—elections, appointments, or conventions—for selecting them. These arrangements have often been the occasion for tugging and hauling among various groups, local and city-wide, for controlling influence. (2) Residents should participate as staff. These programs, generally referred to as the employment of indigenous or nonprofessional workers, are among the most widely used of the poverty program strategies. (3) Residents should be formed into active constituent groups. These groups are sometimes recommended as a program resource for professional staff, providing feedback for program evaluation, or they may be regarded as pressure groups that properly influence the project in its activities." [7a] Piven then raises some fundamental questions: "Whatever patterns developed in the anti-poverty projects for resident participation will reflect answers to two sets of questions: (1) Who should participate? In what action should they participate? Where should this participation be located in the organizational structure? What conditions should govern this action? (2) How can participation by the specified group, and in the prescribed forms, be elicited and maintained; i.e., what are the effectuating mechanisms for the forms of participation prescribed by the answers to the first set of questions above?" [7b]

The welfare rights movement born in the mid-1960s has become a force of some importance in the social welfare field. As Paull points out, "The new welfare rights movement is a recent organizing attempt by public assistance recipients to protect their civil rights and improve conditions in the welfare system. Starting with isolated client groups that are generally coalescing, this movement is a spontaneous combustion of the festering grievances and indignities of welfare clients—the rock bottom of the nation's poor." [8a]

In evaluating the rise of the welfare rights movement, Paull then says, "Social workers as individuals have been aiding the organizing efforts of the new group, but professionals have not been the prime movers, and taken as a whole, professional response has not crystallized. Two interesting questions are raised, however, by the development of the new movement: (1) What will be the response of social workers who are also administrators, supervisors, or otherwise within the structure maintaining the public programs? (2) How will social workers in a community organization and the profession as a whole respond to a movement that is controlled by clients, reserves no endowed status roles for the professional, and frequently collides with the professional operating in the program under attack? The public responses of social workers in administrative and leadership roles of public agencies so far offer no clear-cut answers to the first question. Some have welcomed the protest, explained the nature of their own limited authority to the groups, and helped them to identify the appropriate sources for change. They have managed to fulfill their institutional stewardship responsibilities while leaving no doubt of their support for change. Others have developed a defensive stance and have justified the existing system. For the profession as a whole, the issue has not been sharpened as yet to confrontation and decision." [8b]

In reviewing their experiences with organizations of welfare clients, Rabagliati and Birnbaum say, "It seems clear that a neighborhood-based organization of welfare clients acting alone can do very little to change the welfare system. A nation-wide organization of welfare clients now exists which hopes ultimately to put such pressure on the total welfare system that it will ultimately have to change. It remains to be seen what changes such an organization will bring about. Although it would probably extract from the welfare system much more than is now given to clients, such a strategy also tends to overlook the possibility that repressive measures will be taken against individual clients as well as against the agency that sponsors such welfare organizations." [9]

Client Complaints and Pressures

Among the complaints registered by clients of social welfare agencies is that they are often treated routinely rather than as individuals. In addition, they complain of excessive red tape complicated by obsolete rules and regulations. Frequently, they see the agency as an inflexible instrument unable to meet their particular needs. Now and then, because services are poorly organized, the client feels that he is getting a "run-around" because jurisdictions between agencies are confused. Very often the client feels that he is treated with indifference and abruptness because workers are so frequently under pressure. In addition, the client sometimes feels that the staff is not really interested in his problem and is more interested in the problems of other people. Of course, a major complaint is the inadequacy of welfare grants, which are frequently so low that clients cannot live at even a minimum standard of decency and health.

Client pressure groups have emerged in a number of cities. The protest demonstration, the sit-in, and other tactics have been used. Administrators have had to cope with these disruptive pressure tactics. In one state, policy guidelines have been formulated by the central administration of the state welfare department. These guidelines are reproduced below.

CONNECTICUT STATE WELFARE DEPARTMENT

GUIDELINES FOR EMERGENCY CONDITIONS
IN DISTRICT WELFARE OFFICES DURING DEMONSTRATIONS

1. It shall be a policy of the State Welfare Department to seek out and initiate, wherever possible, positive avenues of communications between the Welfare recipient and the Welfare Department.

2. Meetings with Welfare recipients will be encouraged at neutral meeting sites.

3. If meetings with Welfare recipients cannot be accomplished at a neutral meeting site, the meeting will be held in a meeting room separated from the office area.

4. In the event of a demonstration by an organization of Welfare recipients or any other organization protesting Welfare policy every effort will be made by the Welfare administration to persuade the group to meet with the Department at a neutral meeting site or in one of the aforementioned meeting areas.

5. If the group refuses to meet with the administration under these conditions, the Welfare employees will be vacated from the interview and reception areas to the inner office area.

6. The doors to the inner office area will be locked to prohibit admission of any demonstrating group.

7. In all situations where it is known that groups are preparing to gather or when they have gathered in District Office waiting rooms or interview areas and are threatening to sit in or invade staff work areas, the District Director is to advise the local police chief and request that he be prepared to provide protection for staff and assure the orderly behavior of such groups.

If it is evident that groups gathered in District Office waiting rooms and interview areas are about to attempt or are attempting to gain access to staff work areas, the District Director is to advise such group that he will request the assistance of the local police department to prevent access. If the group persists in attempting to enter off limit areas assistance from local police will be immediately requested.

Should the demonstrating group gain admission to the staff area and present a clear and present danger to the safety and well-being of the staff, administrative action will be taken to assure that the health and safety of the employees is safeguarded.

If it is clearly indicated, the District Director shall, with the approval of the Chief of the Bureau of Social Services, instruct the staff to leave the work area.

On the basis of such factors as the size and composition of the group, their attitude, the time of the day, and the condition of the work area, the District

Director is to advise staff through whatever means available, of the time that staff is to return to work. No leave is to be charged against an employee when released under these conditions by the District Director.

The District Director may request the stationing of uniformed security officers within District Offices at any time it is clearly indicated. Durational approval may be granted considering the intensity and frequency of the demonstrations and the capability to physically secure the District Office.

The Need to Work Together

Ortof discusses "the need for board, staff and the users of agency services to find new ways of communicating and working together. If we are really to become relevant and change our view, we must simultaneously understand that the sponsors, whoever they may be, public or private, and the professionals—whether they are trained or untrained—and the users of the service, cannot all be jaunty, jolly partners in an enterprise. We must face the fact that these different estates have different angles, different perceptions, different views, different needs, and that indeed there is not peace and harmony between and amongst these estates. There has to be conflict, clash, controversy, and difference. Those of us who would rather see everything peaceful and quiet will never truly and honestly engage and join the issues, or the sponsors, the ones who give the funds; or the staff of the agency, either trained or untrained; nor the users of the service. Our experiences, whether we be lay or professional, should make us realize that the categories mentioned above do not see the service, nor the function of the agency in the same way. There are differences and if we pooh-pooh them and sweep them under the rug and try to find mental hygiene approaches for working everything out, it may very well continue to lead us nowhere with respect to steps forward and progress. My experience in the last three years of working with the poverty program has only sharpened my awareness of this situation, and, in my opinion, we must come to terms with it and not be frightened by it. Controversy, conflict, and differences must be accepted as a beginning basis for making our agencies more relevant through changing their function and truly involving the users of the services." [10]

Out of his rich experience in the juvenile delinquency area, Mogulof observes:

Projects must make clear to those involved what their function is and what authority they have with regard to developing policy. The poor may be involved in policy groups as representatives of the different groups the project seeks as constituents. Or groups of target area residents may be involved on an ad hoc or continuing basis fof the purpose of advice and/or sanction. The difference between advice and sanction in dealing with neighborhood representatives is critical. In many of the delinquency projects, neighborhood groups were established on levels subordinate to the projects' top policy group. In some instances the program planners wanted to develop and test ideas by using target area residents as advisors. However, members of the locally based group thought (or were led to think) that they had the authority to sanction as well as to give advice. Sometimes demonstration projects were not honest with neighborhood residents because they thought they could engineer their consent without giving them any real sanction over policy. Often, of course, they were successful. When they were not successful and yet did not intend to have policy sanction rest with a local group, neighborhood residents often became hostile to the project. Whether or not neighborhood representatives are to have policy sanction must be decided individually by each community. But it *must* be decided and this decision must be communicated to those involved. Needless to say, it is easier for neighborhood groups to accept a decision denying their right to sanction policy when their representatives are part of the project's top policy echelon. This does not mean that projects ought to deny sanctioning authority to local groups. In a specific community, target populations may be the most relevant source of power for a project and any program decided upon that did not have the sanction of significant target community groups could not be implemented.[11]

NOTES

1. Arnold Gurin and Robert Perlman, "Current Conceptions of Planning and Their Implications for Public Welfare" in David G. French, ed., *Planning Responsibilities of State Departments of Public Welfare* (Chicago: American Public Welfare Association, 1967), pp. 19–20.
2. Winslow Carlton, "Agency Policy—Who Makes It—Who Controls It?" in *Twenty-Fifth Board Members' Institute Report* (New York: Federation of Protestant Welfare Agencies, 1967), p. 3.
3. Jerome L. Schwartz and Milton Chernin, "Participation of Recipients in Public Welfare Planning and Administration," *Social Service Review,* March 1967, p. 13 and p. 22.
4. "Economic Opportunity Act of 1964," Public Law 88–452, 88th Congress, S. 2642, August 20, 1964, p. 9.
5. Ralph M. Kramer, *Participation of the Poor—Comparative Community Case Studies in the War on Poverty* (Englewood Cliffs, N.J.: Prentice-Hall, Inc., 1969), pp. 6–18.
6. Edward C. Sylvester, Jr., "The Limited Response of Governmental Institutions to Rapid Social Change—and Some Alternatives" in "Achievements and Challenges," *The H.E.W. Forum Papers,* Second Series, 1968–69 (Washington, D.C.: U.S. Department of Health, Education and Welfare, 1969), pp. 31–33.
7. Frances Piven, "Participation of Residents in Neighborhood Community Action Programs," *Social Work,* January 1966, a p. 79; b 80.
8. Joseph E. Paull, "Recipients Aroused: The New Welfare Rights Movement," *Social Work,* April, 1967, a p. 101; b 106.
9. Mary Rabagliati and Ezra Birnbaum, "Organizations of Welfare Clients" in Harold H. Weissman, ed., *Community Development in the Mobilization for Youth Experience* (New York: Association Press, 1969), p. 1351.
10. Murray E. Ortof, "Agency Policy—Who Makes It—Who Controls It?" in *Twenty-Fifth Board Members' Institute Report* (New York: Federation of Protestant Welfare Agencies, 1967), p. 8.
11. Melvin B. Mogulof, "Involving Low-Income Neighborhoods in Antidelinquency Programs," *Social Work,* October 1965, pp. 53–54.

8 Effective Administrative Communication

The social work administrator must understand the importance of establishing and maintaining good communication channels within his agency and between his agency and the community. The administrator has primary responsibility for seeing to it that people are in communication with each other all of the time.

Based on their research, Ronken and Lawrence say, "The administrator needs primarily to be concerned with facilitating communication in the organization. This is a different way of thinking about the job of the administrator from one that is commonly encountered. Administrators frequently think of their job as being one of solving problems, formulating policy, making decisions, delegating authority and checking up to make sure that their subordinates are living up to their delegated responsibilities. It follows from their concept of their job, that they spend considerable time in making value judgments about their subordinates and trying to find the individual who was to blame for some trouble, in giving orders to subordinates and in trying to please their superiors so that they will give favorable judgments. On the other hand, could not the administrator more usefully hold the following assumptions about his job? 'I am best performing my job when I am maintaining the conditions for clear and candid communication with my associates. If I am doing my job well, it will follow that my associates and I, in fact, will be spending our time defining, clarifying and solving our mutual problems.' Instead of thinking it was up to him, the administrator, to supply the answers, the administrator would then be searching with others for answers in the situation itself."[1a]

Definition of Communication

Communication has been defined by many authorities. For example, Albers says: "Communication may be defined as the transfer of meaning from one person to another through signs, signals or symbols from a mutually understood language system." [2a]

Bellows says: "Communication determines quality and climate of human relationships and pervades work activity throughout an organization. Communication is intercourse by words, letters, symbols or messages; it is interchange of thoughts, opinions or prejudices; it is a way that one organization member shares meaning and understanding with another. It is a two-way channel for transmitting ideas, plans, commands, reports and suggestions among all appropriate tasks with an organization. It is the link that unites executives, employees and customers in a common enterprise and establishes a liaison between business, government and the public." [3]

Tead says, "Communication, beyond its techniques, is always the touching of mind to mind, of person to person, whether it is one man to a thousand diverse individuals, or one man to thirty in a single department. This process can be many things, including conversation, interview, dialogue, visual impress—all if they yield an interaction of one personality upon another. Hopefully the interaction will be affirmative and new agreements will be achieved. *Active consent is the important end.*" [4]

The Administrator and the Communications System

The social agency as pictured in Figure 8 is a system of inputs, relationships and outputs. The administrator as the central person in the system is responsible for seeing to it that the various persons within the agency are so organized that a communication system is always operating. As Hungate says, "Communication is a primary administrative tool; thus purposive communication must be studied in relationship to functional aspects of administration. Communication occurs in all organizations, whether or not it is purposefully considered by the administrator. However, it becomes more effective when it is given clarity by having a specific purpose. The broad purposes of communication are: (1) to secure action or cooperation; (2) to solve problems and facilitate decision-making; and (3) to keep all elements within the administrative structure informed. The purposes of administrative communication include: (1) to clarify what is to be done, how, and by whom. (2) to reinforce identity with agency purposes. (3) to transmit problems, suggestions, ideas. (4) to report progress. (5) to promote participation. (6) to promote social interchange or provide recognition. When communication fails, frequently it is because the originator did not have the specific purpose of the communication clearly in mind and did not know precisely enough the results to be achieved. Communication

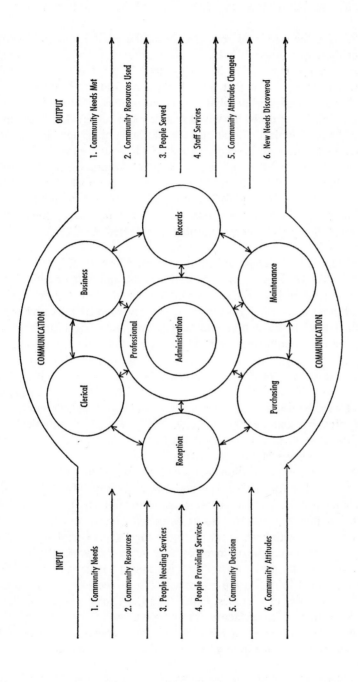

INPUT

1. Community Needs

2. Community Resources

3. People Needing Services

4. People Providing Services

5. Community Decision

6. Community Attitudes

OUTPUT

1. Community Needs Met

2. Community Resources Used

3. People Served

4. Staff Services

5. Community Attitudes Changed

6. New Needs Discovered

COMMUNICATION

COMMUNICATION

Business

Records

Clerical

Professional

Administration

Maintenance

Reception

Purchasing

Figure 8
Social Agency Inputs and Outputs

must be thought out clearly and logically and have a sharply defined purpose." [5]

In establishing the system of communication the administrator must ask and answer these questions: 1. Who are the communicators? Or who must be in continuous communication in our agency? 2. What is the content of communication or what is it that must be communicated? 3. Why is this content being communicated or what is the goal or reason for communicating this material? What decisions will it enable us to reach? 4. When must this content be communicated in terms of total timing of agency operations? 5. How should this content be communicated? Or what means or methods of communicating do we have at our disposal? 6. Where are the channels or networks both formal and informal in our organization which should be used to facilitate communication? The ways and means of communication must be based upon a clear understanding of the purposes sought, the nature of the material to be communicated or solicited, and, of course, the persons involved.

With reference to the communication system, Clegg says, "One of the necessary qualities of the successful executive is the ability to communicate ideas and information. In a welfare office, the dissemination of information is of utmost importance. Welfare programs are governed by laws and regulations which tend to be voluminous and which are subject to frequent change. It is a rare month when some change does not occur in regulations which alters welfare policies and procedures. The Welfare Administrator should treat the subject of communications with the importance it merits. He should express his ideas with clarity and precision and be able to get to the heart of what he wants to say or write. Having mastered these essentials, he should organize and develop an efficient system of communications within his department and devise methods to test systematically and periodically the effectiveness of the system itself." [6]

The test of the communication system is the extent to which the staff really works together for, as Ronken and Lawrence say, "In order to do their jobs effectively, . . . people must learn to perform their technical operations, but they must learn also to work with one another—to communicate effectively with each other and with their superiors. This process of learning how to communicate involves not merely the words that people use but even more the meanings that people assign to the spoken words. And each individual brings to the communication process certain personal equipment in the form of attitudes, expectations, feelings, and social skills or the lack of them. These factors must be taken into account by the administrator whose responsibility it is to develop teamwork in his organization, or to protect a functioning group against the disruptive effects of change." [1b]

As the chief architect of the communication system, the administrator must consider the communications he is receiving from others. He must evaluate this material and, as Albers says, "The executive should look beyond words in listening and reading. He should attempt to evaluate the information he receives from subordinates and others by asking himself questions. Are these the real facts? Does the communicator have direct access to the facts? To what extent is he relying upon information received from others? Does the message contain purely subjective judgments that may vary from person to person? In what respects may the message reflect individual or group vested interests? To what extent might the personality of the communicator have given the message a particular bias? These and similar questions can be helpful in determining the distortion that may be present in a message. Although deliberate distortion may also be involved, the present discussion is concerned with non-deliberate distortions evolving from semantic problems. In other words, the person doing the communicating is not consciously aware that his message is distorted." [2b]

Agency Structure and Communication

The structure of the agency should make for easy communication. Unfortunately, in the large hierarchical agency communication is often slow and incomplete. There are many decision centers and many types of information that must be passed along. As Albers sees it, "The management hierarchy may be viewed as a structure of communication centers through which decisional and control information is transmitted to and from the performance level. The volume of information that flows through this system is closely related to the extent to which decision making is centralized. Decisions made at the apex of the hierarchy involve more communication centers than those originating at lower levels. Too much centralization can easily overload the system and create bottlenecks in the flow of information. This problem is amplified with increases in the size of the management hierarchy, and it may significantly reduce the speed of decision making and the ability to adapt to dynamic operating conditions. A further difficulty is that information is frequently distorted as it passes through a long maze of hierarchical positions." [2c]

In Chapter 9, which deals with organization, the matter of structure will be examined with criteria for facilitating comunication spelled out.

Criteria of Effective Communication

Some of the criteria of effective communication are: 1. The purpose of the communication must be clear and must be understood by the person making it and by the person receiving it. 2. Both spoken and written material must be as clear as possible and subject to one and only one interpretation. If it is not possible to be this precise, every effort should be made to reduce the number of exceptions or options that are left open at the point of interpretation. 3. Effective communication is a series of consistent acts. In other words, subsequent communications are consistently related to earlier communications and avoid the hazard of nullification. 4. Good communication is adequate to accomplish its purpose; it is neither too much nor too little; it has a sharp focus and is selective as to content. 5. Good communication is timely in that thought is given to the timing at point of issue and the readiness on the part of the recipient. 6. In good communication, thought is given to the channels to be utilized and to the distribution, so that the right persons will receive the material. This usually requires a system which will make for not only downward and upward communication but for lateral communication as well.

NOTES

1. Harriet O. Ronken and Paul R. Lawrence, *Administering Changes* (Cambridge: Harvard University, Graduate School of Business Administration, 1952), a p. 315; b 291.
2. Henry H. Albers, *Principles of Organization and Management,* 2nd ed., (New York: John Wiley and Sons, Inc., 1965), a p. 71; b 442; c 193.
3. Roger Bellows, "Communication and Conformity," *Personnel Administration.* September–October 1960, pp. 21–28.
4. Ordway Tead, "Reflections on the Art of Administration," *Hospital Administration,* Winter 1959, p. 14.
5. Joseph I. Hungate, Jr., *A Guide for Training Local Public Welfare Administrators* (Washington: U.S. Department of Health, Education and Welfare—Welfare Administration—Bureau of Family Services, Division of Technical Training, 1964), p. 74.
6. Reed K. Clegg, *The Administrator in Public Welfare* (Springfield, Ill.: Charles C. Thomas, Publisher, 1966), p. 79.

9 Organization, Planning, and Coordination

The social work administrator must have skill in the areas of organization, planning, and coordination. While all social workers must also function effectively in these realms as well, their efforts tend to concentrate on their respective jobs. But for the administrator his point of focus is the *total agency*. He must be responsible for the over-all organization of the agency; he must lead the over-all planning process; he must coordinate the efforts of the entire staff, the board, and others.

As Vasey says, "When a law is enacted establishing a program, machinery must be provided for making the authorized services available, and a structure must be created. This structure may be located in an existing agency, or it may require establishment of a new organization. The outlines of the organization at any rate must be specified in the law. Procedures must be set in motion for the recruitment, selection, and employment of staff. The agency must be organized into divisions, sections, and units, each performing some particular part of the work. In the agency of today, specialization of function is a common feature of organization as the services rendered demand more and more technical skills and processes. The administrative process must be developed to insure the flow of work and the coordination of activities of the organization so that the purposes of the program will be fulfilled. The relationships of boards of advisory or governing committees to the agency executive and to the political authority must develop, as well as that of executive to staff. Personnel policies and procedures must be established, and responsibilities of staff positions clearly delineated." [1]

What Is Organization?

A review of the literature of administration reveals that organization is defined in various ways. Usually emphasis is placed on the formal structural arrangements created between people so that they can work together to accomplish their purposes. As Millett says, "Organization for public service is people working together for a common purpose. People working together create a reaction system, a behavior pattern of individual and group relationships. Organization is supposed to establish relationships among people in terms of work assignments, duties, and responsibilities. But organization does more than this. It provides opportunities and limitations, it encourages ambitions and frustrates the role some individuals believe they should achieve. In spite of political and technical considerations organization quickly becomes also a problem in human relations." [2a]

Friedlander affirms the fact that organization is the means by which staff members' duties are defined and clarified. He says, "Setting up the organizational structure of the agency leads to a distribution of duties to the members of the staff with a clear definition of responsibilities concerning their work, delegation of authority, and supervision; a description of staff and line services, and the establishment of standardized operations. It includes the delegation of everyone's authority, so that each member of the staff knows exactly what his assignment and responsibilities are." [3]

Pfiffner and Sherwood say, "The formal structure of an organization represents as closely as possible the deliberate intention of its framers for the processes of interaction that will take place among its members. In the typical work organization this takes the form of a definition of task specialities, and their arrangement in levels of authority with clearly defined lines of communication from one level to the next." [4]

Peterson relates organization to purposes as he observes: "Organization is the act of putting into systematic relationships those elements essential to the satisfaction of purpose. Organization serves as a faciliating agency in the achievement of a purpose." [5]

Barnard also sees purpose as one of the elements in organization when he writes: "An organization comes into being when (1) there are persons able to communicate with each other, (2) who are willing to contribute action, (3) to accomplish a common purpose. The elements of an organization are therefore (1) communication; (2) willingness to serve; and (3) common purpose. These elements are necessary and sufficient conditions initially and they are found in all such organizations. The third element, purpose, is implicit in the definition. Willingness to serve, and communication, and the interdependence of these three elements in general, and their mutual dependence in specific cooperative systems, are matters of experience and observation." [6a]

Hierarchy, Bureaucracy, and Power

The prevailing organization of large social welfare agencies is hierarchical, bureaucratic, and often times power-dominated. These elements must be understood, for if the administrator fails to recognize them serious problems may arise.

Moore observes, "Every organization is a hierarchical system in which each individual, with the exception of the man at the top and the people at the very bottom, operates within an interacting triad of relationships in which some people are viewed as being in higher positions to him, some as being in lower, subordinate positions, and some as being at the same level. Dealing with these various levels and modifying behavior in appropriate ways in terms of the hierarchical system is one of the important skills of the executive. He has to learn how to get things done through the boss, how to approach him at the right time, how to avoid getting a definite *no,* how to sell ideas to him, how to motivate him, and so on. The executive who doesn't have these skills doesn't get much done. Every executive has to be a promoter of ideas; he has to be selling all of the time. By the same token, the executive has to learn how to deal with subordinates as well as with those at his own level. With his subordinates, he has to learn how to sell the sometimes unpopular notion of work; he has to learn how to translate organizational ideas into goals that have meaning to those under him; he has to learn to balance the impersonal demands of the organization against the personal needs of his people. Above all, he has to learn how to deal with people in sympathetic but not emotionally involved ways. He has to avoid the sense of guilt that haunts many executives who cannot bring themselves to ask others to get the job done. He has to learn to exercise the power given him without projecting his own emotional needs into the situation. Any power position is potentially tyrannical, and the individual with power has to be either self-disciplined or, of necessity, outwardly controlled." [7]

In his discussion of administration as a social process, Getzels suggests, "Let me say then that we may conceive of administration structurally as the hierarchy of subordinate-superordinate relationships within a social system. Functionally, this hierarchy of relationships is the locus for allocating and integrating roles and facilities in order to achieve the goals of the social system. It is here, in these relationships, that the assignment of statuses, the provision of facilities, the organization of procedures, the regulation of activity, and the evaluation of performance takes place." [8]

Since bureaucracy is a prominent feature of all governmental organizations, it is necessary that one understand the characteristics of it. Weber says, "The distinctive characteristics of the bureaucracy are: 1) The organization operates according to a body of laws or rules, which are consistent and have normally been intentionally established. 2) Every official is subject to an impersonal order by which he guides his actions. In turn, his instructions have authority only insofar as they conform with this generally understood body of rules; obedience is due to his office, not to him as an individual. 3) Each incumbent of an office has a specified sphere of competence, with obligations, authority, and power to compel obedience strictly defined. 4) The organization of offices follows the principle of hierarchy; that is, each lower office is under the control and supervision of a higher one. 5) The supreme head of the organization, and only he, occupies his position by appropriation, by election, or by being designated as successor. Other offices are filled, in principle, by free selection, and candidates are selected on the basis of 'technical' qualifications. They are appointed not elected. 6) The system also serves as a career ladder. There is promotion according to seniority of achievement. Promotion is dependent upon the judgment of superiors. 7) The official who, in principle, is excluded from any ownership rights in the concern, or in his position, is subject to discipline and control in the conduct of his office." [9]

But, as Green points out, "often the professional worker may see the requirements of the bureaucracy as impediments to service. The emphasis on procedure, the fact that so many public welfare programs are limited by law, the public accountability of the organizations supported by taxes— these factors stimulate insecurity and rigidity which may clash with the standards of service the social worker professes." Green elaborates as he observes: "when organization requires standards of eligibility for service, the client is automatically categorized. This process conflicts with the social worker's goal of unlimited service to the particular client on the basis of his individual needs. This problem is accentuated in those settings in which the administrative framework was established long before professional social workers were employed by the organization—e.g., in many public aid and correctional settings. The statutes under which the bureaucracy operates set patterns which are not easily modified by 'experts' who move into a structure that is already well-established." [10]

Quite often the administrator has very little chance to change his organization because much of the structure is mandated by higher authority. As Millett says, "Organization for public service establishes a structure for the exercise of administrative power. This structure and this exercise of administrative power are usually subject to determination in the first instance by the political organs of decision-making in our government, and then subject to periodic review by the legislative, executive, and judicial branches of government. This situation necessarily means that organization for public service is a political problem." [2b]

Creating the Effective Organization

The job of the social work administrator is to create an *effective* organization, effective in the sense that purposes are achieved insofar as possible. As Miller and Form have observed, the theory of organization may be simple but there are always problems in making the organization work. They say, "The theory of formal organization is . . . quite simple. It holds that throughout the organization there is a strict definition of authority and responsibility. Similarly, there is an equally precise definition of the functions of every department. . . . Formal organization is necessary to achieve organizational goals. It is necessary because it is by nature impersonal, logical, and efficient. . . . Although formal organization is designed to subject production to logical planning, things never seem to go 'according to plan.' This is evidenced by the many 'problems' managers encounter. They find that no matter how carefully they organize, despite the concern in anticipating problems, unanticipated ones always arise. For these eventualities formal organization offers little guidance because it is created as a guide-post for the routine, the typical, and the foreseeable." [11]

Communication problems seem to rank high in many large social welfare agencies. These problems may result from the rigid, steep hierarchy so common among massive governmental operations. Albers observes that a flat structure is apt to reduce communication difficulties: "A flat structure has fewer hierarchical levels, thereby tending to reduce the 'administrative distance' between top and bottom levels. The concept of administrative distance has reference to the understanding and intimacy which characterizes the relationship between persons at different levels of the organizational structure. Too much administrative distance can create communication difficulties. . . . Many hierarchical levels or 'layering' increases impersonality and reduces understanding between higher and lower levels. The personal touch is lost and informal ties become tenuous." [12a]

By grouping functions in departments it is possible for the administrator to create specialized units which can have a high degree of autonomy. Barnard observes, "the bases of specialization of organizations (and of individuals also) are five: (a) the place where work is done; (b) the time at which work is done; (c) the persons with whom work is done; (d) the things upon which work is done; and (e) the method or process by which work is done." [6b]

Albers, in his discussion of work division, notes: "Departmentation divides the work of the organization into semi-autonomous units or departments. The consequence of departmentation is a delineation of executive responsibilities and a grouping of operating activities. Every level in the hierarchy below the apex is departmentalized, and each succeeding lower level involves further departmental differentiation. The activities necessary to achieve the organizational objective are a basic consideration in organizing. The nature of such activities may differ significantly with such diverse objectives as making steel, waging war, selling insurance, and educating students. However, the types of departmentation have general applicability and can be applied in many different situations. The types most commonly used are as follows: (1) Functional, (2) Product, (3) Service, (4) Territorial, (5) Time, (6) Equipment, and (7) Alpha-numerical." [12b]

As Hungate says,

There is no one absolutely correct organizational structure for a welfare agency. However, in planning the "best" structure to facilitate the particular program being administered and to make "the policy" effective, the following should be considered: (1) Organization provides framework and environment; the goal of organization in a welfare agency is to create a situation in which workers can meet the objectives of the program most effectively. Therefore, some type of formal organization must be established to carry out the purposes of the agency program. (2) The organizational chart is an abstraction of administration. It represents an ideal organization of authority, and functions as a description of actual operations. How far these operations depart from "the chart" will vary with the complexities of the functions being performed. However, if the actual organization departs too widely from the formal chart, the program may be moving informally rather than by adequate planning under a responsible director. (3) The objectives or organization should be clear and, to be effective, must be positive considerations—that is, the orientation should be toward constructive achievement rather than preventive or defensive measures. (4) All individuals within the organization influence the program, and in turn the organization molds and influences the activity and responses of individuals. It follows that any new program that changes established organizational lines and relationships may produce emotional reactions. It is difficult to compensate for losses of prestige, authority, or independence of action if these have been considered the prerogatives of individuals within the organization. In this connection it is helpful if a system of recognition and incentives can be made an integral part of organizational structure. (5) The organizational structure should be established on the premise that the people being served have a *right* to the services of the agency. However, the right to service is based on the law establishing the program rather than in the need of the client. (6) The more programs in functional services a single organization involves, the more differences are encountered and the more the administrator must coordinate and integrate all aspects of service. (7) The organization must not be allowed to become an end in itself but must be a means for achieving agency goals.[13a]

The key to organizational effectiveness rests in the quality of the personnel being organized. As Likert says, "The productive capability of a human organization can be illustrated by thinking of two firms in the same business. Both are of the same size and have identical equipment and technology. One, however, produces more and earns more than the other, because its personnel is superior to the other's with regard to such variables as the following: (1) Level of intelligence and aptitudes. (2) Level of training. (3) Level of performance goals and motivation to achieve organizational success. (4) Quality of leadership. (5) Capacity to use differences for purposes of innovation and improvement, rather than allowing differences to develop into bitter, irreconcilable, interpersonal conflict. (6) Quality of communication upward, downward, and laterally. (7) Quality of decision-making. (8) Capacity to achieve cooperative teamwork versus competitive striving for personal success at the expense of the organization. (9) Quality of the control processes of the organization and the levels of self-responsibility which exists. (10) Capacity to achieve effective co-ordination. (11) Capacity to use experience and measurements to guide decisions, improve operations, and introduce innovations." [14a]

The Responsibility of the Administrator for Planning

The social work administrator has a continuing responsibility for giving leadership to the process of planning. A good plan indicates what is to be accomplished, who is responsible, what are the resource requirements and what are the methods of evaluation and review. As Seider observes: "Planning in a direct-service agency such as the state department of public welfare takes the form of (1) the projection of program and concomitant administrative support to meet anticipated future goals; (2) planning for the coordination of the multiple categorical service programs, internal and subject to the direct authority of the department; (3) planning for the coordination of specialized departmental services and programs with those of related public and voluntary agencies and organizations; (4) planning for the initiation of new or changed services operating under the aegis of the department; (5) planning of new or changed community resources to be operated under other auspices; and (6) planning for societal changes through changing the environmental or social institutions causing or contributing to social breakdown or blocks in the fulfillment of individual and community potential. Although these types of planning may have different goals, and use differing constellations of staff and community involvement, they generally are carried out through the use of one or more of three inter-related and progressively more complex community work processes: inter-organizational exchange, mobilization of community support, and change of community resources." [15]

Hungate says,

The prime requisite of planning is relevance. The following consideration should be borne in mind during the planning phase of any welfare program: (1) The plans devised should be geared to the provision of service—not just to meet the legal requirements of compliance with State and Federal standards. (2) Plans to achieve program objectives are *substantive;* those for the organizational structure are *procedural.* Substantive planning calls for formulations of broad issues confronting the program, whereas procedural planning reflects concern for day-to-day details. (3) A program is a unit of planned purposive action.

Program planning is the preparation for program activity, and purposeful activity to achieve goals must be preceded by adequate planning. (4) Agency planning should directly involve all agency personnel who will be closely affected by the plans developed, and should be integrated with all phases of the agency administration. (5) Plans to achieve the objectives of the welfare program should be: a. consistent with immediate and anticipated human needs. b. soundly rooted in agency philosophy and consistent with the philosophy of the welfare professions. c. based on accurate, imaginative statistical and community research. d. flexible; flexible enough to allow for the unexpected; consistent with available or providable funds and personnel; acceptable to the community. e. communicable; simple enough to be interpreted easily to the staff and to the public. f. progressive; designed to improve, strengthen, or focus the service in such a way that each planning point leads to improvement of performance or sharpens relationship to needs. (6) The concept that plans are always geared to purpose must be stressed pervasively. Plans cannot be calculated without a knowledge and thorough understanding of agency purpose. (7) The range of maneuverability in relation to achieving objectives is always a factor in planning. Capability and creativity are enhanced by flexibility in planning; plans that impose a strict uniformity are certain to result in a rigid, unimaginative approach to welfare. There must be a certain degree of uniformity in any program, but there should be left enough room for adjusting the plans to new ways of doing the job, and to the individuals who are expected to make the program effective, as well as to statutory requirements, cultural conditions, and society's goals. (8) Agency achievements are concrete manifestations of objectives well planned.[13b]

In his work on comparative administrative theory LeBreton offers a model of the planning process which consists of the following fourteen steps:

1) Becoming aware of a possible need for formulating a plan.
2) Formulating a precise statement of the objective of the plan to be prepared.
3) Preparing a broad outline of the proposal or plan.
4) Obtaining approval of the proposal.
5) Organizing planning staff and assigning responsibility.
6) Determining the specific outline of the plan.
7) Establishing contact with all cooperating units.
8) Obtaining necessary data.
9) Evaluating data.
10) Formulating tentative conclusions and preparing tentative plans.
11) Testing components of tentative plans and making adjustment where appropriate.
12) Preparing the final plans.
13) Testing the plan and making adjustments where necessary.
14) Submitting the plan for approval.[16]

Moss says, "Planning in the social service department in the hospital includes consideration of both the over-all purpose and plans of the institution and the specific goal and plans of the social service department.

The social service department must be identified with the over-all objectives in the hospital in which it operates. The structure and functions of the institution will largely determine the planning of the social service department; that is, the planning of program and formulation of policy must reflect the fact that social service is only one part of the total medical care program. The objectives of the institution may change according to the needs of the community or within its own organization. Planning is, therefore, a dynamic process and responds to changes in the institution, in the community and in the social service department, itself. . . . In addition to planning the social work services in the hospital, the social work administrator has a responsibility to participate through appropriate channels in planning hospital policies and procedures and to contribute his knowledge along with other administrative staff in planning specific programs, such as home care program or a program for care of premature infants. The administrator of the social service department can contribute to hospital planning the philosophy of social work concerning the rights of the individual, his awareness of the social needs of patients and his knowledge of their reactions to existing policies and procedures. The extent of social service participation will depend upon the acceptance of the team concept in planning by the hospital administrator or the department head responsible for over-all planning." [17]

Osborn stresses the importance of broad participation in planning: "If each person caring for any aspect of agency program has an opportunity to share in a manner appropriate to this function, in the promulgation of the plan and in the subsequent evaluation process carried on under it, agency administration and programs will in all likelihood be greatly strengthened." [18]

The Responsibility of the Administrator for Coordination

Coordination is one of the continuing responsibiilties of the social work administrator. Coordination is an activity that interrelates the various parts of the agency so that it functions as a whole. Walton says, "Coordination is referred to as the activity that allocates and directs various persons, functions, specialtites, and spaces with a view to their reciprocal relations in such a way that they contribute maximally to the accomplishment of an organization's purposes." [19]

Georgopoulos and Mann says, "Organizational coordination is defined as the extent to which the various interdependent parts of an organization function each according to the needs and requirements of the other parts and of the total system." [20]

Simon distinguishes between procedural and substantive coordination: "Coordination may be exercised in both a procedural and a substantive sense. By procedural coordination is meant the specifications of the organization itself—that is the generalized description of the behaviors and relationships of the members of the organization. Procedural coordination establishes the lines of authority, and outlines the sphere of activity and authority of each member of the organization. Substantive coordination is concerned with the content of the organization's activities." [21]

Basing his findings on many years of study of human organizations, Likert notes: "At least four conditions must be met by an organization if it is to achieve a satisfactory solution to the coordination-functional problem. (1) It must provide high levels of cooperative behavior between superiors and subordinates and especially among peers. (2) Favorable attitudes and confidence and trust are needed among its members. (3) It must have the organizational structure and the interaction skill required to solve differences and conflicts and to attain creative solutions. (4) It must possess the capacity to exert influence and to create motivation and coordination without traditional forms of line authority. (5) Its decision-making processes and superior-subordinate relationships must be such as to enable a person to perform his job well and without hazard when he has two or more superiors." [14b]

Likert then specifies a major ingredient of effective coordination: "To perform the intended coordination well a fundamental requirement must be met. The entire organization must consist of the multiple, overlapping group structure with *every* work group using group decision-making processes skillfully. This requirement applies to the functional, product and service departments. An organization meeting this requirement will have an effective interaction-influence system through which the relevant communications flow readily, the required influence is exerted laterally, upward, and downward, and the motivational forces needed for coordination are created." [14c]

NOTES

1. Wayne Vasey, *Government and Social Welfare* (New York: Holt, Rinehart and Winston, Inc., 1958), p. 257.
2. John D. Millett, *Organization for the Public Service* (Princeton: D. Van Nostrand Co., Inc., 1966), a p. 102; b 28.
3. Walter A. Friedlander, *Introduction to Social Welfare,* 3rd ed., (Englewood Cliffs, N.J.: Prentice-Hall, Inc., © 1968), p. 203.
4. John M. Pfiffner and Frank P. Sherwood, *Administrative Organization* (Englewood Cliffs, N.J.: Prentice-Hall, Inc., © 1960), p. 18.
5. Elmore Peterson, E. Grosvenor Plowman, and Joseph M. Trickett, *Business Organization and Management* (Homewood, Ill.: Richard D. Irwin, Inc., 1961), p. 27.
6. Chester I. Barnard, *The Functions of the Executive,* Thirtieth Aniversary Edition (Cambridge: Harvard University Press, © copyright 1938, 1968 by the President and Fellows of Harvard College; © copyright 1966 by Grace F. Noera Barnard), a p. 82; b 128–129.
7. David G. Moore, "What Makes a Top Executive?" in Robert T. Golembiewski and Frank Gibson, eds., *Managerial Behavior and Organization Demands.* (Chicago: Rand McNally & Company, 1967), pp. 331–332.

8. Jacob W. Getzels, "Administration as a Social Process" in Andrew W. Halpin, ed., *Administrative Theory in Education* (Chicago: Midwest Administration Center, University of Chicago, 1958), p. 151.

9. Max Weber, *The Theory of Social and Economic Organization,* trans. Henderson and Parson (London: William Hodge and Co., Ltd., 1947), pp. 329–34.

10. A.D. Green, "The Professional Worker in the Bureaucracy," *Social Service Review,* March 1966, p. 72.

11. D.C. Miller and W.H. Form, *Industrial Sociology* (New York: Harper and Row, 1951), pp. 159–160.

12. Henry H. Albers, *Principles of Management* 3rd ed., (New York: John Wiley & Sons, Inc., 1969), a p. 113; b 120.

13. Joseph I. Hungate, Jr. *A Guide for Training Local Public Welfare Administrators* (Washington: U.S. Department of Health, Education and Welfare—Welfare Administration, Bureau of Family Services, Division of Technical Training, 1964), a pp. 19–20; b 21–22.

14. Rensis Likert, *The Human Organization* (New York: McGraw-Hill Book Company, © 1967), a p. 148; b 158; c 167.

15. Violet M. Seider, "Organizing the State Welfare Department for Community Planning" in David E. French, ed., *Planning Responsibilities of State Departments of Public Welfare* (Chicago: American Public Welfare Association 1967), p. 37.

16. Preston P. LeBreton, "A Model of the Administrative Process" in *Comparative Administrative Theory* (Seattle: University of Washington Press, 1968), p. 170.

17. Celia R. Moss, *Administering a Hospital Social Service Department* (Washington, D.C.: American Association of Medical Social Workers, 1955), pp. 12–13.

18. Phyllis R. Osborn, "Meeting the Needs of People: An Administrator Responsibility," *Social Work,* July 1959, p. 75.

19. John Walton, *Administration and Policy-Making in Education* (Baltimore: The Johns Hopkins Press, 1959), p. 86.

20. Basil Georgopoulos and Floyd Mann, *The Community General Hospital* (New York: The Macmillan Company, 1962), p. 273.

21. Herbert A. Simon, *Administrative Behavior: A Study of the Decision-Making Processes in Administrative Organizations* (New York: The Macmillan Co., 1955), pp. 140–141.

10 Decision-making

Social work administrators, like all administrators, have a major responsibility for the decision-making processes of their agency. They must understand the meaning of decision, the types of decisions, and the steps in the process of decision-making. They must know whom to involve in the decisions that must be made. They must be willing to make difficult decisions and above all they must strive for decision-making that enhances the purposes of the agency and furthers the meeting of client needs. Albers makes the point that, "An important function of executives is decision-making or choosing from alternatives. Decision-making is partly a matter of planning organizational objectives and the methods that will be used to achieve them." [1]

Morris observes, "Large organizations can be managed not by a single brain but through coordinated decisions made by many. Just how decisions are to be thus delegated and the resulting actions coordinated is the central question in organization design." [2]

The Meaning of the Term "Decision"

A number of authorities have developed helpful definitions of the term "decision." For example, Albers says, "Decision-making may be narrowly defined as the making of a choice from among alternative courses of action. More broadly, decision-making also involves all of the actions that must take place before a final choice can be made. Probably the most important of these is to determine whether something needs to be done. This aspect of decision making is similar to the initial step in a scientific investigation. Neither decisional nor scientific endeavor can begin unless there is a problem that requires solution. . . . After a decisional problem has been identified, alternative strategies for the solution of the problem may

148

be developed. This aspect of decision-making generally involves both the questions of ends and means. Are the ends presently sought by the organization appropriate in terms of changing environmental conditions? Are the means now being utilized adequate for existing or changed ideas? The final step in decision making is to make a choice from among two or more alternatives. Strictly speaking, at least some of the alternatives must appear to be equally appropriate. If such were not the case, there would be no real problem of choice. The best alternative would be obvious and automatically eliminate the other alternatives." [3]

Gore says, "The term 'decision' may refer to the choice of picking up the telephone ('I decided to answer the phone'); it may just as well refer to a momentous and unprecedented international act. . . . Generically, decision refers to the consideration of the consequences of some act before undertaking it. Purposive behavior, behavior organized by means of goals projected by individuals as a means of meeting their needs, tends to extend beyond the resources of a behavioral system. In this situation, the decision becomes a mechanism for selecting both goals to be undertaken first and those that must wait. One of the meanings that decision has come to have is a choosing, not between alternative courses of action, but between alternative goals, each offering benefits prized by someone." [4a]

According to Thompson and Tuden, "Choices from among alternatives seem to be the end-point of decision-making, but the term 'decision' will not be confined simply to ultimate choice. Rather, 'decision' will refer to those activities which contribute to choice, including recognizing or delimiting and evaluating alternatives as well as the final selection. Thus an individual may have responsibility for making a final choice on behalf of an organization, but if others help him delimit or evaluate alternatives, we will not describe that individual as *the* decider." [5]

As Walton observes: "Administrative decisions contain three elements. First, there is a continuing element of purpose that gives direction to the decision about means. Second, there is the actual decision about the choice of means to accomplish the accepted purpose. And third, there is usually a concomitant value choice in the selection of means that does not materially effect the end." [6]

Hungate says, "A decision is a specific course of action selected from the alternative courses available. It provides a way to design action to solve a problem. The setting for decision is a human situation, and an understanding of the human elements is necessary to the problem-solving process. A problem must be confronted, fully grasped, and understood in all of its behavioral complexities before a decision can be made. A decision cannot be effective unless it is accepted by those to whom it applies. . . . The acceptance must come (1) from those within the organization who will be called upon to implement the decision, (2) from the public groups affected by the decision, and (3) from the superiors of the administrator making the decision. By the same reasoning, a decision must appear right and correct to those who are expected to accept it. . . . Decision-making rests upon the assumption that there is adequate competence and skill available to implement the decision effectively; decisions are of no consequence unless there is a probability that they can be carried out. No decision rests in isolation. Any decision has effect upon other areas not specifically covered by the particular decision; therefore, carrying out decisions is a matter for participation by all organizational staff. Decisions are made at all levels and by all personnel within an organization." [7]

Types of Decisions

When one reviews the number and types of decisions that must be made by an agency in the course of its work, it is evident that there are many variations and differences. Some decisions are simple; other decisions are complicated and far-reaching. As Gore says: "Decision serves so many purposes in the processes of an organization that it is difficult to characterize their functions in a word or a phrase. Most frequently they serve as devices for triggering action, but they may serve as both blueprints for and catalysts of action in a single stroke. Major decisions set off such rambling discussions that they serve many more objects than can be counted. Like radiation, some of the effects of a sustained decision process may appear only long after the process has run its course." [4b]

Simon states, "Decisions are programmed to the extent that they are repetitive and routine, to the extent that a definite procedure has been worked out for handling them so that they don't have to be treated de novo each time they occur. . . . If a particular problem recurs often enough—a routine procedure will usually be worked out for solving it. Decisions are nonprogrammed to the extent that they are novel, unstructured, and consequential. There is no cut and dried method for handling the problem because it hasn't arisen before, or because its precise nature and structure are illusive or complex, or because it is so important that it deserves a custom-tailored treatment." [8]

Steps in the Decision-making Process

A number of writers have analyzed the decision-making process and have come to the conclusion that it is a step-by-step matter.

Jensen and Clark say, "Regardless of how the procedure is viewed or defined—decision-making or administrative process—it is a process involving sequential steps. These are orderly stages in a continuum, however, interrelated; that is, one cannot start with the resultant and work backward; the direction is toward the resultant. . . . One very significant component of the procedure lies in the deliberate phase of the procedure, the recognition of the problem, gathering and organizing facts and data, weighing alternatives, and eventually coming to a point of decision on a course of action to be taken. To stop at this point, which unfortunately happens in some cases, totally ignores the implementation and assessment of the continuum." [9]

Griffiths says, "In practically any discussion of the process of decision-making, steps similar to the following will be presented and described:

1) Recognize, define, limit the problem.
2) Analyze and evaluate the problem.
3) Establish criteria or standards by which a solution will be evaluated or judged as acceptable and adequate to the need.
4) Collect data.
5) Formulate and select the preferred solution or solutions. Test them in advance.
6) Put into effect the preferred solution.

The preparation for making a particular decision becomes known, and the decision-maker goes through a process of defining and limiting the problem. He attempts to state the problem in terms of either his goals or the goals of the enterprise, and he also attempts to state the problem in such a way that he can grasp its significance." [10]

In discussing White House decision-making, Sorensen says, "It is not hard to state the ideal, but it is hard to state it with conviction. Theoretically it would be desirable to take, for each important decision, a series of carefully designed, carefully spaced steps, including ideally the following: First: agreement on the facts; second: agreement on the overall policy objectives; third: a precise definition of the problem; fourth: a canvassing of all possible solutions, with all their shades and variations; fifth: a list of all the possible consequences that would flow from each solution; sixth: a recommendation and final choice of each alternative; seventh: the communication of that decision; and eighth: provision for its execution. In these ideal and mechanical terms, White House decision-making sounds easy, if somewhat elaborate. It is simply the interaction of desire and fact—simply a determination of what the national interest requires in a given situation. But unfortunately it is neither mechanical nor easy; nor, it should be added, is the amount of care and thought devoted to a particular decision necessarily proportionate to the formality and regularity of the decision-making process." [11]

Participation in Decision-making

In professional social work administration it is important for many people to have a part in the decision-making. In the large social welfare agency there are many decisions to be made and it is impossible for the administrator to make them by himself. As Cleveland says, "[The] extent to which each individual is personally responsible to others is most notice-able in a large bureaucracy. No one person 'decides' anything; each 'de-cision' of any importance is the product of an intricate process of broker-age involving individuals inside and outside the organization who feel some reason to be affected by the decision, or who have special knowledge to contribute to it. The more varied the organization's constituency, the more its decisions affect 'the public,' the more outside 'veto-groups' will need to be taken into account. But even if no outside consultations were involved, sheer size would produce a complex process of decision. For a large organization is a deliberately created system of tensions into which each individual is expected to bring work ways, viewpoints, and outside rela-tionships markedly different from those of his colleagues. It is the admin-istrator's task to draw from these disparate forces the elements of wise action from day to day, consistent with the purposes of the organization as a whole." [12]

Bennis declares, "The leader does not abdicate from the tough decisions of management but attempts to deal with them by exploring with his group or organization the facts at hand, involving his people directly with the solution of the problem. His style is problem-oriented leadership and relies not solely on organizational power or status but rather on situational de-mands. . . . He tries to mobilize his people, to activate them to explore mutually the job or problem that has to be accomplished. He does so by communicating the problem, by insisting on involvement and participation, and by jointly working on the problem. His is management by objective, not management by control." [13]

Millett observes, "If communication is to be a two-way street in an or-ganization, then various persons and groups must be invited to participate in the decision-making process." [14]

Administrators who believe in the importance of involving people in decision-making have to decide *which* persons to involve in which de-cisions and at what time and in what ways.

Ripley points out in discussing hospital administration: "It is unwise . . . to think everyone must contribute to all decisions, because many of the personnel may be incompetent to make such decisions. For example, the housekeeper cannot be expected to express a valid opinion of a candidate for the hospital fiscal officer, and the chaplain is not qualified to advise on the purchase of x-ray equipment." [15] Similar observations can be made with reference to the social welfare field. The criterion of competence is basic to the choice of who should participate in what decisions.

The Administrator's Role in Decision-making

Decision-making is often difficult and always hard work. The administra-tor is at the center of the decision-making process and is ultimately responsible for the decisions made. Barnard offers a penetrating analysis of the problems of the executive along with suggestions on how to cope with the inevitable strains of the job. He says, "The making of decisions, as everyone knows from personal experience, is a burdensome task. Offsetting the exhilaration that may result from correct and successful decision and the relief that follows the terminating of a struggle to determine issues is the depression that comes from failure or error of decision and the frustration which ensues from uncertainty. Accordingly, it will be observed that men generally try to avoid making decisions, beyond a limited degree when they are rather uncritical responses to conditions. The capacity of most men to make decisions is quite narrow, although it is a capacity that may be considerably developed by training and especially by experience. The executive is under the obligation of making decisions usually within approximately defined limits related to the position he has accepted; and is under the necessity of keeping within the limits of his capacity if he is continuously to discharge this obligation. He must, therefore, to be successful, distinguish between the occasions of decision in order to avoid the acceptance of more than he can undertake without neglecting the field to which his position relates. For the natural reluctance of other men to decide, their persistent disposition to avoid responsibility, and their fear of criticism, will lead them to overwhelm the executive who does not protect himself from excessive burdens of decision if he is not already protected by a well regulated and habitual distribution of responsibilities." [16]

When the administrator has developed an agency structure and organization which is working effectively there are many decision-making persons and points. Under these circumstances the administrator does not have to make all the decisions but, as Thompson and Tuden point out, his role "is to *manage* the decision process as distinct from *making the decision*." [5b]

Griffiths and his colleagues sum it up by saying, "1) The role of the administrative staff in an institution is to create an organization within which the decision-making process can operate effectively. The organization should permit decisions to be made as close to the source of effective action as possible. 2) The administrative staff of an educational institution should be organized to provide individual staff members with as much freedom for initiative as is consistent with efficient operation and prudential controls. Hierarchical levels should be added to the organization with caution, and only when deemed imperative to maintain reasonable control over the institution. 3) The administrative functions and the sources of decision-making in an institution should be organized to provide the machinery for democratic operation and decentralized decision-making. 4) The purpose of organization is to clarify and distribute responsibilities and authority among individuals and groups in an orderly fashion consistent with the purposes of the institution. The structure of the institution is determined by the nature of its decision-making process and the organization of the institution should be established to provide for the most effective operation of this process. 5) An institution should be organized with a unitary source of decision-making at its head. Authority and responsibility delegated by the chief administrator should result in a unitary pattern of decision-making levels all subordinate in the institution. 6) The administrative organization, by its very structure, should provide for the continuous and cooperative evaluation and redirection of the organization from the standpoint of adequacy (the degree to which goals are reached) and efficiency (the degree to which goals are reached relative to the available resources)." [17]

NOTES

1. Henry H. Albers, *Principles of Organization and Management,* 2nd ed., (New York: John Wiley and Sons, Inc., 1965), p. 71.
2. William T. Morris, *Decentralization in Management Systems* (Columbus: Ohio State University Press, 1968), p. 3.
3. Henry H. Albers, *Principles of Management,* 3rd ed., (New York: John Wiley & Sons, Inc., 1969), pp. 78–79.
4. William J. Gore, *Administrative Decision-Making: A Heuristic Model* (New York: John Wiley & Sons, Inc., 1964), a p. 19; b 113.
5. James D. Thompson and Arthur Tuden, "Strategies, Structures, and Pressures of Organizational Decision" in James D. Thompson, ed., *Comparative Studies of Administration* (Pittsburgh: University of Pittsburgh Press, 1959), a p. 196; b 209.
6. John Walton, *Administration and Policy-Making in Education* (Baltimore: The Johns Hopkins Press, 1959), p. 52.
7. Joseph I. Hungate, Jr., *A Guide for Training Local Public Welfare Administrators* (Washington: U.S. Department of Health, Education and Welfare—Welfare Administration, Bureau of Family Services, Division of Technical Training, 1964), pp. 55–56.
8. Herbert A. Simon, *The New Science of Management Decision* (New York: Harper and Row, 1960), pp. 5–6.
9. Theodore Jensen and David L. Clark, *Educational Administration* (New York: The Center for Applied Research in Education, Inc., 1964), p. 53.
10. Daniel E. Griffiths, "Administration as Decision-making," in Andrew M. Halpin, *Administration Theory in Education* (Chicago: Midwest Administration Center, University of Chicago, 1958), pp. 132–133.
11. Theodore C. Sorensen, *Decision Making in the White House* (New York: Columbia University Press, 1963), pp. 18–19.
12. Harlan Cleveland, "Dinosaurs and Personal Freedom," *Saturday Review,* February 28, 1959, p. 38. Copyright © 1959 by Saturday Review, Inc.
13. Warren G. Bennis, "Problem-oriented Administration," *Hospital Administration,* Winter 1960, p. 64.
14. John D. Millett, *Organization for the Public Service,* p. 116. Copyright © 1966 by Litton Educational Publishing, Inc. by permission of Van Nostrand Reinhold Company.
15. Herbert S. Ripley, M.D., "Human Problems in Hospital Administration and the Care of Patients" in Preston P. LeBreton, *Comparative Administrative Theory,* (Seattle: University of Washington Press, 1968), p. 247.
16. Chester I. Barnard, *The Functions of the Executive,* Thirtieth Anniversary Edition (Cambridge: Harvard University Press, © copyright 1938, 1969 by the President and Fellows of Harvard College; © copyright 1966 by Grace F. Noera Barnard), pp. 189–190.
17. Daniel Griffiths et al., *Organizing Schools for Effective Education* (Danville, Ill.: The Interstate Printers and Publishers, Inc., 1962), pp. 71–72.

11 Policy Determination

Administrative leadership is responsible for developing and guiding the process of policy determination for the agency. A policy is a stated course of action adopted and followed by the agency in doing its work. Policy in action becomes practice. While many persons are involved at various points in the policy determination process, the administrator has a special role as does the agency board (see Chapter 6).

It is the function of the administrator to develop and present to the board proposals concerning policies, taking into account community, constituency, and staff thinking and consensus. Then it is necessary for the administration to assist the board as it makes policy decisions. Once the policy decision has been made, it is the job of the administrator to administer the policy effectively with the staff.

Policy Defined

A policy is a stated course of conduct, a statement of intentions. Agency policies are written statements formally adopted by the board or legal authority and made public so that persons will know the conditions under which services will be rendered. The community, the constituency, and the staff should be clear on the nature and purpose of the specific policy and its interpretation. Policies are tools for administrators, staff, and constituents to use in providing service. Good policy statements are positive affirmations of what the agency exists to do and how it is to be done. Policies give focus and direction to the work of the staff especially in terms of decision-making. As Griffiths points out: "An effective set of policies should indicate *who* is to make a decision, *what* the decision is to be concerned with, and some information as to *how* the decision is to be made. Members of an organization should have the security which well-written policy affords

155

them. One of the chief causes of confusion in the network of human relationships in an organization is the lack of clear policy." [1]

Areas Where Policies Are Needed

Policy determination within a framework of defined agency purpose tends to evolve in a number of interrelated categories. *First,* there is a need for policy regarding whom the agency is to service and the kinds of services to be offered. To a great extent the legislative body determines broad purposes and eligibility policies for public agencies, but there are many details of service policies which must be worked out at the agency level. Policies regarding evolution of services and termination of services are also needed. *Second,* policies are needed in the area of personnel. These include standards of employment, salaries, workloads, promotion, and evaluation. *Third,* the area of financial arrangements requires policy formulations especially when fees for services are charged. *Fourth,* the area of community relationships should have policy pronouncements to guide the agency in its work with other agencies. In addition to these broad policy areas the agency must work out procedures which constitute uniform ways of carrying out operations. Ordinarily procedures are chiefly internal and do not require the breadth of participation in formulation necessary for policies.

The Policy Determination Process

In Figure 9 policy-making is presented in a series of steps. Policy-making in social work administration is a process through which communities, constituencies, staffs, and boards with the leadership of social work administrators contribute facts, experiences, views, and preferences so that statements of intention will be adopted by the board and will be implemented by administration and staff to achieve the agency goals of services to people uniformly provided.

In Specht's model of stages of policy formulation, he identifies eight stages. They are: (1) identification of the problem, (2) analysis, (3) informing the public, (4) development of policy goals including the involvement of other agencies, (5) building public support, (6) legislation, (7) implementation and administration, (8) evaluation and assessment.[2]

In working out professional social service policies the staff must be given an important role. The same principle applies in all professional fields. With reference to policy-making in the public schools, a commission said, "Teachers should play a major role in initiating and formulating administrative and policy decisions. In the interest of the advancement of education, the staff should seek such a role and the superintendent should welcome it. Most school policies and administrative plans are successful only insofar as they foster improved interaction between teacher and pupil, for

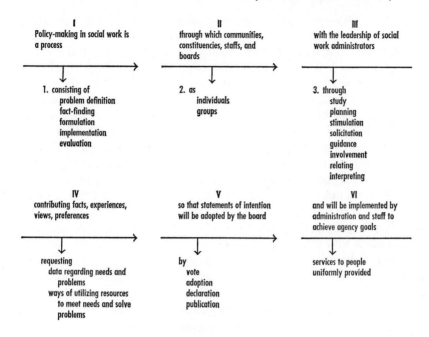

Figure 9
The Policy-making Process

classroom instruction is the most important function of the school. Policy-making and administrative direction which ignores the professional knowledge of specific situations are likely to result in poor policies and poor directives. Decisions should therefore reflect the pooled intelligence of the professional staff. In the interests of education this is necessity, not a mere matter of professional courtesy." [3]

Moore and Walters in their work on personnel administration in education say: "Policy formation by the staff, subject to approval by the governing board, is a responsibility of the entire group, and those that are affected by a given policy should have a part in its development." [4]

Basing her conclusions on experience in hospital social work, Moss says, "Direction in a social service department is facilitated when established policies and procedures are set down and made available to the entire staff. To operate on the basis of a separate decision on each situation would become a complicated and trying ordeal for director and staff alike. When it becomes necessary to change an established policy or procedure, everyone should have a common body of knowledge and a common starting point. Where the staff is informed of the reason for a new procedure before it becomes a directive, they accept it more readily. Consultative direction, in which the staff participated in planning for and formulating the actual instruction, produces more cooperative effort and professional growth on the part of the staff." [5]

Utz says, *"The administration should make provision for the staff to participate in policy formulation.* This undertaking, is particularly challenging for both the administration and the staff. The challenge for the administration lies in deciding what kinds of policy formulation the staff can participate in appropriately and in being clear about the issues at stake. The challenge for staff members lies in learning how to participate effectively. Effective participation requires the caseworker to behave quite differently from the way he behaves in casework practice, where 'the waiting game' is the appropriate one. He must be prepared to state his views promptly. The administration has a responsibility to give casework staff members guidance and direction in how to prepare themselves in how to participate responsibly in policy formation. Their eventual responsibility in this sphere can be discussed with potential staff members during employment interviews, and later it should be brought up for discussion in supervisory conferences. Moreover, although it is not appropriate to encourage the expression of differences for its own sake, the atmosphere of the agency should be conducive to the kind of free expression in which genuine differences in opinion can be aired. Along with this it is important to realize that in a complex agency operation refinement and progress come more from the combination of one person's bits of ideas with another's than from one person's 'pearls of wisdom.' " [6]

Lack of clarity about roles and responsibilities is one of the usual problems in the policy-making process. While various groups must participate in the process of defining the policy, only one group, usually the board, can adopt policy legally, and only one group, usually the professional staff, can carry out policy. Writing from the hospital field, Hennessey says, "In a hospital there is an apparent conflict surrounding policy-making represented by these three observations: (1) The legally responsible group in the hospital, charged with legislating policy, is the board of trustees: therefore, these men must be the policy-makers. (2) The essential activity of the hospital is medical care for the sick, a specialty of physicians; therefore, they should determine the policies of the organization. (3) The person most knowledgeable about all phases of life in the hospital, the only full-time professional with wide perspective, is the administrator; therefore, he should decide policy. The fact of multiple interest and involvement in policy-making causes the process to be complex and ambiguous. In this sense it is like policy processes in the federal government implying a balance of contending powers. Thus, the relationships among the three principal groups have a crucial effect on hospital policy." [7]

Hungate repeats, "There are a number of problems inherent in the policy-making process." He lists:

(1) *Policy Too Strictly Defined.*—The tendency to think of policy in terms of law, charter, or legal order has created a problem in the failure to focus upon policy as a facilitative device of administration to accomplish established objectives. Administration, all too frequently, is not seen clearly in the policy role. The administrator may consider himself as an executor of policy with no part in formulation, but legal mandates only establish the broad general limits of policy. The administrator must assume the responsibility for policy within the realm of legal prescription. (2) *Policy Too Rigidly Detailed.*—The attempt to cover every detail of agency service in a policy directive can pose serious problems. Policy must be sufficiently flexible to allow for some variation as unique situations are encountered. Detailed policy that spells outwith excessive rigidity every phase of operation undermines worker confidence. Attempts to ensure uniformity of attention to details can produce stagnation and stultify imaginative efforts. Details are necessary in certain instances, but they can become the center of concern at the expense of good service. (3) *Emotional Subjectivity of Individuals.*—Emotional involvement in the policy process is a problem which must be considered. It is not easy to carry out a policy that impinges upon emotions or is contrary to beliefs. The administrator may not face the policy decision at all if what must be decided causes too severe discomfort. (4) *Variety of Training and Experience Levels.*—Policy formulations for a widely diverse staff are exceedingly difficult. With a fully trained staff more flexibility and discretion can be permitted at the point of application of the broad policy. For the less experienced workers policy formulations need to be more elementarily stated. A heterogeneous staff produces problems in the policy process. Obviously administration faces a difficulty in meeting a wide range of competences. (5) *Variety of Disciplines.*—If an agency has a staff composed of several disciplines it is difficult to find a generally acceptable frame of reference for the policy decisions. Each discipline's particular professional expertise may stoutly defend its own interpretation of policy as it pertains to its own realm of practice. (6) *Segmentalized Participation.*—An individual may invest only a part of himself in the organization, leaving the remainder of himself to work outside of the policy controls of the program. The part of the policy which is in accord with his beliefs he supports, but he segments himself and simply ignores the elements he disagrees with, or leaves them to chance. (7) *Geographical Distances or Specialization of Work Load.*—The policy process faces problems if units widely separated geographically are implementing the same policy without close coordinating efforts. The distances between program specialization can also create difficulty. If work assignments are narrowly specialized by units the problem of finding conformity in policy and assuring uniformity is greatly increased.[8]

Principles of Policy Determination

In an earlier publication [9] the author summarized some general principles of policy determinations as follows:

1. Policy must be based on and develop out of agency purpose.
2. Policies must be soundly based on adequately evaluated facts and

experience. Persons affected by policy should share in the creation of it.

3. Policy implies focus and direction for the achieving of the agency purpose.
4. Unity and consistency between the various policies of the agency and between policies and purposes is essential.
5. Although the board is responsible for the *enactment* of policy, the entire agency should participate in the policy formulation process.
6. Policy should relate the agency purpose to the realities of the community setting (including other agencies and special needs) and of the agency's own facilities and resources.
7. Policy-making, planning, and operations are integrally related and cannot be separated.
8. New policies should develop out of an evaulation of the existing policies in practice as they are systematically reviewed and studied.
9. Thorough knowledge of policy on the part of every staff member is essential. It is the administrator's responsibility to make policy statements available to staff in written form.
10. Policies should be expressed in positive forms; expressed in this way their constructive use is emphasized.
11. The carrying out of policies in the spirit of their intent is a major responsibility of administration.
12. Conflict between statement of policy and actual practice are a signal to the administrator of a need to evaluate both.

NOTES

1. Daniel E. Griffiths, "Administration as Decision-making" in Andrew M. Halpin, *Administrative Theory in Education* (Chicago: Midwest Administrative Center, University of Chicago, 1959), p. 140.
2. Harry Specht, "Casework Practice and Social Policy Formulation," *Social Work,* January 1968, p. 44.
3. National Education Association and American Association of School Administrators, Educational Policies Commission, *The Unique Role of the Superintendent of Schools.* Washington, D.C.: The Commission, 1965, pp. 21–22.
4. Harold E. Moore and Newell B. Walters, *Personnel Administration in Education* (New York: Harper and Row, 1955), p. 19.
5. Celia R. Moss, *Administering a Hospital Social Service Department* (Washington, D.C.: American Association of Medical Social Workers, 1955), p. 39.
6. Cornelius Utz, "The Responsibility of Administration for Maximizing the Contribution of the Casework Staff," *Social Casework,* March 1964, p. 139.
7. John W. Hennessey, Jr. "The Administrator and Policy Processes," *Hospital Administration,* Fall 1965, p. 66.
8. Joseph I. Hungate, Jr., *A Guide for Training Local Public Welfare Administrators.* (Washington, D.C.: U.S. Department of Health, Education and Welfare— Welfare Administration, Bureau of Family Services, Division of Technical Training, 1964), pp. 93–94.
9. Harleigh B. Trecker, *Group Process in Administration* (New York: Association Press, 1950), pp. 275–276.

12 Financial Management

Every administrator is concerned about the financing of his agency. He has to secure the funds from legislative appropriation, from private giving, or from fees charged clients. He has to determine what needs are to be met and how the budget must be set up to meet these needs. He has to interpret his budgetary needs to various groups who decide how much will be appropriated. In addition, the executive must control the spending of the budget in terms of the law and in relation to the declared objectives. He must pay attention to sound business practices and must be ready to be held accountable at all times. Furthermore, he must evaluate the results of his spending program in terms of the objectives that have been set up. Most administrators would agree that securing, spending, and evaluating the use of funds is a most important part of their work. As Friedlander says: "The mobilization of the financial resources of the agency depends upon its nature and structure. In public agencies, the administration of the budget requires negotiations for the allocation of funds with the Federal, state or local government; in private welfare organizations, money from special campaigns or the Community Chest is relied upon for funds. Budget controls guarantee that the money received is spent economically and in accordance with the policies and rules of the agency. Budgeting also describes the allocation of the funds available to the branches and divisions of the agency so that each of them can operate most effectively." [1]

Large amounts of money are now needed to finance existing social welfare programs. As new programs are authorized and as the nation grows in population more funds will be required. Programs are possible only when money is available. Held says, "Since every governmental program is only as extensive as the money put into it, the place where the decisions—whether rational or not—over how to divide up the national effort are most apparent, is in the federal budget. The budget is the central expression of how the government's finite resources will be allocated, the terms of the annual cease-fire, as it were, within the executive branch, between the competing claims of different advocates for more money for defense, or agriculture, or new welfare programs. . . . William Gorham, an Assistant Secretary in the Department of Health, Education and Welfare and an economist who recently moved up from the Defense Department to introduce into HEW the kind of analyses that have been helpful in resolving defense decision problems, finds non-quantifiable considerations already so profuse in an agency such as HEW that there is hardly a danger for some time of introducing too much calculation." [2]

The Budget and Its Preparation

The agency budget is the annual estimate of the financial needs of the organization for the year to come. It is one of the most important documents in the agency. Its preparation is a demanding task. Its utilization is a matter of trusteeship. Wildavsky says, "In the most literal sense a budget is a document containing words and figures, which proposes expenditures for certain items and purposes. The words describe items of expenditure (salaries, equipment, travel) or purposes (preventing war, improving mental health, providing low-income housing), and the figures are attached to each item or purpose. Presumably, those who make a budget intend that there will be a direct connection between what is written in it and future events. Hence, we might conceive of a budget as intended behavior, as a prediction. If the requests for funds are granted, and if they are spent in accordance with instructions, and if the actions involved lead to the desired consequences, then the purposes stated in the document will be achieved. The budget thus becomes a link between financial resources and human behavior to accomplish policy objectives. Only through observation, however, is it possible to determine the degree to which the predictions postulated in the budget document turn out to be correct." [3a]

A first step in budget preparation is to look again at the purposes of the agency and the needs it is designed to meet. Then a decision is made as to what resources are required to achieve the purposes. As Wildavsky states, "In the most general definition, budgeting is concerned with the translation of financial resources into human purposes. A budget, therefore, may be characterized as a series of goals with price tags attached. Since funds are limited and have to be divided in one way or another, the budget becomes a mechanism for making choice among alternative expenditures. When the choices are coordinated so as to achieve desired goals, a budget may be called a plan. Should [the administrator] include a detailed specification of how its objectives are to be achieved, a budget may serve as a plan of work for those who assume the task of implementing it. If emphasis is placed on achieving the most policy returns for a given sum of money, or on obtaining the desired objectives at the lowest cost, a budget may become an instrument for ensuring efficiency." [3b]

How the administrator regards the budget and its preparation is crucial to the matter of whom he involves in the preparation process. According to Clegg, "The preparation of the annual budget is one of the most important tasks performed by the Welfare Administrator. The budget sets the pattern for what can be accomplished by the department in the fiscal year which the budget covers. The budget also acts in a limiting manner, for that which is not anticipated in its preparation cannot be initiated and accomplished during the year." [4a] Moss comments on the budget of the social service department in the hospital: "The social service director is responsible for helping to plan the departmental budget and for administering it during its period of operation. Obtaining capital and income for the social service department may be a serious problem in hospitals where the values of the social service activities have not been recognized. However, the social service department is a segment of the hospital program, and its method of obtaining funds must be the same as that used by the hospital itself. The director of the department will play little or no part in raising of funds, but in preparing and administering the budget of his department he is participating in the assembling of financial resources." [5]

Heads of departments and other key staff members have a contribution to make to the budget preparation process. As Clegg says, "While the actual preparation of the budget may be centered in a few individuals, it is helpful to enlist the estimates of personnel in the department who are close to a particular operation. For example, the supervisor of Aid to the Aged may have a first-hand knowledge of trends which will be helpful. When staff members are called upon for estimates, they develop a better knowledge and understanding of the budget than they would otherwise. This, also, is in a small way an opportunity for administrative growth on the supervisory level and should be considered for that reason." [4b]

When the budget estimate has been drawn up it must be presented to the board of the voluntary agency or to the executive branch of the governmental agency. The administrator, often assisted by department heads and fiscal officers, must interpret the budget request pointing out why the funds are needed. Wildavsky makes some interesting points about the several purposes served by budgets: "It should now be apparent that the purposes of budgets are as varied as the purposes of men. One budget may be designed to coordinate diverse activities so that they complement one another in the achievement of common goals. Another budget may be put together primarily to discipline subordinate officials within a governmental agency by reducing amounts for their salaries and their pet projects. And a third budget may be directed essentially to mobilizing the support of the clientele groups who benefit by the services that the agency provides. Nothing is gained, therefore, by insisting that a budget is only one of these things when it may well be all of them or many other kinds of things as well." [3c]

In stating and discussing the services to be provided if the budget is adopted and funds provided, the administrator is committing the agency to a course of action which must be faithfully pursued. As Clegg points out: "Regardless of who does the actual work of [budget] preparation, the director of the Welfare Department is held responsible for it. He may take credit for its accuracies, but he must also answer for its deficiencies. He must present it to the board of local supervisors or commissioners charged with the responsibility of adopting it, and he must return to that same governing board to request additional funds for any deficiencies which may occur." [4c]

Budget Management and Evaluation

Living within the budget becomes the responsibility of the administrator once allocations have been made. Controls have to be set up on a monthly basis and care must be taken to see to it that expenditures conform to the intentions expressed under the budget prepared and submitted. When budget adjustments must be made, approval has to be sought from higher authority especially if the charges are major in scope. If deficiency appropriations are required to meet emergencies or unanticipated needs, these requests must go through the regular process.

Schottland makes a point about the power and responsibility of the administrator who controls the budget: "Too frequently, the fund allocation process is looked upon as one in which the legislative body appropriates the funds. As we have pointed out, however, administrative decisions may be as important as legislative appropriations. Decisions made prior to submission of budgets to the legislature usually set over-all feelings while the subsequent decisions of budget officers or administrators may curtail expenditures or channel them into certain program areas rather than others. In many jurisdictions, considerable flexibility is given administrative officials in expending appropriated funds. Occasionally, legislative committees will appropriate additional sums and leave to the discretion of administrators their allocation to programs. In effect, this relegates a fund allocation role to administrators." [6a]

Schottland observes in addition, "Many of us are beginning to learn that good laws may be sabotaged by inadequate appropriations, and good programs may be hampered by bad administrative decisions; that sound administrative decisions may be useless if inadequate fund allocations prevent their implementation or that even adequate fund allocations may be ineffective if their proper use is blocked by inept administrative decisions." [6b]

In recent years the Federal government has developed what has become known as Program, Planning, Budgeting Systems (PPBS).[2] This approach has merit and helpful features for the administrator. As Greenberg says, "PPBS starts with the assumption that an organization rarely finds its resources adequate to finance all of the valid programs which are urgently needed. The program, planning, budgeting systems approach deliberately pits one program proposal against another—or more properly against all the others—and tries to assess the relative merits of each in achieving the organization's objectives. . . . Its practitioners hoped to achieve these gains through its use: First, to find some ways of achieving 'order' when faced with tons of data about large numbers of people, complex activities, interrelated programs, high-powered demands for money, et cetera. Second, to make rational decisions wherever it is appropriate to be rational and to identify the value decisions which need to be made—and their consequences. . . . There are several basic operations in PPBS. The more you observe them, the closer you come to achieving the full potential of the method. These elements are: 1. Keep your eye on the 'end product'—not just on the specific activity: 2. Take a long-range view, looking five or even ten years in the future—rather than just a year-to-year review; 3. Identify alternative courses of action—and if none exists invent some; 4. Analyze each alternative course of action in terms of both its contribution toward achieving the 'end product' and its costs; 5. Keep tabs on what is happening in the system; and 6. Be flexible." [7]

Another approach of considerable value to the administrator who wishes to evaluate the extent to which the budget is achieving its objectives is the "cost-benefit" method. Levine says, "By 'cost-benefit' is meant the relationship of the resources required—the cost—to attain certain goals—the benefits. It is based on the economic concept that many executive decisions involve the allocation, or best use, of limited resources among competing requirements. The allocation of available resources is determined by a comparative analysis of the current system with presumably practicable alternative systems. Thus conceived, cost-benefit analysis is a tool for the administrator confronted with the need to make choices among viable competing programs designed to achieve certain objectives. It is not a substitute for the educated judgment of the decision-maker. Rather it provides a package of relevant information on which to base certain kinds of decisions. Also, it does not favor the 'cheapest' or even the 'best' program, but the optimal program in terms of the available resources—money, trained personnel, facilities." [8a]

Levine then points out: "As generally used, cost-benefit analysis provides the administrator with a package of information to assist him in making a choice among alternative programs which are competing for that scarce resource—even in an affluent society—money. Actually the uses to which such an analysis can be put by administrators vary with the level of the administrator. For the local administrator it can serve as a guide to the improvement of project operations: to remind him of the objectives and to raise the question of whether project operations have strayed from the original objectives. . . . For the administrator of a state or national program such an analysis provides the basis for choice among programs to accomplish either the same or other important objectives in terms of the relative returns on investment." [8b]

When one considers the fact that expenditures for social welfare are generally modest when compared with expenditures for defense and space exploration, it can be argued that the nation receives a substantial return from whatever it invests in the welfare of its people. Because the returns are intangible and often hidden, it is difficult to make the public understand how important it is to help people with special needs. The administrator faces a never-ending task of interpreting the need for and importance of adequate resources for the work of his agency.

NOTES

1. Walter A. Friedlander, *Introduction to Social Welfare,* 3rd ed., (Englewood Cliffs, N.J.: Prentice-Hall, Inc., © 1968), p. 203.
2. Virginia Held, "PPBS Comes to Washington," *The Public Interest,* Summer 1966, p. 104.
3. Aaron Wildavsky, *The Politics of the Budgetary Process* (Boston: Little, Brown and Company, 1964), a p. 1; b 1–2; c 4.
4. Reed K. Clegg, *The Administrator in Public Welfare* (Springfield, Ill.: Charles C. Thomas, Publisher, 1966), a p. 52; b 53; c 52.
5. Celia R. Moss, *Administering a Hospital Social Service Department* (Washington, D.C.: American Association of Medical Social Workers, 1955), p. 31.
6. Charles I. Schottland, "Administrator Decisions and Fund Allocations in Social Welfare," Social Welfare Reprint Series 22, Brandeis University, The Florence Heller Graduate School for Advanced Studies in Social Welfare. Reprinted from *Economic Progress and Social Welfare,* ed., Leonard H. Goodman. Published for the National Conference on Social Welfare by Columbia University Press, 1966, a pp. 85–86; b 65–66.
7. Martin Greenberg, "Program, Planning, Budgeting Systems," *Research Reports,* Council of Jewish Federations and Welfare Funds, New York, N.Y. Paper presented at the Annual Meeting of the National Conference of Jewish Communal Service, Atlantic City, New Jersey, May 26, 1967, pp. 1–2.
8. Abraham S. Levine, "Cost-Benefit Analysis and Social Welfare Program Evaluation," *The Social Service Review,* July 1968, a p. 174; b 182.

13 Agency Evaluation, Change, and Growth

In this chapter attention will be given to the evaluation of administration, the role of the administrator in providing leadership for the process of change, and ways of facilitating the growth of administrators and staffs.

The Importance of Evaluation

For many reasons it is important to evaluate administration. The quality of administration has a considerable influence on the quality of services rendered. Because the agency is held in trust by the community, it has a moral obligation to appraise the extent to which it is fulfilling its role. The community has a right to expect that the agency will evaluate itself. As Coughlin observes, "A social welfare agency is a public trust. Unlike a profit-making business or industry, but rather like a university, a welfare institution springs out of the culture and value and needs of the community, and offers to the community its service. In turn, it is financed and supported by the community, so that in a certain real sense the right to ownership is the community's, even though direct administrative responsibility is in the hands of a private group." [1]

The changing nature of the community and the changes in social service programs make administrative evaluation increasingly important. As President Nixon said, "A third of a century of unprecedented growth and change has strained our institutions, and raised serious questions about whether they are still adequate to the times." [2]

Continuous and regular evaluation of administration is of significant benefit to the agency as a whole. It gets a picture of itself and sees points where it needs to be strengthened. It becomes more flexible and more able to modify its administrative practices.

When an agency evaluates its administration it sets the tone for evaluation elsewhere. If it never looks at administration it is less likely to attempt appraisal of other aspects of its work.

Evaluation is valuable to administrators because they need to know how well they are doing their jobs. When they know their strengths and limitations they can work out programs of personal growth and self-improvement. Furthermore, administrators get a real sense of satisfaction when accomplishments are revealed through evaluation.

Criteria and Standards of Evaluation

A vital step in the evaluation of administration is the formulation of criteria and standards to be used by the person who is making the evaluation. This is not easy, for, as Moss says, "Social workers have sometimes been guilty of resisting standardized procedures in administration. The importance of individualization which is the primary tenet of casework, is often misconstrued when applied in administration. It is applicable in administration but the unit individualized is not always a person. Often it is a form of organization in relation to a function to be performed. One of the differences between business and social work is that of measurement. The social service department in the hospital does not operate on a profit motive that can be translated into financial gain. Its activities are essentially cooperative rather than competitive. It, therefore, has difficulty in evaluating the degree of success of its service, since for the most part success consists of enabling the persons served to achieve personally satisfying and socially useful lives within the limits of their illness. The skills of professional personnel which make this result possible are not often easily interpreted." [3]

In spite of the difficulty in formulating and applying criteria, more and more agencies are publishing helpful guides.[4] Gladieux lists eight elements of good administration of welfare: "1. A sharp distinction between the legislative powers and policy leadership of the governing board and the executive authorities of the chief administrator; with scrupulous observance of these respective roles by both parties. 2. Well-understood goals and well-defined programs arrived at through a process of intensive planning based on a perceptive evaluation of changing conditions and need. 3. The provision of a sound structural organization which divides the work to be performed into manageable functional units based on purposes to be served. 4. The clear fixing of administrative responsibility and the delegation and redelegation of authority to points of competence in the hierarchy. 5. The establishment of coordinating and control mechanisms at the level of top responsibility and the provision of effective processes of consultation and decision-making. 6. A system of personnel management which recruits and maintains a staff corps that performs to the limit of its capacity and that is satisfied as to the equity and justness of its conditions of employment. 7. The provision of a rational budgetary and fiscal system that scrupulously controls expenditures and assures the balanced allocation of resources. 8. Sound business practices which take advantage of the multifarious and striking advances of modern management in procedural and mechanical techniques." [5]

A workshop group listed twelve administrative yardsticks:

1. the agency's objectives and functions should be clearly defined. 2. The agency's program should be based upon actual needs: it should be limited in scope and territory to a field in which the agency can operate effectively; it should be related to the social welfare needs, patterns, and resources of the community; it should be regarded as dynamic rather than static; and the program should change to meet changing needs. 3. The agency should be soundly organized. This would include a clear distinction between policy-making and execution; cooperative and creative relationships between board, executive, and staff; unity of command, that is, administrative direction by a single executive; logical allocation of functions in accordance with a general plan of administration; clear and definite assignments of authority and responsibility; and effective co-ordination of all organization units and staff members. 4. Staff members should be employed on the basis of qualifications for their jobs. Staff personnel should be adequate in quantity and quality to the needs of the agency. Employees should be paid adequate salaries. The agency should operate on the basis of good working conditions and sound personnel policies. 5. The agency should be located effectively from the standpoint of its function; it should have adequate space, and equipment and supplies should be adequate in quantity and quality to its needs. 6. The agency's funds should be regarded as trust funds, to be administered in a sense of stewardship to those from whom the funds are received and to the community. The agency should operate on the basis of an annual budget; it should have an adequate accounting system; its accounts should be audited annually by a competent disinterested professional accountant; the sources of funds and methods of money raising should be appropriate to the nature and needs of the agency. 7. The agency should maintain adequate records. Records should be accurate, as comprehensive as necessary for the purpose yet as simple as possible, filed so as to be readily accessible when needed, and properly protected and safeguarded. 8. Clerical and maintenance services and facilities should be adequate in quantity and quality and efficient in operation. The agency should have an office or organization manual as a textbook for new staff members and a handbook of operation. 9. The agency should avoid isolation and should be an active and contributing participant in the social welfare services of the community. It should have constructive working relationships with appropriate local, state, and national bodies. 10. All who are connected with the agency should develop attitudes and methods of working which will build sound public relations. The agency should have a definite program of education and interpretation. The agency should seek to develop a constituency which will have a real understanding of the needs which it is trying to meet, and of its objectives, services, and problems. 11. The work of the agency should be characterized by a basic desire to serve human beings; an understand-

ing of the individuals whom it seeks to serve, and of their needs; a spirit of freedom, unity, and democratic participation in a common adventure in human service; and a sense of creativeness, movement, and growth. 12. At appropriate intervals, probably once a year, the agency should put itself to the test of a self-appraisal which would take stock of such matters as the successes and failures of the past year, the present status of the agency and its program, its performance as measured by objectives and established criteria, its strengths and weaknesses, its current problems, and the next steps that it ought to take.[6]

In an earlier volume [7] the author presented criteria which might be used in an evaluation of the effectiveness of administrative leaders. These criteria have been revised and are offered below:

1. Effective administrative leaders advance the organization toward its goals of providing high-quality programs and services. Barker and Briggs say, "Without a clear notion of what the organization's function is, there can be no way of determining whether manpower deployment has achieved its optimum level, but defining this function is an impressive challenge. This is so because every organization has many different functions, some of which are continually being modified, many of which are inconsistent with other functions, and most of which are not clear to the organization members. Furthermore, for every function there is a variety of possible means that may be used to fulfill it, and these different means must also be identified. Organization members may compete among themselves for the institution of means that are relevant to their own capacities. Pressures from a variety of sources, including other organizations, present barriers to the fulfillment of functions. Finally, members of the organization continually change in their capacities and interests and are subject to outside pressures that require behavior of them that may not be in harmony with the organization's functions." [8]

2. Effective administrative leaders have a deep and growing understanding of the culture and character of the agency. Moore's discussion of business organizations has pertinence for social agencies as well. He notes: "Each company has a history, a way of doing things, a set of conventions, customs, and social habits that constitute its character as a business. Executive development in many organizations represents a kind of acculturation process whereby the young executive is taught how this particular company operates—what its way is, what its character is, what kinds of things it will do, what kinds of things it positively will not do, what its policies, common symbols, ceremonials, and heroic figures are. The difference between the young, immature executive, the fellow who doesn't know his way around, and the older one is often simply a difference in the degree of acculturation that has occurred. The latter knows the ins and outs of the organization, how to get things done, what symbols and conventions to invoke under varying circumstances; he looks, speaks, and acts the part. The other man doesn't even know how to write a letter; he doesn't know busi-

ness parlance, the lingo; he is unaware of all the sacred cows around the organization; he has no sense of the tempo of the place, how people dress, how they act, and how they get things done. There is an uneasiness about him because he has not yet learned the culture, symbols, and values of the organization. The culture or character of a business and the understanding that executives and employees within the organization have of this culture are important controls. As a consequence, determining the character of an organization, which really means determining who you are, where you are going, and how you operate in this complex world, is likely to absorb a great deal of the attention of top management." [9]

3. Effective administrative leaders give vigorous, continuous, and stimulating leadership to the people with whom they work.

4. Effective administrative leaders establish and maintain cooperative, productive, working relationships with their community, and their regional and national affiliate groups.

5. Effective administrative leaders achieve a balance in relationships with the board, the staff, the constituency, and the community.

6. Effective administrative leaders state and project challenging goals for the period ahead and encourage people to work toward those goals. As Dimock puts it, this calls for an administrator "who can rise above his daily tasks and see his institution with a fresh eye; he is the one capable of providing energy and drive and preventing the onset of decline. Unfortunately, many administrators are limited to trouble-shooting, to the settling of immediate and often petty crises, and to keeping their noses to the grindstone; as a result, they have no time or energies left over to devote to questions of morale, inspiration, and vitality." [10]

7. Effective administrative leaders strive to create a sense of organization wholeness and unity. They place accent on the importance of coordination of human effort.

8. Effective administrative leaders strive to establish good channels of communication within which all members of the organization feel free to contribute their thoughts and energies. This makes for the growth of a responsive staff with high morale.

9. Effective administrative leaders give evidence of getting satisfaction out of their work and try to see that others also receive satisfaction.

10. Effective administrators plan their work carefully, they review their accomplishments and their shortcomings, and they set goals for themselves.

11. Effective administrators think ahead. They concentrate attention on forecasting trends and needs so that the organization will not get caught short.

12. Effective administrators predict and anticipate behavior. As a result of their sensitive timing, they avoid the creating of situations that arouse misunderstanding and conflict because people are not ready.

13. Effective administrators make good choices in terms of priorities and sequence of items that need to be done at a certain time.

14. Effective administrators select competent and qualified people and see to it that they are clear on their duties and responsibilities. They surround themselves with the best people they can get.

15. Effective administrators delegate responsibility to people and show faith in the ability of these people to carry through successfully the assignments they have accepted.

16. Effective administrative leaders keep people informed about plans, changes, problems, and other important areas of knowledge needed by the total work force.

17. Effective administrators seek to understand the continual changing forces of the community, the nation, and the world and keep in mind their over-all responsibility to their community.

18. Effective administrators exhibit a spirit and attitude which is buoyant, hopeful, positive, and contagious because they know this is an important factor in helping other people achieve their maximum potentials.

19. Effective administrative leaders have worked out a theory and a philosophy of administration grounded in conviction about democratic values.

20. Effective administrators are oriented toward the future and have learned how to facilitate change within their organization.

21. Effective administrators know how to handle the unexpected, emergency, crisis situation and know how to deal with the inevitable pressures of work. They are flexible and adaptable and give evidence of being able to respond to the challenge of the moment.

22. Effective administrative leaders concentrate attention upon the growth of persons and the development of leadership. As has been pointed out, "The continued vigor of any institution is dependent in large measure upon its ability to provide a continuous supply of creative leadership to its critical points of control." [11]

23. Effective leadership places emphasis on research and evaluation as means of helping them discover better ways of performing their tasks.

24. Effective administrative leaders spot emerging problems and move in on these problems before they become seriously advanced.

25. Effective administrative leaders know how to release the energy of people. As Schlesinger says, "The true test of an administrator may be, not his ability to design and respect organization charts, not his ability to keep within channels, but his ability to concert and release the energies of men for the attainment of public objectives. It might be argued that the essence of successful administration is: first, to acquire the ideas and information necessary for wise decisions; second, to maintain control over the actual making of the decision; and, third, to mobilize men and women who can make the first two things possible . . ." [12]

26. Effective administrative leaders handle the mechanics of their job with confidence and dispatch.

27. Effective administrators are conscious of the importance of careful and close control of all finances.

28. Effective administrators build good understanding of the services and programs their agency offers through wide and continuous interpretation.

29. Effective administrative leaders make good use of technical resource experts to provide special help on special problems.

30. Effective administrative leaders have worked out a thoughtful program of self-development including reading, participation in conferences, seminars, and the like.

The Administrator's Role in Facilitating Change

The social work administrator must assume considerable responsibility for facilitating change. *First,* he must be expert in diagnosing and determining the need for change. This is another way of saying that he locates agency problems and spots points at which changes are needed in the agency's operations. *Second,* the administrator must be an expert in assessing the motivation, the capacity, and the readiness on the part of people to change. *Third,* the administrator must have an understanding of his own motivation for change, his own capacity to change, and an awareness of what change is going to do to him. All too often administrators expect other people to change without being willing to change themselves. *Fourth,* the administrator must have skill in selecting appropriate change objectives and in relating those objectives to a time span. Changes that might be suitable at one time are not necessarily suitable at another time. Changes that require months to accomplish are different from changes that may require years to accomplish. *Fifth,* the administrator has the responsibility of choosing the appropriate type of helping role within the change situation. He may take leadership in gathering, collating, and interpreting needed factual materials. He may give leadership to the formulation of change plans and objectives. *Sixth,* the administrator must establish and maintain a helping relationship or helping role in the change process. He must be willing to modify his role as new and different needs emerge.

Years ago Vasey pointed out: "The concept of social welfare in the United States of America is not constant but rather it alters with changing conditions. Most recently, social welfare has been defined as encompassing the development and administration of (1) social insurance, (2) social assistance, and (3) other social services designed to strengthen family life and to provide care and protection for special groups such as children, the aged, and mentally, socially or physically handicapped persons." [13]

In 1969 President Nixon offered "a new set of reforms—a new set of proposals—a new and drastically different approach to the way in which government cares for those in need, and to the way the responsibilities are shared between the State and the Federal Government." [2] While the Nixon proposals had not been enacted by the end of 1970, if they are adopted they will make for major changes in the administration of public welfare services. Also, as society changes, it is likely that there will be continuous innovation in the welfare field calling for continuous adjustment on the part of administrators.

As Titmuss says, "The inescapable fact, regardless of whether we like the world as it is today, is that we are all living in a period of startlingly rapid change. In the past, economic and social changes were effected only at the price of immense hardship. The amount and rate of change under way today, and affecting all countries in varying degrees, may in some areas be less crudely evident in strictly economic terms but the consequences as a whole may be no less profound—though more subtly expressed —in generating social frustration and psychological stress. In other respects, economic and industrial changes dominate the problems of societies in transition. In all countries, the question of 'how to live together in society' is made more insistent by the widespread and pervasive effects of technological change. Yet little is known about how all these factors of change are affecting levels of poverty and need, patterns of family living, and community relations. Change, however induced, cannot take place without people being hurt. In consequence, new and different social needs are constantly arising, many of which are (or should be) the direct concern of social workers and social welfare programs. To identify and meet these needs and to minimize and prevent the hardships caused by change, social policy should be better informed. More and better data about the human condition, constructive and critical, should be at the disposal of policy-makers and administrators." [14]

Critics of society's institutions frequently level the charge that the human services are not changing fast enough to meet the new needs and rising demands for service. As Marien says: "Although there is evidence of a trend toward humanistic organization, it is also clear that organizations —especially those facing little competition—have not changed fast enough to meet new demands for new services and the growing norm of participation. Indeed, every public institution is under attack today for obsolete personnel, structure, and processes: police and welfare departments, schools and colleges, planning agencies and post offices, foreign policy-makers and political parties, churches and labor unions, the construction and transportation industries, Congress and state legislatures, hospitals and mental hospitals, and prisons and courts. Ironically, the institutions most responsive to human needs—those producing toothpaste, tires, and television sets— are probably the least important to our 'progress' or survival." [15]

Specht feels that at least some of the blame for failure to change rests with the administrators. He observes: "The basis for institutional policy change is in some problems identified as an unrecognized or unmet need in the community, a need the originator of the policy goal believes that the institution is responsible for meeting. The perception of the problem and the institution's responsibility are related to the policial, economic, social and institutional forces that come to bear on the perceiver; what is perceived to be a problem will depend on the institutional position of the initiator. So, for example, it is possible that concerns for institutional maintenance might guide the perceptions of professional administrators more than their feelings of responsibility for providing better service to clients." [16]

The administrator must realize that every agency is always undergoing change and that in every agency there are forces that resist change. Likert says, "Every organization is in a continuous state of change. Sometimes the changes are great, sometimes small, but change is always taking place. The conditions requiring these changes arise from both within and without. As a consequence, there is never-ending need for decisions which guide adjustments to change. The adequacy of these decisions for meeting an organization's current and developing internal and external situations determine the well-being, power, and future of that organization. We are coming to recognize with increasing clarity that the capacity of an organization to function well depends both upon the quality of its decision-making processes and upon the adequacy and accuracy of the information used. Sound decisions require accurate information about relevant dimensions of the problem as well as correct interpretation of that information. If the information available for decision-making is inaccurate or is incorrectly interpreted, the diagnostic decisions are likely to be in error and the actions taken, inappropriate." [17]

Dalton says, "The forces for change represented by tension and the desire for change must be mobilized, however, and given direction. Those forces acting to resist change in some given direction must be overcome, neutralized, or enlisted. In an organization, unless there is to be protracted resistance, someone must gain the acceptance and possible support of individuals not seeking change and even of those who feel threatened by it. The initiator of change gains support and overcomes resistance in proportion to his power and the relevance of his power to the objectives of the organization. His power in turn stems in large measure from the multiple sources of authority attached to his position in the structure." [18a]

The social work administrator who takes leadership in the change process may be helped by Kahn and Katz, who list four suggestions for facilitating change: "(1) In every attempt to create change, specify the target for change—change in individual behavior, in individual personality, in some interpersonal relationship, in family arrangements, or whatever it may be. . . . (2) Remember that no method of change is uniquely powerful and appropriate to all situations. Learn to use more than one approach, to judge the indicators favoring one or another. Above all, learn to use them in combination. . . . (3) Learn to work with the natural groups in which the individual functions—family, friends, organizations, work groups. Use them to learn of his life situation from observers besides himself, and use them to reinforce and secure and assist the process of change. . . . (4) Social workers [should] acknowledge the importance of and attempt to utilize . . . direct systematic changes—changes which involve altering formal procedures, policies, and structural arrangements." [19a]

While it is true that no one knows nearly enough about how to facilitate change, some studies have been enormously helpful. As Ginzberg and Reilley put it, "Effecting change in large organizations is primarily a question of alterations in the behavior of various groups who carry major responsibility. Top management must recognize, therefore, that its success in carrying out the major changes will largely depend on how well it mobilizes the psychological forces that can facilitate acceptance of the new and how well it diminishes those forces which reinforce people's adherence to the existing pattern. The major approaches available to management are effective communication, the control of anxiety, and the learning of new skills." [20]

There is substantial agreement that when staff members are involved in the change process and in the decision to change there is a much greater chance that the change will be accepted. As Guest notes: "Controls imposed by persons at the top of the hierarchy do not assure either efficiency or the cooperation of subordinates. There must be some kind of involvement from below which makes it possible for subordinates to accept changes and even to initiate a certain amount of change themselves. Put in the form of a general hypothesis: In a complex organization tension and stress will diminish and performance will improve with the introduction of social mechanisms which permit those in subordinate positions to participate in making decisions affecting their present and future roles in the organization." [21]

Dalton agrees: "In instances of successful change, there is a movement over time toward increased self-regard as the person finds himself capable of making the changes in behavior or attitude. He experiences a sense of accomplishment, a relief from tension, and a reintegration around a new pattern of activity and thought." [18b]

As administrators evaluate the change process in their agencies they come to realize that change in one part of the organization is likely to call for changes in other parts. As Kahn and Katz observe, "The degree of control and regulation of the activities of an organization cannot be changed at one level without affecting the whole organization. In fact, there is a characteristic of the properties of a system. If we are dealing with an organizational or system variable, we are working with something which applies to the entire organization. Change of such organizational characteristics is regarded as inherently difficult because it means changing so much and of course, this is correct. What is overlooked, however, is that less ambitious attempts to modify organizational processes by working with non-organizational variables is infinitely more difficult from the point of view of organization outcome, though it may entail less effort on the part of the change agent." [19b]

Administration has to understand the feelings of individuals who will be affected by agency changes. This requires a thorough knowledge and a careful evaluation of the effect change will have on the total organization before action is taken. As Selznick says,

The art of the creative leader is the art of institution building, the reworking of human and technological material to fashion an organism that embodies a new and enduring view. The opportunity to do this depends on a considerable sensitivity to the politics of internal change. This is more than a struggle for power among contending groups and leaders. It is equally a matter of avoiding recalcitrance and releasing energies. Thus winning consent to new directions depends on how secure the participants feel. When many routine problems of technical and human organization remain to be solved, when the minimum conditions for holding the organization together are only precariously met, it is difficult to expend energy on long-range planning and even harder to risk experimental programs. When the organization is in good shape from an engineering standpoint, it is easier to put ideals into practice. Old activities can be abandoned without excessive strain, for example, the costs of relatively inefficient but morale-saving transfer and termination can be absorbed. Security is bartered for consent. Since this bargain is seldom sensed as truly urgent, a default of leadership is the more common experience. On the same theme, security can be granted, thereby releasing energies for creative change, but examining established procedures to distinguish those important to a sense of security from those essential to the aims of the enterprise. Change should focus on the latter; stability can be assured to practices that do not really matter so far as objectives are concerned but which do satisfy the need to be free from threatening change. Many useless industrial conflicts have been fought to protect prerogative and deny security, with but little effect on the ultimate competence of the firm. If one of the great functions of administration is the exertion of cohesive forces in the direction of institutional security, another great function is the creating of conditions that will make possible in the future what is excluded in the present. This requires a strategy of change that looks to the attainment of new capability more nearly fulfilling the truly felt needs and aspirations of the institution leadership.[22]

The individual is likely to react positively toward change when he feels that it will strengthen the organization and his important place in it. As Dalton says, "Increasing self-esteem also appears to be an integral part of the phenomenon of behavioral and attitudinal change. Interestingly, moving toward greater self-esteem seems to be a facilitating factor not only in establishing new patterns of thought and action, but also in unfreezing old patterns. Abandoning previous patterns of behavior and thought is less difficult when an individual is moving toward an increased sense of his own worth. Movement along this continuum is away from a sense of self-doubt toward a feeling of positive worth, from a feeling of partial inadequacy toward a confirmed sense of personal capacity. The increased sense of one's own potential is evident all along this continuum, not merely at the end." [18e]

Principles of Institutional Change

The best formulation of principles of institutional change was prepared by Sorenson and Dimock. They developed ten principles as a result of their extensive research:

1. Policy making or legislation by the official Board of Directors is a developmental process in planned change. Policy control by citizen groups is a cardinal principle of institutional life. Technical contributions by staff are essential in proper combination with citizen policy control. Keeping these two factors in proper relation through periods of change is important, and it is not easy. Neglect of either principle blocks permanent change. The hard fact in policy making is that voting by a board does not necessarily change the attitudes, habits and practices of the organization. A new policy must be undergirded with enough understanding, commitment, and ability to carry it out or it will be only a good resolution on the books. This means that some change must actually take place before official policy becomes really governing policy. . . .

2. Planned change in an institution takes time and occurs by stages. Only significant changes are effected quickly. A considerable span of years is required to change attitudes, generate motivation, create new methods, materials, and facilities, get new habits for old, and establish new ways as accepted policy. Willing it, voting it, exhorting for it, does not bring significant change. Recognizing in advance that it will take time and projecting some scheme of stages (even though they cannot be firmly scheduled) has strong advantages. It relieves anxieties on the part of the participants, thereby lessens resistance and encourages positive attitudes toward the undertaking. It saves the administrative leadership from frustration arising from trying to accomplish everything all at once, releasing them to take each stage in stride. It also insures against certain failure if too short a time expectancy is assumed.

3. Planned institutional change must reckon with the strength and resilience of established patterns. If this were not so, institutions would die more easily. It is a common observation that ten years, and often twenty years, of mismanagement do not kill an old organization. The complex attitudes and habits in all the parts hold an agency together and cause it to persist even when administrative leadership is lacking or blundering. This fact, which protects an institution and which permits its body to live on even when the head is missing, is what makes changing an institution so difficult and so slow. . . .

4. Determined and persistent administrative leadership is required for planned institutional change. Because the whole agency is involved, in all its policy-making, administration, financial, building, personnel, and program aspects, it

is not possible for the executive officer to delegate program modernization to some staff member. Unmistakable commitment by the board and the executive to achieving the planned change is essential to give the effort the force of full "company policy." The administrative leadership must be continuing, persistent yet patient, and confident rather than sporadic, intermittent, easily discouraged with blocks, resistances, and time consumed, or threatened by hostility and failures. . . . The executive's job is always a twofold one: to administer change and to achieve cooperation in organization. These tend to pull in opposite directions. There is conflict between newer ways and newer policies that can be voted on and declared quickly and the old habits of men and institutions which change slowly. Beyond a certain point the processes of change cannot be hurried. Management involves a wide gamut of interpersonal and inter-group relations. It is not a technical but a human matter. Change without attention to cooperation in the social system is, ultimately, to fail to change. . . .

5. Planned institutional change proceeds from centralized to distributed operations and from external to internal motivation. At the outset, administrative leadership supplies the initiative, sets up meetings, does the bulk of the document formulation, enlists participation and cooperation, and gets the early steps in motion. In this early stage it is necessary as well as inevitable that such operations as get under way are centralized and that for most of the staff and constituency the motivation for the project is chiefly external, that is, in the administrative leadership. This does not mean that they are not for it, but that they have not participated in and agreed to, the decision, or that they are not anxious to see it succeed. But such commitment is permissive, not propulsive, in the early stages. As the project proceeds, the involvement of staff, advisors, and officers becomes deeper. Satisfactions come from new ways of doing things. As new skills are gained, confidence, security, and further commitment to the new ways develop. They are then more ready to take responsibility and leadership in their own branch and group. Persuading and training others speeds the process of internalizing motivation. . . .

6. Planned change in an institution calls for detecting and dealing with blocks. There will be blocks in the form of specific difficulties, fallacies in early assumptions, resistance, and specific need for additional processes and skills. It is impossible to foresee the whole route, the detours, the engine trouble, the poor roads and obstacles, or the number of miles ahead. No complete map or report of road conditions is available in advance. Knowing and accepting the fact that there will be difficulties is some preparation for them. Skill in diagnosing them as they arise grows with practice. The reasons for resistance to change must be discerned beneath the symptoms. Remedies for some difficulties must await more insights and motivation in the persons. Some problems call for administrative changes; some, for additional training; others, for revision in materials and methods; and still others yield with some catharsis or talking it out.

7. Institutional change is basically in persons and human relations. Institutional change is personality change. An organization is the sum of the attitudes, habits, and practices of the people in its leadership. Therefore, the deeper the institutional changes desired, the deeper the changes must be in staff. Logically, institutional change could come more quickly if the re-education of the staff came first. Practically, this is not possible. Staff realization of the need for

change comes enroute, as they become more involved. The need for staff re-education comes only as the need for it is discovered by them in the process of undertaking program change.

8. Administrative changes go with program change. As new ways of work are tried, blocks become apparent which are involved in building design or building usage, staff organization and assignments, and finance. Again, it would be logical to tackle these essentials first. But such changes usually require the pitchfork of necessity. New ways of working, when blocked by older administrative arrangements, generate readiness for undertaking difficult changes in structure, finance, and buildings. Budgets, organization, buildings, and administrative procedures are means to ends. They exist to support functions. When functions change, the means must change. However, so devoted do people become to the outer forms of structure, budgets, and buildings that their continued operation almost becomes ends. Functions are squeezed and adjusted to the inherited forms, rather than the forms being adjusted to changes in functions. When people come to care most about the vital functions, they are ready to change the inherited forms. This is what happens at the stage in planned change where the inherited structure, budget, and buildings get in the way of what people are enthusiastic to do. Changing the institution is a by-product of changing what the institution does. A new concept of function with its goals and methods set new directions. The blueprint for institutional change grows out of changes in function. Program changes fashion changes in every other part of the institution.

9. Institutions have not been changed until the changes have been consolidated, rooted, or established as normal. This is the fact too often overlooked in short-term experiments. No matter how sound or how effective has been a short demonstration, the institution itself will be relatively unchanged by the novel interlude unless the new is rooted in regular procedures and habits as established in normal ways. This means that enough people must understand and approve the changes. The new ways must be established as policy in the organization. And the new practices must be established in harmony with the new policies as normal operating habits. The "new" must no longer be new. It must have become the usual.

10. Institutions have not really changed until the members are undergoing a different experience. Real institutional change is not petty manicuring of the externals or just rearranging machinery or even an exciting professional exercise by the staff. Real change is measured at the heart, in the experience of the members for which it exists. Until that happens, all else is prelude.[23]

Growth of Administrators and Staffs

One of the vital areas of need in all social agencies is an educational program designed to further the growth of administrators and their staffs. If persons are to develop their skills and achieve higher levels of competence they must engage in programs of study developed by the agency or by a group of agencies or by institutions of higher education in cooperation with the agencies. As Clegg points out: "Welfare departments should have an on-going training program for all employees who are working in the social service program. The program should be designed to increase the competency of the staff, and to provide a continuing training program for efficient operation of new programs and changes in existing programs. The programs must take into consideration the levels of performance of administrative, social work, technical and clerical staff, and be geared to upgrading performance at all levels." [24a]

What is involved when the social work administrator seeks to develop his skills and competences? *First,* he should accept the fact that this is an individual matter. No two administrators have exactly the same needs at any given time. Consequently, each administrator should frame his own program by self-development. *Second,* to formulate such a program the administrator must analyze the job he is doing and focus upon the skills required to do it well. He will discover that in some areas he is strong and in other areas less so. *Third,* as discussed earlier in this chapter, evolution of the agency will reveal points where improvements are needed. *Fourth,* the administrator must try to set aside time for reading and for attending conferences, institutes, workshops, and seminars. In so doing he sets a tone for the agency and encourages others on the staff to do likewise. *Fifth,* the administrator can learn much about the community by participating actively in community affairs. *Sixth,* in his supervision of his key aides the administrator can locate areas of development important for all. In addition, he can spot persons who show good potential for growth and the ability to assume more complicated administrative tasks. *Seventh,* by participating in research efforts the administrator has the opportunity to learn much about the extent to which his leadership of the agency is resulting in good achievement. *Eighth,* by formulating a comprehensive program of in-service training, the administrator locates common growth needs of everyone who works for the agency.

Staff Development and In-service Training

Many agencies have directors of staff development and in-service training who are responsible to the executive. As Clegg says: "Staff development is a widely used term which relates to any process or program whereby an agency or department seeks to improve staff performance during the period of time they remain with the agency or department as employees. It includes all efforts to increase knowledge through planned instruction, reading or academic training, technical skills basic to job performance and improvement in work habits and attitudes. It includes training on the job and participation in training activities outside the scope of regular working hours. . . . All supervisory staff must share responsibility for staff development. Much of the encouragement and necessary inspiration for participation in staff development programs will spring from supervisory conferences with individual employees and from group discussions in unit meetings." [24b]

As Schroeder says: "Staff development is important because it serves to strengthen an agency and provides for improvement of staff services to clientele. In order for educational activities to be successful within the agency, it is essential that this belief be implemented by administrative sanction and support, by planning for this part of the program as systematically as for the other necessary parts of the program. Four principles are identified as basic to the planning of an educational program: 1. Staff development should be continuous and ongoing. 2. Staff development should be planned. Plans should include the educational assessment of staff members, which, along with the needs and problem areas in the agency, forms the basis for the formulation of objectives. Educational objectives should always be service oriented. 3. A variety of techniques can be used in carrying out the educational program. The particular combination of agency needs, staff needs, and immediate goal will determine which techniques are applicable at any particular time. 4. Staff development must be an integral part of the total program." [25]

Taylor and associates observe that: "To be successful, a staff development program must ensure—1. identification of training needs on a long-term and current basis for groups of staff as well as for individuals; 2. use of the administratively planned and implemented methods of training available within the State agency and its subdivisions; 3. use of educational resources outside the agency in accordance with the special needs of individual staff members; and 4. establishment of policies concerning the rights and obligations of personnel with respect to training and technical and professional education, the educational requirements for various positions, training, leave for short-time study, and attendance at professional conferences and meetings." [26]

In her brilliant formulation of criteria and guidelines for the evaluation of in-service training, Heyman sees the agency's administrative structure and policy as basic. She says: "In-service training is an essential component of administration. . . . The goals, content, and methods of training are necessarily determined by the continually developing and shifting agency goals and programs. In addition, training holds implications for organizational change. Frequently, the need for organizational change is identified during in-service training by the trainers themselves and brought to the attention of program administrators. Frequently, organizational change is identified as a result of the training through the trainee's increased knowledge and skill and appropriate attitudes toward the client. The trainee reflects these changes in a new perception of his job which in turn may call for structural and policy change within the agency. To implement the integral relationship between in-service training and administration, there is a constant flow of intelligence between them. This is made effective by locating the position of Director of Staff Development among the policy-making staff positions of the agency." [27]

The principles of social work administration which are summarized in the next chapter can be used as a guide for the formulation of educational programs.

NOTES

1. Bernard J. Coughlin, S.J., "Interrelationships of Governmental and Voluntary Welfare Services," *The Social Welfare Forum*, 1966 (Published for the National Conference on Social Welfare by Columbia University Press, New York), p. 95.
2. President Richard M. Nixon, "Address of the President" on nationwide radio and television, August 8, 1969.
3. Celia R. Moss, *Administering a Hospital Social Service Department* (Washington, D.C.: American Association of Medical Social Workers, 1955), p. 57.
4. In this connection the National Federation of Settlements and Neighborhood Centers has prepared a checklist for rating neighborhood centers entitled *Measuring Up!* (1967) Also the Midwest Region of the National Jewish Welfare Board has developed *A Guide for Creating Tools for Program Evaluation* (1968).
5. Bernard L. Gladieux, "Management Imperatives for Welfare Administrations in the Future." New York: National Social Welfare Assembly, December 12, 1957, p. 4.
6. *Proccedings of Workshop on Social Agency Administration—Leadership and the Social Welfare Executive.* Richmond Professional Institute—School of Social Work, Richmond, Va. April 12–14, 1967, pp. 27–28.
7. Harleigh B. Trecker, *New Understandings of Administration* (New York: Association Press, 1961), pp. 193–197.
8. Robert L. Barker and Thomas L. Briggs, *Differential Use of Social Work Manpower.* (New York: National Association of Social Workers, 1968), p. 57.
9. David G. Moore, "What Makes a Top Executive?" in Robert T. Golembiewski and Frank Gibson, eds., *Managerial Behavior and Organizational Demands* (Chicago: Rand McNally & Company, 1967), pp. 330–331.
10. Marshall E. Dimock, *Administrative Vitality* (New York: Harper, 1959), p. 59.
11. *Professional Administrators for America's Schools,* 38th Yearbook, 1960 (Washington, D.C.: American Association of School Administration, National Education Association), p. 143.
12. Arthur M. Schlesinger, Jr., *The Age of Roosevelt—The Coming of the New Deal,* Vol. II (Boston: Houghton-Mifflin Co., 1959), p. 522.
13. Wayne Vasey, *Government and Social Welfare* (New York: Holt, Rinehart and Winston, Inc., 1958), p. 10, quoted from "Social Welfare Administration in the United States," a report prepared at the request of the United Nations for incorporation in its international study of social welfare administration.
14. Richard M. Titmuss, *Commitment to Welfare* (New York: Pantheon Books—A Division of Random House, © 1968), pp. 42–43.
15. Michael Marien, "Irrepressible Revolt," *The New Republic,* February 22, 1969, p. 31.
16. Harry Specht, "Casework Practice and Social Policy Formulation," *Social Work,* January 1968, p. 45.
17. Rensis Likert, *The Human Organization* (New York: McGraw-Hill Book Co., © 1967), p. 128.
18. Gene W. Dalton, Louis B. Barnes and Abraham Zaleznik, *The Distribution of Authority in Formal Organizations* (Harvard University, Division of Research, Graduate School of Business Administration, 1968), a pp. 114–115; b 132; c 129–130.
19. Robert L. Kahn and Daniel Katz, "Social Work and Organizational Change," *The Social Welfare Forum,* 1965 (Published for the National Conference on Social Welfare by Columbia University Press, New York), a pp. 179–181; b 179.

20. Eli Ginzberg and Ewing W. Reilley, *Effecting Change in Large Organizations* (New York: Columbia University Press, 1957), p. 60.
21. Robert H. Guest, *Organizational Change—The Effect of Successful Leadership* (Homewood, Ill.: Dorsey-Irwin, 1962), pp. 153–154.
22. Philip Selznick, *Leadership in Administration* (New York: Harper & Row, 1957), pp. 22–28, 33–43, 62–64, 149–154.
23. Roy Sorenson and Hedley S. Dimock, *Designing Education in Values—A Case Study in Institutional Change* (New York: Association Press, 1955), pp. 204–210.
24. Reed K. Clegg, *The Administrator in Public Welfare* (Springfield, Ill.: Charles C. Thomas, Publisher, 1966), a p. 105; b 107.
25. Dorothy Schroeder, "Basic Principles of Staff Development and Their Implementation" in *Staff Development in Mental Health Services,* ed. George W. Wagner and Thomas L. Briggs (New York: National Association of Social Workers, 1966), pp. 45–46.
26. Eleanor K. Taylor, Eulene Hawkins, and Hilda P. Tebow, *Administrative Approaches to Staff Development in Public Welfare Agencies* (Washington, D.C.: U.S. Department of Health, Education and Welfare, Social and Rehabilitation Service, 1968), pp. 16–17.
27. Margaret M. Heyman, *Criteria and Guidelines for the Evaluation of In-Service Training* (Washington: U.S. Department of Health, Education and Welfare, Social and Rehabilitation Service), pp. 5–6.

14 Basic Principles

In this concluding chapter the principles of social work administration will be presented. In a sense, the chapter is a summary of the book in that the principles grow out of what has been discussed in Chapters 1 through 13.

Principles Defined

One dictionary declares that a principle is "an accepted or professed rule of action or conduct" and "a fundamental, primary, or general law or truth from which others are derived" and "an adopted rule or method for application in action." [1]

White says that "a principle must be understood to mean a hypothesis so adequately tested by observation and/or experiment that it may intelligently be put forward as a guide to action, or as a means of understanding." [2]

Barr observes that "a principle is a verbalized statement of an observed uniformity relative to some class of objects. . . . Principles—that is, general rules or laws, concepts, fundamental truths, generally accepted tenets —are the means by which we proceed from one situation to another. . . . Principles may arise from either critically analyzed experience or from systematic investigation." [3]

The principles of social work administration are generalized statements for use by the administrator as he does his job. These statements of good practice in administration have grown out of observation, analysis, and research. They are separate ideas but they are also interrelated and, taken as a composite, constitute a philosophy of administration.

The Importance of Principles

The administrator who has an understanding of basic principles and who uses these principles to guide him in the action he takes is behaving professionally. He makes his choices and decisions not in terms of technique but rather in terms of his broad beliefs as to what social work is, the values that undergird it, and the purposes it serves in society. His professional skill rests upon his knowledge of how people behave and how they work together.

The social work administrator who is guided by principle works planfully and consistently. His methods and his goals are closely related. He strives for excellence in his work and encourages others to perform to the best of their ability. When confronted with situations where values are in conflict he makes decisions in terms of what is regarded as being best for the clients. In evaluating his work the principle-oriented administrator takes the long view rather than the short view.

Principles are the most useful tools the administrator has. They are tools for the analysis of problems, the determination of goals, the choice of methods, the assignment of responsibilities, and the evaluation of results. When the administrator pays serious attention to principles, he finds that his efforts are creatively productive in terms of the growth of persons and the advancement of the agency to high levels of accomplishment.

Basic Principles of Social Work Administration

The eighteen principles offered and discussed below represent a beginning formulation. It is hoped that they will be useful and will lead administrators to their own formulations of principles as they see them.

1. *The Principle of Social Work Values.*

In social work administration the values of the profession are the foundations upon which services are developed and made available to persons who need them. The administrator and everyone in the agency responsible for providing service must accept these values and be guided by them.

Central to this principle is our belief in the dignity and worth of all people and their right to participate in making decisions about matters which affect them. Administrators who accept social work values and are guided by them believe deeply in freedom of expression and respect the rights of individuals in this regard. The human personality is considered to be the prime source of energy and influence in administrative work. The way administrators accept individuals as persons and release their energies and talents is reflected in the tone of the agency and in the way it does its work. The individual and his needs is always the primary concern of the administrator. He is responsible for the indvidual's basic well-being. An essential attribute of social work administration is the realization by each individual of his full potential to serve society through his participation in the purposeful work of the agency. The administration is obligated to find ways by which individuals can achieve self-realization. What happens to people is always of central importance.

2. The Principle of Community and Client Needs.

In social work administration the needs of the community and the individuals within it are always the basis for the existence of social agencies and the provision of programs. The administrator along with the others who make up the agency must accept the fact that the meeting of needs is their primary obligation.

The principle of community and client needs implies that the administrator will seek always to understand the condition out of which needs arise and that he will work to remove such conditions insofar as is possible. He will have a method of studying the community to discover points of stress and he will anticipate emerging needs to be better prepared to meet them. He will seek to relate his agency to all of the forces making for the enrichment of community life and the strengthening of community services. He will be an active participant in the community development process.

3. The Principle of Agency Purpose.

In social work administration the social purposes of the agency must be clearly formulated, stated, understood, and utilized. The administrator along with others makes decisions and takes action in terms of the extent to which the decisions and actions will further the achievements of the stated objectives of the agency.

The administrator who recognizes the need for consciously formulated specific objectives for his agency becomes a purposeful leader who influences the course of the agency in terms of agreed-upon goals. Skillful administrators make wise and continuous use of agency *purpose*. It should be their primary point of reference. It should influence and guide every move they make.

The administrator, therefore, must be increasingly clear about the nature and meaning of purpose. He must give leadership to the process by which purposes are determined and utilized.

When purposes are clear, the administrator is able to mobilize, focus, and coordinate individual and group energy in relation to priorities logically set up and systematically implemented.

4. *The Principle of Cultural Setting.*

In social work administration the culture of the community must be understood inasmuch as it influences the way needs are expressed, services are authorized and supported and utilized by people who need them. The administrator must have an ever-increasing knowledge of the culture of his community.

Every social agency exists in a cultural setting which in itself is always changing. The beliefs, views, values, prejudices, experiences, and feelings of the people in a given situation constitute the basis for their behavior. The administrator who recognizes this fact seeks to sharpen his awareness of the nuances of cultural determinations and diligently tries to work in ways that will utilize the cultural strengths in his setting. Programs and services should be in harmony with the prevailing cultural forms and should be carried forward in ways which support the growth of positive cultural change.

5. *The Principle of Purposeful Relationships.*

In social work administration effective, purposeful working relationships must be established between the administrator, the board, the staff, and the constituency. The administrator must concentrate his attention on helping people relate to him and to each other so that their joint efforts will result in a program of services.

This principle assumes that it is both possible and necessary to create the conditions under which effective relationships may develop. It assumes that the teamwork character of effective working relationships can be experienced and felt. Effective working relationships grow out of the mutual acceptance of the administrator and others in the agency who seek to cooperate and work in harmony. The quality and strength of the administrator's relationships with his people determines in large measure the extent to which they will be motivated to their highest levels of productivity. Relationships based on acceptance, cooperation, mutual respect, shared responsibility, and broad participation are the foundation of democratic administration.

6. *The Principle of Agency Totality.*

In social work administration the agency must be understood in its totality and wholeness. It must be seen as a living instrumentality made up of interrelated parts which constitute a system of energy output and resource deployment to meet defined needs and render defined services through the united efforts of people.

The administrator must strive to create a sense of unity in his agency and must strive for balance, continuity, stability, and relatedness so that the impact will be as efficient as possible.

When the administrator accepts the totality of the agency and sees it in its wholeness, his leadership and energy output is distributed across the spectrum of ongoing programs to the advantage of all and the favoritism of none. Resources are properly allocated and services are appropriately underwritten in terms of their value to the agency as a whole and the needs of the people to be met.

The approach of wholeness and total agency understanding and development makes for unity and reduces the forces of devisiveness. The administrator more than any other person must regard the agency as a totality.

7. *The Principle of Professional Responsibility.*

In social work administration the administrator is responsible for the provision of high-quality professional services based on standards of professional practice which have been carefully formulated and rigorously applied.

The professional social work agency is made up of persons who have specialized knowledge and skill that they have acquired by means of professional education and experience. It is the task of the administration to help provide the conditions under which professional people can render professional services. The way the agency is set up and regarded as a system of *professional responsibility* is largely determined by the administrator who is himself a major model of professional behavior to be followed by his colleagues. It is scarcely possible to develop a staff that behaves with professional judgment and skill unless the administrator exhibits the highest form of professional, responsible leadership. The accountability of the administrator is basically to the clientele who have need for the professional services the agency is designed to provide.

8. *The Principle of Participation.*

In social work administration appropriate contributions of board, staff, and constituency are sought and utilized through the continuous process of dynamic participation structured and encouraged by the administrator who seeks to involve people in agency decision-making and problem-solving.

This principle is based on the dual proposition that agency members have both the *right* and the *responsibility* to take part in the administration of the agency. Participation is a key concept in the democratic process. It assumes that the product which emerges from the joint efforts of many competent people is superior at what any one person can produce by himself. In addition, the issues of administrative situations come alive when people are involved in solving problems and in making decisions. Furthermore, decisions made this way are more certain of implementation. It is the interaction of persons with each other that makes the agency a corporate force for furthering the agreed-upon objectives.

9. *The Principle of Communication.*

In social work administration open channels of communication are essential to the complete functioning of people. The administration is responsible for creating the communication channels and for seeing to it that they are kept open and utilized to the fullest possible extent.

Communication is, of course, basic to the principle of participation. Unless people are in communication with one another there can be no organized human effort. Unless the communication is focused on objectives, problems, and tasks to be done, it will be random and will not produce the agreements required. The social work administrator, therefore, has a responsibility to give direction to the communication efforts of the people for whom he is responsible. In addition, he must be in communication with his board, staff, and constituency and must constantly assess the extent to which his communication skills are being effective.

10. *The Principle of Leadership.*

In social work administration the administrator must carry major responsibility for the leadership of the agency in terms of goal attainment and the provision of professional services.

In his leadership role the administrator by example, by stimulation, and by encouragement and support seeks to create a climate where innovation is sought and regarded as essential to the ability of the agency to meet changing needs with the utmost of effectiveness.

Good leadership is basic to all productive group experience. In social work administration it is apparent that the administrator carries a heavy leadership responsibility which must be taken seriously. In his leadership of the agency the administrator skillfully solicits the contributors of his board, staff, and constituency and creates new patterns of synthesis from these contributions. He sets high but reasonable goals and offers direction and guidance to people who join him in efforts to achieve these goals. He encourages others to develop and display their leadership abilities and provides opportunities for them to assume progressively more responsible roles in the agency.

11. *The Principle of Planning.*

In social work administration the process of continuous planning is fundamental to the development of meaningful services. The administra-

tion must give leadership to the planning process and must enable others to plan their work as individuals and in relation to the total task of the agency.

The principle of planning assumes that the agency must have some method or system for determining policies and programs and that the administrator is a key element in the formulation and operation of the planning mechanisms and processes. Sound administration is necessarily planned action rather than sporadic or haphazard. When action is planned it has a logical quality about it. There are steps which can be taken in a serial way in the planning process and each phase of the plan being made grows out of previous moves. Planning does not guarantee the complete success of every venture but without planning most ventures have little chance of succeeding. The skill of planning is an essential quality for the social work administrator.

12. *The Principle of Organization.*

In social work administration the work of many people must be arranged in an organized manner and must be structured so that responsibilities and relationships are clearly defined.

The administration is responsible for developing the form of organization most suitable for the kind of agency it is. The administrator must check on the effectiveness of the organization in terms of maximum energy release and output focused upon the tasks of service provision.

The principle of organized human effort is fundamental to both individual and group accomplishment. When administration is viewed as a process of interaction and as a situation within which interpersonal relationships provide the energy for the agency to use in pursuing its goals, it is clear that the administrator must concentrate upon organizing for productivity. Unless there is good organization energy will be wasted and efficiency will become illusive, if not impossible.

13. *The Principle of Delegation.*

In social work administration the delegation of responsibility and authority to other professional persons is essential inasmuch as no one executive can possibly perform all of the specialized tasks that must be undertaken.

The administrator delegates work assignments and responsibilities to colleagues in terms of their competence and then assumes that they have the authority to make decisions within defined realms and according to agreed-upon policies and practices.

The act of delegation is symbolic of the confidence shown by a person who trusts someone else to carry a responsibility to him. When one delegates a task he assumes that the person to whom it is assigned has the ability to perform it. This implies that when personnel are selected to do various jobs they meet qualifications essential to the doing of the work. Delegation is itself a matter of administrative judgment. The decision to delegate or to retain a task is one of the vital ones an administrator makes in his day-to-day work.

14. *The Principle of Coordination.*

In social work administration the work delegated to many people must be properly coordinated so that specific contributions are brought to bear upon the major tasks of the agency and that all energy is rightly focused upon the mission to be accomplished.

The administrator as the central person around whom and with whom work gets done must understand and give leadership to the continuous process of coordination of effort.

The larger the agency, the more work divisions it has, and the more specialized its delegation format, the greater is the need for coordination. Coordination must take place on divisional and department levels and must occur within the agency as a whole and between the agency and community. Without effective means and processes of coordination the agency administrator cannot hope to integrate the contributions of the many people who carry specific parts of the total agency load.

15. *The Principle of Resource Utilization.*

In social work administration the resources of money, facilities, and personnel must be carefully fostered, conserved, and utilized in keeping with the trust granted to the agency by society.

The administrator as the custodian of resources is responsible for seeing to it that they are properly controlled and carefully accounted for.

It is assumed that for an agency to serve people it must have sufficient resources and these resources must be economically deployed. The administrator keeps an inventory of all resources, and he projects the resource requirements essential for the expansion of services when it becomes necessary to meet new or changed needs. The skill with which the administrator extracts maximum value from the resources at his disposal is a matter of signal importance.

16. *The Principle of Change.*

In social work administration the process of change is continuous both within the community and within the agency. The administrator has the responsibility to guide the change process and to assist people to implement necessary changes democratically decided.

The world, the community, and the agency are always changing. In the well-administered agency the director seeks to guide, to influence, and to direct the change process along lines that will enhance the contributions of all concerned. Planned institutional change becomes a matter for the continuous and wide involvement of board, staff, constituency, and community, with the administrator taking major responsibility for leadership. As new needs arise, new services are offered. As new patterns of administration are required, they are developed consciously and planfully. Change becomes a goal of innovation and growth.

17. *The Principle of Evaluation.*

In social work administration continuous evaluation of processes and programs is essential to the fulfillment of the agency's objectives.

The administrator, the staff, the board, and the constituency have roles to play in the evaluation process, with the administrator assuming primary responsibility for guiding it.

It is assumed that evaluation is not only desirable but necessary if one is to know the extent to which objectives have been achieved. The administrator must evaluate his own work as well as the work of others. The climate within which evaluation flourishes is open, critical, secure, and future-oriented. The ruts of routine operations are avoided when regular evaluation procedures assess the continuing advisability of programs, procedures, and policies and when there is a willingness to subject every act to thoughtful appraisal and scrutiny.

18. *The Principle of Growth.*

In social work administration the growth and development of all participants is furthered by the administrator who provides challenging work assignments, thoughtful supervision, and opportunities for individual and group learning.

The growth needs of persons can and must be met by administration. In so doing the administrator helps each person to render greater service to the agency and in addition he enriches the life experience of the person concerned.

The growth of the administrator himself is essential if his skills and competence are to broaden. Consequently, he seeks experiences which will widen his horizons, deeper his insights, and make more firm the grasp he has over himself and his duties.

Learning and growth are essential to life. Without them there can be no progress and no fulfillment.

When one reflects on the eighteen principles listed above, it should be apparent that social work administration is a coming together of ideals and methods deeply rooted in the values of the profession of social work. As Moss says: "Effective administration requires a fusion of ethical and operational principles. Neither is sufficient without the other. Individuals attain their richest fulfillment through participation in democratically organized and effectively productive enterprises. Democratic organization and effective production are the twin and inseparable goals of successful administrators." [4]

As social work administrators continue their vital labors in service to people, they will discover that *what* they do is less important than *how* they do it. They will learn that administration has many rewards, the greatest of which is the fact that through their efforts people have been helped to a fuller life.

NOTES

1. *The Random House Dictionary of the English Language* (Unabridged Edition). (New York: Random House, 1966, 1967), p. 1144.
2. J.M. Gaus and Leonard D. White, *The Frontiers of Public Administration* (Chicago: University of Chicago Press, 1936), p. 21.
3. A.S. Barr, William H. Burton, and Leo J. Brueckner, *Supervision—Principles and Practices in the Improvement of Instruction* (New York: Appleton-Century-Crofts, Educational Division, Meredith Corporation, 1938), pp. 32–33.
4. Celia R. Moss, *Administering a Hospital Social Service Department* (Washington, D.C.: American Association of Medical Social Workers, 1955), p. 9.

PART TWO

PRACTICES

Resolving Typical
Administrative Problems

The cases included in this section of the book are offered as brief examples which may be useful in the teaching of social work administration either in schools of social work or in social agency staff development programs. They have been tested in the classroom and in numerous institutes throughout the country. Naturally, names and agencies and locations have been disguised and editorial changes have been made to further the anonymity of the material. However, they are real situations or combinations of real situations. Most of these documents have never before been published. In selecting these particular cases from the many that have been turned in by students and practitioners, an effort has been made to offer a variety of social work settings and problems. About half of the cases represent governmental agencies and half depict voluntary agencies. Some of the cases come from agencies that work primarily with individuals, and some come from agencies that work primarily with groups. Some of the cases show the place of social service in a host setting.

The cases do not necessarily represent either good or poor practice of social work or social work administration. Instead, they are offered to illustrate some of the problems of administrative leadership at work. The questions at the end of each example may serve as a springboard for group discussion.

CASE 1

Working Together to Provide Medical Care

Ever since Mrs. Johns, the Rural Division Welfare chief, had taken over the job, there had seemed to her to be a conspicuous gap in the service offered by the Division: provision of medical care for the clientele. Those living nearest the County Hospital were thirty-five miles from it, and those living farthest away were two hundred miles from both outpatient and in-patient facilities. Some local doctors did not want to serve public assistance clients; some required "cash-on-the-line" before treatment; only a few gave adequate prompt service. It was a pretty bad situation. Mrs. Johns did not know how to tackle it; she was a comparative newcomer to the staff, and she was fearful of jeopardizing possible success by making the wrong moves. She felt fairly sure of support in her staff and, with the right approach, would have the County Welfare Director's approval, but she was doubtful of the community.

One of the staff supervisors, during her weekly conference with Mrs. Johns, commented that working in a rural area certainly had its drawbacks. She wondered if she could get a transfer to the main office. This was a shock to Mrs. Johns; Miss Edwards was one of her most competent staff members. She said a transfer could be arranged in time, but she wondered just which of the drawbacks loomed the largest. Miss Edwards said she felt harried; she was always behind in her work and, even so, she put in more time than she had any right to. There was a pause. She went on to say that it was nobody's fault, of course, but there seemed to be a great deal of sickness in her caseloads, and it took so much of the worker's time away from the regular job, getting these people down to the County Hospital many miles away. In the Main Office in the city, all a worker had to do was to walk down the hall with a Form 16R to the Accounting Division and get the carfare to send the client to the hospital. Even driving a client out to a clinic in a staff car was a fairly quick and simple affair. Here, it meant giving a whole day of a worker's time to get a client down to the hospital and back, and then look what happened to the deadlines on applications and renewals!

Mrs. Johns said she was very glad Miss Edwards had brought this up; it was something that had been on her mind, too. Maybe it would be a good idea to bring this up in the staff meeting and see what the group thought about it. Miss Edwards said she was glad that she didn't have Mrs. Johns' job; she was thinking of what it would mean in tangling with County Supervisor Harris on a thing like this. Had Mrs. Johns heard about the Grange meeting last night? Supervisor Harris got the floor, as usual, but this time he had really gone after the Welfare Department. It seemed that the new increase in Aid to Needy Children budgets was bothering him most. He wound up on his favorite topic, "chiselers." Miss Edwards looked really discouraged, but Mrs. Johns thought there was a gleam of interest when she said she realized there were bad moments in this and every job worth having; but, at least, here there was always a chance to talk things through and maybe plan a way out together. Miss Edwards left the con-ference without mentioning the transfer; it was never brought up again.

At the next staff meeting, Mrs. Johns said that Miss Edwards had brought up a problem that kept recurring in her caseload and she knew it must be a problem to others in the group. She nodded at Miss Edwards who spoke warmly on the subject. Mrs. Vinson, another supervisor, spoke up then to say that it was nothing new to her; there was plenty of sickness in her case-loads, too. She hadn't mentioned it before because she felt there wasn't anything to be done about it. She had been in that office longer than anybody else and they'd seen the problem years ago, but what could you do?

That "broke the ice." Everybody wanted to talk at once. Someone mentioned the famous Brown case where the client died en route to the hospital after waiting all day for a county ambulance, while the Welfare Department and the hospital argued over diagnosis and eligibility. Some thought that only extreme cases needed help; a policy should be worked out only for ambulance service. Some thought a plan was needed, but it was a bad time to try anything new; the Taxpayers' Association was carrying on a campaign against rising costs. Some thought the problem was outside the department's function; it should be dumped into the hospital's lap. There seemed to be quite a bit of insecurity on the part of some of the staff. Perhaps fear of the unknown, dislike of having to learn new procedures, apprehension about going too fast for the community, might be on their minds. Mrs. Johns found a good deal of positive feeling, too, for wanting to take some action to relieve the frustration that was evident and to realize the best possible service to needy clients.

In bringing the discussion together, Mrs. Johns said she realized that everybody recognized the problem. Perhaps what the group wanted was to see how much of a problem it was, how badly some kind of local policy on medical care was needed. There was agreement on this and from there the decision came that the workers would send in reports showing each trip to the hospital, including date, case name and number, clinic or ward, and the hours consumed for the round trip. The supervising steongrapher said that if the reports were routed to her, she would make a weekly tally. At the end of a month there would be some facts to go on.

Shortly after that staff meeting, when the Director of the Welfare Department, Mr. Miller, was on the long-distance line, Mrs. Johns decided to broach the subject to him. She said that the staff had been thinking lately about that old problem (Mr. Miller had been with the department for twenty years), medical care for the rural clients. Would there be time during her conference hour next week to go over some of their ideas? There was a long pause and she went on to say that the staff had, on its own initiative, compiled some facts and figures for him to mull over; would he like to have them first? Mr. Miller said yes, he'd better have the facts for a starter, but on the other hand, maybe he would take a run out to the country some staff meeting day, and look the situation over himself with the group. Any kind of medical program would have to be worked out with the hospital and right now, it would be a pretty "hot potato"; they hadn't got over the bad publicity on the Brown case yet. He'd keep in touch with Mrs. Johns on the thing.

Mrs. Johns wondered how she had bungled so badly as to put Mr. Miller on the defensive. She thought perhaps he felt his authority challenged or felt the lack of opportunity for participation in the planning. He might have been realistic, on the other hand, in thinking that it was an inopportune time, that it might be going too fast for the community, or that the hospital was not ready for change at this point.

About a month later another fatality occurred, this time in a staff car en route to the hospital. Mr. Miller called for a report. In discussing it with Mrs. Johns, he said he thought the hospital staff would be interested in working something out. Supervisor Harris had swung around to a different point of view, and Mr. Miller thought the decks were really clear for action. Plans were made in this conference for the workers on the Rural Division staff to call on each local physician asking for suggestions of how to meet the need, in cooperation with the Department. The approach would be the doctors' professional interest and ideals of service to the community. The material, when gathered, would be summarized and presented to the Hospital Board. Meanwhile, Director Miller would get in a little "spadework," he said.

When Mrs. Johns brought this to her staff, she could present it as the fruit of their own planning. They saw it as their own project, and although extra time and work had to be put in, they seemed to take that in stride.

After the twenty-five doctors had been interviewed, a solution began to take shape in staff meetings. The workers found that seven doctors wished to be relieved of all responsibility for agency clientele. These doctors believed that the county should establish mobile clinics, bus service, better ambulance service, or branch hospitals. Eighteen doctors thought their services should be used, but at public expense. Some wanted the proposed policy cleared with the County Medical Society. Some wished to deal only with the local branch of the Welfare Department, fearing red tape and control by the hospital. Fees suggested were from nominal charges to maximum city fee schedules, plus mileage for some home calls. The Division Chief's secretary worked overtime on summarizing the report, which was forwarded to Director Miller after staff approval.

One morning Mrs. Johns received a telephone call from Director Miller. He asked her how long it would take her to get to the city. He and Mr. Arthur, the Assistant Superintendent of the hospital, had been conferring all morning, and Mr. Miller thought they might take up the rural staff's report over lunch. There was a possibility that Judge Dawson of the District Attorney's office might join them as Mr. Miller wanted his opinion on the legal aspects of the plan.

Mrs. Johns said she could make it in an hour. What would Mr. Miller think of including Dr. Williams, whose office was right across the street from the restaurant; he seemed to have considerable influence on the Hospital Committee and besides, he was President of the County Medical Society. Mr. Miller said he would try to get him. Mrs. Johns asked if she should bring along some copies of the report. Mr. Miller thought not; this would be a preliminary discussion, time enough to get the facts later. Let it be an orientation, he said. He cautioned Mrs. Johns to go slowly; this was a conservative group.

At luncheon it developed that Mr. Arthur had been thinking for some time about the rural medical problem, but it had been his impression that the hospital could not legally pay private practitioners for service the hospital staff was responsible to provide. Judge Dawson was doubtful, but it was brought out that the county paid morticians on a fee schedule, by ancillary contracts. He said he would ask somebody to study that question and get an opinion. Dr. Williams said if an ordinance was involved, the County Medical Society would bow out of the picture; it sounded too much like government control. Mr. Arthur wondered what kind of fees the rural doctors thought they should receive. He thought, too, that it would be difficult to fit the scheme into the hospital's organizational structure: delegation of responsibility to so many physicians sounded almost impossible, and he did not think the superintendent, Dr. Ryan, who was out of town on vacation, would take kindly to the idea. Mrs. Johns asked if anybody knew what they were doing in Lincoln County; there must be a terrific problem up there, with such a scattered and large population. Mr. Arthur said he was going up soon, and would look into it. They had a plan, but he wasn't sure just how it operated. Dr. Williams said he knew only that most of the doctors here didn't like Lincoln County's plan. Mrs. Johns suggested that if the patient's right to choose his own doctor and the doctor's right to limit his practice were guaranteed, perhaps the Medical Society would approve it. It seemed as if they were really in agreement with her because everybody was interested in some way of getting a needed service to the community. Dr. Williams smiled and said that was true, but that was about the only thing they had in common. Mr. Arthur thought it was worth following through, and Mr. Miller suggested that each bring what additional facts he could muster to the next hospital board meeting.

Medical service for the rural area was fifth on the agenda of the hospital board meeting some six weeks after the luncheon conference. One doctor left after the third item of business. Supervisor Harris, during the fourth item, kept his eye on his wrist watch, and finally got up to telephone his office that he would be late for an appointment.

Dr. Ryan, the superintendent, said he had heard that Mr. Miller had something on his mind about the rural area; what was it? Mr. Miller laughed and said he really had, but he wanted to bring it up for discussion rather than make a report. He went on to approach the plan from the standpoint of meeting a need and the joint responsibility of the two agencies involved to find some solution to the problem. He summarized the rural staff's report, indicating that copies would be sent each member before any formal consideration of the problem need be tackled. He turned to Mrs. Johns for elaboration and then to Mr. Arthur for an outline of Lincoln County's experience. Noticing Dr. Williams' obvious uneasiness, he summed up by saying that he felt certain Sawyer County could do better than that, but it was helpful to have some experience to go by. He had in a mind a possible way of using the best features of Lincoln County's scheme but, because of the smaller population here, individual doctors could be freer and, he thought, the Sawyer plan would be more economical.

Mr. Keller, a newspaper editor on the board, mentioned the notorious Brown case, and commented that both the hospital and the Welfare Department could use some good publicity right now. One of the doctors wanted to know if the rural group of physicians was going to be paid for what the city doctors did on a voluntary basis in the hospital's clinics. Dr. Ryan, the superintendent, growled that he couldn't be responsible for the kind of medicine those "horse doctors" up in the country practiced. Everyone laughed so much at this that although tension was relieved, Mrs. Johns was afraid that Supervisor Harris, who represented the rural constituents, and Dr. Ryan would lose status with the group. She suggested that the tie-up of private practice with department clientele might promote a more uniform standard throughout the county, since final approval for payment would rest with the hosiptal. She thought, too, that the rural doctors who had shown interest in a plan were indicating pretty high professional ideals of service. It seemed that distance alone would prevent their giving voluntary service at outpatient clinics.

Discussion followed, covering the number of calls a month, a fee schedule, medication, and tie-in with laboratory and visiting nurse service. The last step taken was the request made by Supervisor Harris, agreed on by the whole group, that Mr. Arthur and Mrs. Johns work out definite policies in cooperation with both hospital and Welfare Department accounting units and that a sample ancillary contract be requested from the district attorney's office. Both were to be sent to Dr. Williams for the County Medical Society and to Dr. Ryan for administrative consideration. Material prepared by the rural staff and by Mr. Arthur was to be sent each board member and all would be reviewed at the next Hospital Board meeting.

On the way back to the office Mrs. Johns tried to see where the group was and where the policy had got to. One thing was clear: the committee wanted something done about medical care for rural clients. There was a real cohesiveness in the group, mutual confidence, and recognition of one another's ability. The Superintendent had a stake in any extension of medical service but the group protected his status and made him the controlling figure in the plan. Mr. Arthur was given scope for creative activity in designing the policy. Supervisor Harris stood to gain in prestige through benefits to his rural constituents. Dr. Williams had accepted his role of interpretation to his professional colleagues, as long as he could protect their interests. Director Miller's greatest stimulus to action, she felt, had been the staff's confidence in him.

Shortly thereafter, notice was received from Director Miller that the County Board of Supervisors had taken official action and that funds were available for the Rural Medical Service Program. In the staff, Mrs. Johns had seen the doubts and the discouragements, the extra work, and the frequent disagreements about the way the policy should be formulated. But when it was ready to be put into effect, she saw, too, the feeling of achievement the group had. In the staff discussion of the procedures to be used, no one seemed to think of orders given. It sounded more like tracing the policy through to its last stage, because the group knew step by step how the policy had evolved. The important thing about it was that it was essentially their creation. They were eager to interpret it to the community because they genuinely needed to make it work; they had a stake in its outcome. It seemed almost on the order of a miracle to Mrs. Johns that a concrete aim of the agency had been realized and had every chance of success. It had been a unique and illuminating experience.

QUESTIONS

1. Who are some of the key individuals involved in working on this problem?
2. What are the responsibilities of Mrs. Johns and Mr. Miller? What do you think of the way they work together?
3. As you trace the chronology of this case, what, in your opinion, were some of the key turning points?
4. Evaluate the informal and formal group meetings that took place during the period of time covered by this document.
5. What are some examples of administrative leadership in this case?
6. What principles of administration are illustrated by this case?

CASE 2

A Public Welfare Agency Revises Its Manual

In the two years that I had been employed in the agency, I had met only a few of those on the administrative staff. I—along with a very large number of others—had once gone through a receiving line headed by the Commissioner of Welfare, and had been introduced to him and had shaken his hand; all in a matter of seconds. It was not entirely without foundation, therefore, that the workers in our district office (which was situated a short distance from the central office) began to view the administrative unit as poles and poles apart from us. Policy change upon policy change was handed to us with little or no explanation for such changes. We felt that the administration could not possibly understand our position in the agency because of the things that they were asking us to do. And, most frustrating of all, was the fact that we had no way of expressing our feelings and views to those who made policy. True, we could at least discuss "our gripes" with our supervisors; but it was not the same as having direct participation regarding the matter at hand.

In addition to all this, the Welfare Department had been under an almost constant stream of criticism all the while that I had been employed there. Charges of inefficiency, chiselers, and similar items were forever being leveled at the department. Many pressures and crises developed on the job, and for some it was too much to bear; for others it was a stimulating and somewhat strenuous challenge.

In the midst of this situation a new Commissioner of Welfare was appointed to reorganize the department. All members of the agency from the top on down waited anxiously—and cautiously—to see just what could be accomplished. One of the things which the new commissioner did was a very small but, to me, a tremendously important thing. Soon after his appointment he visited each district office to acquaint himself with the personnel and to let the staff become acquainted with him. Imagine! Now many of the staff met the head of their agency for the first time.

The job of reorganizing the Department was started immediately. Yet, the changes which were taking place were sufficiently far removed from the workers in the field as to pass by without much comment. Then a staff letter, written by the Commissioner, was mailed individually to all the staff announcing plans for revising the workers' manual so that it might be more concise, understandable, and usable—all three of which were needed.

Very heartening, indeed, was the fact that a committee of staff members of all levels was selected to participate in the discussions preceding revision. A person from each of the eight district offices was appointed to the committee. In addition to these, there were three members from the administrative section of the Department, and a member from the Property Section— making a total of twelve on the Committee. This group of twelve truly did represent the different levels of agency personnel. There were two district supervisors—both having considerable and varied backgrounds in social work. Some members of the Committee were professionally trained. There were a couple of case supervisors with many years' experience both in this state and in others. One had practiced social work in Great Britain. There were a few members who had been with the department almost since the time of its inception. There were also two senior caseworkers. And, lastly, there were two caseworkers both of whom had less than two full years' experience as social workers—and I was one of the latter. The Commissioner of Welfare was to preside over the committee meetings. Special consultants were to be called in whenever the need for their services was indicated.

It was recognized that an undertaking such as that proposed would be a failure if the entire staff did not participate in the work of revising the manual. Therefore, the letter circulated to the staff acknowledged the fact that many of the staff had ideas concerning manual improvement and it urged staff members to submit their ideas to the member representing their offices.

Three days after the letter mentioned above had been circulated, each committee member received a letter from the Commissioner informing him that a short meeting would be held a week hence. The letter was written to convey the idea that each committee member's services would be greatly appreciated. At this meeting, it was decided that the Committee would meet for a whole day once every week because of the magnitude of the job ahead of us. Plans were formulated whereby the material which the Committee would discuss and write would be mimeographed and sent to the district offices. After the staff had been given sufficient time to digest this material, each committee member would hold group meetings in his own office, at which time the staff would be able to voice their ideas or criticisms, of the material discussed. At the next meeting of the Committee, the material would again be discussed, with the added importance of having the benefit of complete staff participation. The material would then be edited accordingly and submitted to the entire staff again, after which the committee members would again present their findings to the Committee. Minor changes, if any, were to be made and the material was to be distributed in final form.

It is true that the above seems like a long and laborious process. Yet, it was felt that if we took the needed time while we were doing the job, and did not rush through anything for the sake of saving time, it would well be worth our while in time and effort in the long run. It was also felt that here was a time when all of the staff could actively participate in revising the manual—especially the line workers who, after all, were to use it most —and that this would be about the only chance they might ever have to do so.

We were asked to bring in at the next meeting, a week away, the written suggestion of the staff, who were by now acquainted with this fact by means of the circular and by other informal channels of communication. Also, some material had been prepared and we would take the time to discuss it so that it could be relayed to the staff as soon as possible. It was decided at this meeting that each committee member would be given a portion of the manual to rewrite in as clear and concise English as possible. Not only were we to rewrite this material, but we were also to incorporate pertinent staff ideas into the material and change it if we thought it would be best to do so.

At the second meeting, the suggestions of staff were turned in by the committee members. These suggestions were separated according to subject matter and given to the committee member who was to rewrite that special portion of the manual.

We then launched into a discussion of the material which had been prepared. It was the portion of the manual dealing with "Fair Hearings." Each word, sentence, and page was carefully scrutinized. There were many deletions and additions. Material was shifted from one section to another in order to form a more readable whole. The material was logically arranged from the beginning with the quoting of the law providing for fair hearings, down to the last provision for an appeal on the part of a client from a decision rendered by the presiding officer of the fair hearing. Parts of the material—such as the social worker's attitude toward fair hearings— were omitted entirely, as it was felt that this should properly be placed in the in-service training manual. It was to be tied up with purpose and not included in the policy manual.

Out of this committe meeting also came the idea to dispense with stenographic recording of the hearing—which was quite time-consuming and expensive—and to replace the stenographer with a mechanical recorder. Provision was made to make available a stenographic transcript to the court in case of appeal or, if a transcript were needed for any other reason, a copy would also be made available.

Early the next week the revised material on Fair Hearings was distributed to each staff member in all the district offices. I had been in close contact with my district supervisor concerning the proceedings of the committee meetings and with her support we were able to publicize, by means of an interoffice memo, the fact that a meeting would be held for discussion near the end of the week. The staff was again encouraged to make suggestions at this meeting so that these could be taken back to the Manual Revision Committee by their committee member.

The initial response of the staff was very heartening. They immediately took advantage of the opportunity to express themselves on the matter at hand. The committee members were there to guide the discussion, give explanation for certain policy, and express the prevailing philosophy of the Committee, as a whole, in formulating the policy.

Just as the committee meetings, the material—which had already been studied by the staff—was taken up page by page. The new format of the material was especially appealing to the workers. Whereas previously they had to shuffle through a maze of material to locate what they were looking for, now they merely had to consult the table of contents. In this table, material was separated into subject matter and it was also indexed by a numbering system which was a modification of the Dewey Decimal System —thus making it extremely simple to identify specific subject matter for ready reference. The numbering system also served to arrange and coordinate the subject matter in logical order; it served to reduce repetition to a minimum; and lastly, it served to permit easy revision for maintenance of the manual.

The staff liked the way the material was clearly written and defined, showing each and every one's responsibilities in the matter of Fair Hearings. Their general comments were very favorable!

But there were flaws in the material which the staff was able to pick out. Most of the staff, of course, were well-acquainted with Fair Hearings and through their experience they were able to pinpoint certain deficiencies and ambiguities in the material. This also showed that the staff was really interested in participating in the work of manual revision and had enough confidence to know that if their suggestions were well-founded, they would be accepted.

Because the line staff was in such close contact with the clients whom the agency was serving, they kept, as a rule, the best interests of the clients uppermost in mind. To the Committee's question regarding what the staff felt about having a centralized place where fair hearings could be held, the staff decided on a flexible policy—leaving it up to the choice of the client. (And staff's wishes on this matter prevailed.) When a question arose as to who other than the applicant or client could request a Fair Hearing, the Staff unanimously spoke against allowing the applicant's or client's attorney to make such a request unless the attorney had been given written permission to do so.

When the material was too broad and indicated areas where difficulties might arise, the staff asked more definite, concrete limitations. They liked the idea of recording the Hearings by mechanical means because they realized that it was a cost-saving device and that a lot of paperwork would be eliminated. They also liked it because of the fact that by this means of recording, tonal inflections and attitudes of those concerned would not be lost as they had been under the old method.

Throughout, the staff sought to incorporate material into the manual which would enable the district offices to become somewhat more autonomous than they were—which would mean a good deal of saving in time and money with the flow of paper work to the central office being cut down.

The day after this staff meeting, the third committee meeting was held. At this time the committee members presented the suggestions of the staff regarding refinements in the Fair Hearing material. It was interesting to note that many of the same changes proposed were common to a large number of district offices, and it showed that the district offices were sharing a number of common problems, yet had no outlet for discussing these problems with each other. It was also shown at these committee meetings that various district offices were interpreting policy differently thus adding confusion to an already confusing situation. It was unanimously felt that all district offices should be operating in one and the same manner under existing policy and that this could be arranged by the Committee's discussing policy—as we had been doing—in connection with the revision of the manual.

Four days later the revised material on Fair Hearings was distributed throughout the agency. Through staff meetings conducted by committee members this material was further revised and refined. A week later the final draft of the material appeared and in a little less than a month after the Committee had started to meet, the completed section on Fair Hearings and complaints (Chapter VI of the Social Workers' Manual) was issued to the staff.

While the process of completing Chapter VI was being accomplished, each individual member of the Committee had been rewriting the section of the manual assigned to him. These sections dealt with eligibility requirements of the various categorical relief programs. And so, preliminary work in this area was being prepared in connection with the other material—eliminating a void when Chapter VI was finally completed.

Within four months after the Committee had assembled together to discuss plans for the revision of the manual, the preliminary draft of Chapter II, "Social Work Policies: Specific Eligibility Requirements," had been completed and had been issued to the staff for review and for suggestions. This was indeed a very large piece of work covering the "heart" of the categorical relief programs. Included in this work were some changes in policy. Because the legislature had been in session and new laws regarding public welfare had been promulgated, these new revisions were also incorporated in the material. In line with the revision of the manual, much of the old material was included, but it had undergone somewhat of a metamorphosis in that it was written in a much more complete, concise, and explicit manner.

Drafts of portions of Chapter II had been issued to the staff for discussion prior to the issuance of the complete preliminary draft of this chapter, and suggestions made by the staff had been incorporated into the material. Yet, because of the size of the complete preliminary draft, more than one staff meeting was necessary to cover the material thoroughly. Throughout all these months, staff interest in the work of the Committee—which was basically representing the staff—never lagged and staff discussions were almost always stimulating and enlightening. A benefit derived from these staff meetings was that they served as a good vehicle for in-service training and that they provided a forum for a painless way of reviewing policy and getting to know policy better.

During the fifth month after the formation of the Committee, Chapter II was issued in final form. In actual time, it took only four months for Chapters II and VI to be completed, Committee meetings having been disbanded for a month because it was a summer month for which many vacations were scheduled.

Like the staff meetings, the committee meetings were almost always stimulating and exciting to me. As I have mentioned previously, the committee members came to the discussion table with wide and varied backgrounds and experience. Naturally there were times when all members were not in accord with what was being proposed and debate was "hot and heavy." In such instances, compromises had to be reached. At other times the Committee was united in its proposal of certain areas of policy.

The Commissioner of Welfare was Chairman of the Committee. He was sincere and zealous in his efforts to discover from the committee members just how the staff was reacting to the proposals emanating from the Committee. He was extremely interested in knowing the extent to which staff were participating in the whole project.

The Commissioner was gifted with a good sense of humor and he had the knack of turning a tense moment into a relaxing one with his wit. He was able to direct the meetings without dominating them. He made the committee member feel free to present his and his constituents' views even though they might not seem to be generally accepted by the others. He was very attentive to and eager for the suggestions and recommendations of the members of the Committee who were the social workers, who were facing the problems discussed, and who would be the ones who would be putting the policy into practice. He was gifted with the ability of making the Committee function steadily and efficiently. The Commissioner had an open mind and was willing to listen to and act upon the Committee's suggestions. He showed a warmth and real regard for the constituents of the agency.

In the matter of public relations, the Commissioner was doing an excellent job. He showed a willingness to speak, whenever he had a chance, about the agency and about the work of the Committee.

The other members of the Committee each had his own specific contribution to make toward the total performance. And I believe that each committee member always kept in mind the fact that he was not working for himself but was there at the meetings as a representative of a vast number of people who were relying upon him to present their views in the matter.

QUESTIONS

1. What were some of the feelings and attitudes held by the staff that had to be dealt with by the new Commissioner?
2. Evaluate the way the new Commissioner of Welfare got started on his job.
3. What is the purpose of an agency manual, and do you think it was a good vehicle for the Commissioner to use as a means of developing staff participation?
4. Would working this way on manual revision have any impact on staff feelings and attitudes mentioned early in the record?

5. Do you think that it was wise to put so much time on this manual revision project?
6. What are the advantages and disadvantages of this kind of a process of manual revision?
7. If you had served as a staff representative on this Manual Revision Committee, do you think that your time would have been well spent?

CASE 3

A Public Welfare Agency Develops an Orientation Program

This is a study of a large public agency which, aware of the necessity for more effective services to clients and concerned about large staff turnover, recognized the basic relationship of these factors to the need for development of an orientation program and set about to develop such a program.

This agency, with roots deep in the past, had been struggling to meet its responsibility for expanded and new services through an administrative organization and structure which had been set up years ago to serve a program of far less complexity and magnitude. The unsuitable structure and organization resulted in limitations on the agency's ability to realize its goal of prompt and effective services to those who came to it for help, and there were concomitant, interacting factors of public criticism, poor staff morale, and rapid staff turnover.

As a result of increasing dissatisfaction both within and without the agency, a new Executive Director was appointed whose progressive ideas were soon reflected in changes in agency structure and organization based upon a realistic appraisal of the agency's multiple functions, size, and goals. There were reassessment and clarification of job responsibilities and the creation of several important jobs, including that filled by the Supervisor of Staff Development, who plays a central role in this record. With this more dynamic leadership and the improved administrative structure and organization, there resulted a surge ahead in agency planning of which the program presented here is but one part. During the early period of this reorganization, the insecurities of some of those affected in Central Office were reflected in apprehension in the district offices through the strongly developed "grapevine" system of informal communication. No doubt aware of the uneasiness, the new leadership took steps to allay it through releasing written material in which the reorganization was explained and through face-to-face contacts with staff in each district office.

Just as the new Executive Director came to meet and talk with staff in an informal but purposeful way, so other newly appointed leadership from Central Office came to see and be seen, to accredit staff work, acknowledge difficulties, discuss agency goals and their own administrative responsibilities, and to promise staff representation in changes ahead. The Supervisor of Staff Development was no exception to this plan. After she had met the entire staff, she held a series of workshops for casework supervisors. These workshops furthered her acquaintance with these supervisors who were directly responsible for staff training and helped her to understand their problems and needs in respect to the teaching aspect of their jobs. It was apparent from these meetings, conferences with Personnel Department, District Supervisors' reports, statistical data, and other available information, that one of the most basic needs in the area of staff development was a carefully formulated orientation program to prepare workers, most of whom were inexperienced, to meet the complexities of a very demanding job. The steps taken in the formulation of this program are outlined in briefly summarized chronological form in the material which follows. Each step, while part of the whole administrative process, represented a separate unit which could be narrated in much greater detail.

1–15   After the need for a uniform and ordered orientation program had arisen repeatedly in the supervisory workshops and in several Central Office meetings of the Field Director and the District Supervisors directly responsible to him, each District Supervisor received a memo from the Field Director referring to discussion of this subject at the meetings, and requesting that with their monthly reports they include a comprehensive statement of the orientation program presently used in each office together with an evaluation of the strengths and weaknesses of such a program. The memo made clear that these reports would be used as a departure point for formulation of a uniform new program, and suggested that in compiling these statements case supervisors and workers be consulted.

1–17   The District Supervisor in the Thorndale District Office where I was employed as a case supervisor held a case supervisors' meeting at which we discussed the manner in which we oriented new workers, and agreed to hold separate unit meetings with workers to share the fact that the agency was focusing attention on this problem, and to gain their viewpoint on past and current methods. The latter information was particularly important as some of the senior workers had been oriented several years previously when there had been an intense but short-lived centralized orientation program.

1–21   After the unit meetings had been held and the case supervisors had met with the District Supervisor to share the results, the District Supervisor sent her report to the Field Director in which she stated very frankly that there was no carefully formulated orientation program in our office, and that workers were expected to learn amid the pressures of the job with only the varying protection the case supervisor might be able to provide from day to day. The report further stated that senior members of the staff who had participated in the former intensive, centralized program felt it had been very helpful.

2–1   The District Supervisor, who had received a request from the Field Director for a case supervisor to serve as a representative on a committee to work on the orientation problem, asked me to take this assignment. After I agreed to do so, I received a memo from Mrs. Smith, Supervisor of Staff Development, welcoming me to the Committee and stating that information regarding meetings would follow later.

2–5   The Supervisor of Staff Development released mimeographed material to all staff in which she identified the agency's need for an orientation program and related this to effective services, recruitment, and retention of staff. She stated that for formulation of this program it had been decided to appoint a committee consisting of representatives from each office whose functional responsibility related to training new workers, two representatives, including herself, from Central Office with similar though over-all responsibilities, and three ex-officio members from outside the agency who had special competence in necessary content areas. She identified by name and position all members on the Committee including several District Supervisors, outlined the charges made to the Committee, and stated that five meetings would be held. Each Committee member received with this generally circulated material, special material on current orientation practices drawn from District Supervisors' reports, from orientation programs in other states as well as a suggested orientation content outline prepared by Mrs. Smith. She gave the date and agenda for the first half-day meeting and also indicated the time schedule and the general areas to be covered in subsequent full-day meetings.

Staff reaction to this information was moderately enthusiastic, which was really a tribute as, generally in the past, changes issued by Central Office had been greeted by groans or indifference. New workers, facing the impact of assuming job responsibility without training, speculated as to whether they would be included in such a program, and later developments in that area were in themselves another story. Some workers felt it presaged a staff development program for senior staff members, and there were varied reaction to that with some hopeful, some indifferent, and some who expressed feelings that what was needed was not more training but more workers. On the whole the orientation plan was seen as another recognition of staff need on the part of the new administrative leadership and an effort to meet this need.

2–10   At the first half-day meeting of the Committee, which was held at Central Office, Mrs. Smith's planning was apparent in the physical arrangements for the Committee's work, including a room in which reference material was available and in the seating arrangement around a large table. She kept the atmosphere informal and friendly as we met each other, in some instances for the first time. After mutual recognition of the importance of the subject of orientation, the Committee's charges were reviewed and plans were developed for following meetings. Particular stress was placed on each representative's responsibility to report Committee work staff and staff suggestions to the Committee, and ways of accomplishing this were discussed. After discussion led by Mrs. Smith, the orientation period was designated as the first six months of employment, and it was agreed that by the next meeting we would have read pertinent material received from other agencies and would be ready to consider content for the first month of orientation, using as a frame of reference Mrs. Smith's suggested content guide.

2–15   Mrs. Smith forwarded to each of the Committee full minutes of the past meeting prepared by one of the ex-officio members who had been designated by Mrs. Smith for the job, and a copy of a memo received by her from the Executive Director in which he emphasized the importance of an orientation program in the total agency picture and stressed the importance of attitudes as well as materials in any orientation program.

2–17   At a meeting of supervisory staff I reviewed, with the help of the minutes and personal notes, the work of the first Committee meeting. All had read the suggested content outline drawn up by Mrs. Smith which had been previously circulated and they made constructive suggestions, relating the material to the daily job as they saw it from close range.

2–28   At this meeting the Committee, after reviewing informally the suggestions of the respective offices, located with the help of Mrs. Smith, three main content areas. They agreed, as had been suggested by Mrs. Smith at the first meeting, to break up into three subcommittees—each to study the separate content areas to be included in the first month and to reassemble during the last hour for a brief reporting session. They further agreed that each subcommittee would appoint a secretary and share written minutes with other subcommittee members. Mrs. Smith named the chairman and members of each subcommittee, designated its area of study, and stated she would circulate among the subcommittees and at the meeting of the whole would aid in integrating reports.

2–30—6–15   The patterns outlined above were followed in the second meeting and two subsequent meetings, including the reporting between district office and the Committee, and use of the subcommittees as well as the whole Committee. Between meetings Mrs. Smith circulated minutes of each subcommittee and the whole, as well as additional reference material. Members of the subcommittees volunteered for specific reading assignment reports, which they sent to subcommittee chairmen in preparation for each meeting and which were forwarded to Mrs. Smith prior to the meeting for total distribution.

6–15   Mrs. Smith forwarded to the Orientation Committee copies of the work done by the Committee which she had organized into a chronological guide draft with content suitable for orientation of new staff, as well as supplements containing specialized knowledge prepared by the appropriate ex-officio Committee member. In a covering memo she requested that this material be given to all supervisory personnel, and that each Committee member report in writing by 7–25 the comments and suggestions made by the supervisory staff as whole. She further stated that these contributions would be integrated and then distributed to the Committee in preparation for a final meeting on 8–10. She suggested that the material be used with new workers for a testing period of several months which would be valuable in preparing the final edition to be used as a basis for workshop in helping case supervisors assume responsibility for its use.

As in the past, our supervisory unit met for discussion of the material and I then forwarded to Mrs. Smith their suggestions and comments, which were helpful and enthusiastic. At the final meeting of the Committee there was some revision of the material followed by a testing period, and it was then used as a basis for supervisory workshops and, finally, as a uniform agency-wide orientation program.

The following material is an attempt to analyze in part some of the major factors of the administrative process described above as I look at it in retrospect and in terms of social work administration. The steps that were necessary in this process and the number of individuals and groups involved indicate, of course, that this process could be the basis for a much longer and more detailed analysis than I have attempted. No doubt, too, there were negative factors in this process but my over-all experience was a positive one as I recall it now.

In the background description of this problem I have touched on the inadequacy of the structure and organization of this agency prior to the appointment of the new Executive Director. No matter how progressive the Legislature was in passing sound social welfare legislation and in appropriating supporting funds, the administrative process with its goal of prompt, effective services to clients could not be successful because of this basic inadequacy.

Obviously the structure and organization of this agency had not developed out of practice but had remained static, growing more and more outmoded and less and less adequate for the types of group work relationships necessary in fulfilling the agency's purpose. One of the many criticisms made was about the extreme centralization of authority in Central Office and the responsibility without authority given to District Supervisors. This we know is one of the circumstances from which problems of authority often arise. Because of the outmoded structure and organization there were other interrelated difficulties which contributed to problems of authority, including poor lines of communication, job functions not clearly defined, constant work pressure, and rapid change of policy. These factors frequently led to personalization of problems, and the cumulative effect sometimes resulted in negative feelings about the job.

Through the careful planning of the Executive Director, who utilized experts in the field of social work administration, a new administrative structure and organization was designed through which the administration process became a continuation and strengthening of the social work process, making possible the mutual purpose of prompt, effective service to the client. The new design included decentralization of authority with the necessary provisions for over-all coordination and evaluation.

In the process of change in leadership personnel and over-all change in organization and structure, staff did not participate, as these responsibilities were not within the function of their jobs. However, the new leadership showed awareness of the needs of individuals and groups for recognition and participation in decision-making by providing staff with written explanations, and far more important, by visiting each district office, accrediting staff for what it had done under difficulties, and promising staff would be represented in forthcoming changes where decisions directly affecting its work might be made.

In further analysis of the administrative problem I will consider the part played by Mrs. Smith who, as Supervisor of Staff Development, carried major responsibility for formulation of an orientation program. Mrs. Smith's professional training in social work gave her a basic understanding of herself, individuals, groups, the agency, and the community which are necessary, I feel, for anyone filling a role of administrative leadership in a social work agency. Her authority, as she recognized and used it, was not a personal one but a functional one, inherent in her job for which she had been selected because of her larger experience, deeper insight, and more specific education. Some of her professional philosophy of social work administration and her skills in this area are located and described as I view them in retrospect and relate them to recent learning.

Mrs. Smith's basic philosophical concept of social work administration as a group process in which the executive's role is that of an enabler, was apparent throughout the work on this problem. She was well-equipped to prepare an orientation program herself, and undoubtedly this would have conserved time and energy on her part and on the part of all those involved. Thus, in terms of initial outlay of funds, single-handed preparation would have been far more economical. However, Mrs. Smith, understanding some of the basic concepts around change, individual and group needs, and her own responsibility, as an administrative leader, for developing people, knew that to be successful all concerned must be involved in the formulation of a program, that those nearest the operation must have a role in the decision-making process, and that her role was one of partnership or sharing, though not one of equality in terms of responsibility. In other words, in deciding on group sharing and participation while also recognizing responsibility, she showed her conviction as to the importance of the democratic process which the group process supports, and of the precedence which human values must take over material values in the solving of problems.

Mrs. Smith, in her first release of material to the entire staff, showed recognition that all were involved in the problem and should therefore share to the extent indicated by function in plans for solving it. Her definition of the problem and its relationship to agency purpose, together with the basis for Committee selection, identification of membership, function, and general time schedule, demonstrated Mrs. Smith's understanding of the relationship of change and participation to individual and group needs.

Through emphasizing the importance of Committee district office communication, she demonstrated again her recognition of the need to involve, as far as possible, all those affected by change. (This principle was also utilized by the Field Director in his suggestion that supervisory staff and workers be informed as to focus on the current orientation programs and be consulted regarding strengths and weaknesses.) The testing period of the orientation guide draft also showed Mrs. Smith's recognition of the importance of participation.

In deciding where she would start in her job of staff development, Mrs. Smith used the diagnostic approach. She made her decision that the major problem of staff development was the training of new staff only after securing all possible information from agency resources regarding the areas in which staff development was most needed to aid in the agency purpose of service to clients. One of her most important resources here was the original workshop series with supervisory staff who, among other duties, were orienting new staff to their jobs. On the basis of accumulated information, observation, and study, she defined the problem as the need for formulation of an orientation program. She knew that while the problem affected the entire agency, supervisory staff were most involved and that, because of the authority inherent in her job, she must take primary leadership in tackling the job. She was aware that the former outmoded structure and organization of the agency had prevented any consistent orientation program, and that this was not unique to the agency; and she secured information as to how other agencies had solved similar problems. In accepting her functional responsibility for planning and forecasting, she visualized the steps to be taken in view of the time schedule necessary. With the use of this and other diagnostic material available to her, she decided to take hold of the problem at the point of formulation of an orientation program through a committee of supervisory personnel composed mainly of supervisory personnel whose job was directly related to training new workers. Thus Mrs. Smith used a scientific fact-finding approach to the problem and its solution.

Mrs. Smith, in the general announcement of the need and the method by which she proposed to meet it, was showing her ability to use constructively the authority inherent in her job. The same ability to recognize when it was wiser for the leader rather than the group to make the decision was shown in her appointment of subcommittee chairmen and members. She alone was in a position to evaluate the strengths and weaknesses of those present in terms of the job to be done and was therefore best equipped to make those appointments. One of the main problems in administration is the recognition of those areas in which a decision is a group responsibility and those in which it properly belongs within the leader's function. It is clear that if all the decisions made in the solving of this problem had been left to the group, not much would have been accomplished.

Through the supervisory workshops, Mrs. Smith learned where this group was in relationship to their ability to train new staff and what their needs were. She made further progress here by determining, through the Field Director who had immediate responsibility for over-all work done in the district offices, the current plans utilized for orientation. A part of her acceptance of this responsibility was shown in her preparation of a suggested content outline which gave the Committee, with its varying backgrounds of training and experience, a frame of reference and focus. Mrs. Smith's inclusion on the Committee of three specialists in areas where the group needed their help also showed recognition of the leader's responsibility to bring in specialists as needed.

Closely related to Mrs. Smith's recognition of where the group was in its ability to formulate an orientation program was her awareness of the time schedule. The length of time allowed, together with recognition of where the group was in starting its work, determined the type and extent of Mrs. Smith's enabling role. Five meetings over a period of six months did not represent much time in terms of the charges placed on the Committee and its state of readiness. Therefore Mrs. Smith's role as an enabler carried with it heavy responsibilities both within and without the Committee meetings and necessitated greater activity on her part than if her work had been with a Committee whose total background was more adequate for certain aspects of the job.

Mrs. Smith knew that the broad area of staff development was a responsibility inherent in her job, partialized the problem into orientation and subsequent staff training, and, in view of giving emphasis to that part of development which would serve agency purpose best at this particular time, focused on the former. In helping the Committee to work toward a solution of the problem she subdivided it into component parts and assigned subcommittees to work on specific parts. Within the subcommittees she made suggestions for further partialization of the problem and assignment of these smaller sections.

Mrs. Smith showed recognition of responsibility for gathering and communicating information in making available suitable reference materials from district offices within the agency and from other agencies while also stimulating the Committee to independent exploration of the literature through her own example and her use of the ex-officio members of the Committee. One part of the information gathering, recording, and commuicating was provision for preparation and distribution of the minutes.

Mrs. Smith recognized that with division of labor, coordination of effect is imperative, and she accepted responsibility for this through her purposeful visits to each subcommittee where she assisted each in focusing on its job in relationship to the work of the other subcommittees, through her help in integrating each subcommittee's work in meetings of the whole Committee, and, finally, in her integration of all this work into a unified guide draft with attached supplements.

Because she knew so well and accepted so readily her own leadership responsibilities, Mrs. Smith was able to stimulate the group to accept their responsibilities.

At the time I was involved in the administrative process which I have described and analyzed in part, I was impressed with the personal ability of Mrs. Smith to organize and work with the Committee. The over-all tone or atmosphere which she set for the Committee was a result of her application of concepts generic to social work and to the administrative process. These concepts and principles, appropriately used, together with her positive attitude and obvious pride in her work, facilitated the working relationships of the Committee and enabled us to complete our job with positive feelings of accomplishment and growth.

QUESTIONS

1. How would you define the administrative responsibilities of the supervisor of staff development?
2. What did you think of the new Executive Director's way of getting acquainted with his staff?
3. Why it is important that agencies have soundly developed orientation programs for new staff?
4. Trace through the series of meetings presented and outline the development of the orientation program.
5. What is your opinion of the writer's analysis and evaluation of his experience as a part of this administrative process?

CASE 4

Conflict in the Chester County Welfare Department

This is the story of a situation which developed in a large county welfare department where conflict between the casework staff and the clerical staff had come to be accepted as an almost chronic condition.

The casework staff consisted of three assistant supervisors and eighteen workers most of whom were young women who had recently graduated from college. The clerical staff was made up of a receptionist, a telephone operator, a file clerk, three stenographers, two medical clerks, and their supervisor, Mrs. Clancy. All of the clerical employees had been with the agency for more than three years; their education consisted of a high school diploma and some business courses. Mrs. Henry, who supervised both departments, had a background in casework.

There was little interaction of any kind between the two groups either during or after working hours, and there appeared to be no joint effort. Work was individual with little thought given to the role of the others or to total agency purposes and function. They were working separately rather than together with little sharing of job assignments, interests, or goals.

There was also a physical separation of the two groups. The workers were grouped together in one room and the clerical staff occupied another. The supervisors had their individual offices, but the casework group was located in one area, easily accessible to each other, while the clerical supervisor, Mrs. Clancy was several doors away, separated by the workers' interviewing rooms.

Both groups were governed by uniform policies, which were applicable to every district office within the larger county agency, and varied only with the employee's position. There was a great deal of occupational stratification within the agency due to its civil service structure. There was no flexibility in regard to rules, regulations, and personnel policies. There was little vertical sharing in either group between staff and supervisors.

It is not surprising, then, that these groups with all of their difference and seeming incompatibility should arrive at a conflict situation. The matters involved were meaningless and trivial as compared with the real issues of separation or distance.

For the past five or six months the clerical staff had been complaining separately and jointly to Mrs. Clancy. It was their feeling that "the caseworkers were getting away with murder." They were thoughtless and demanding; dictation was not done on scheduled days. When it was finally accomplished, the workers wanted a "rush" job on an unsurmountable amount of material. They were careless writers and terrible spellers; letters were illegible, incorrectly addressed, and often without salutation. Caseworkers were forgetful; they couldn't even remember to put the letters into envelopes for mailing. The clerical workers felt that the caseworkers had a tendency to shirk unpleasant parts of their own job. The receptionist was expected to "get rid of clients" whom the worker did not choose to see. Telephone calls were often avoided with the suggestion that the operator take or give a message. Workers took coffee breaks, overstayed their lunch hours.

Mrs. Clancy had been trying to handle the complaints herself, but feeling that some of the "gripes" were justifiable, she decided to bring them to the attention of Mrs. Henry, the head supervisor. Mrs. Henry, reflecting on her own days as a worker, recognized that they were probably doing about as the clerical staff said. She, therefore, decided to bring it to the attention of the supervisory staff, who, in turn, could discuss it with their individual workers if they felt it necessary.

Following of schedules, meeting of deadlines, correction of letters, and the like were to be emphasized with the workers. Mrs. Clancy also decided to put up signs such as "Place Letters in Envelopes," in an effort to remind the workers of their duties and at the same time give the clerical staff some tangible evidence that something was being done about their complaints. This plan was put into operation shortly after the supervisors' conference. Word spread quickly among the workers and rumors flew as to the initiation of the complaints. Many of the workers were resentful. They wondered among themselves, "What business is it of the clerical staff what we do?" "We don't bother them, why should they bother us?" The signs increased the irritation; ill feeling flourished; habits were unchanged. The workers kept out of the supervisors' and clericals' way, considering both groups "against" them.

The clerical staff sensed the hostility. They saw the lack of results and concluded that the supervisors were allied with the workers. They felt that most workers were snobs whose education and higher salaries went to their heads, and these feelings were verbalized to Mrs. Clancy.

Out of necessity due to the group pressure, Mrs. Clancy again went to Mrs. Henry, who hoped that somehow the conflict would "blow over." During this conference both women discussed possible ways of handling the situation. Since the individual approach did not have the desired effect, it was decided to plan a group staff meeting, where the problem could be brought out into the open.

A staff meeting was scheduled for the following day. Notices were posted in the late afternoon with instruction that everyone must attend and no telephone calls would be taken during the meeting. The casework staff was annoyed; appointments had to be cancelled, and this necessitated visits to the clients who did not have phones. Some workers stated flatly that they would not attend; others saw it as a waste of time; still others thought it would be well to keep quiet and get the meeting over with as soon as possible.

Mrs. Henry opened the meeting with an explanation of the problem and then turned it over to the group for discussion. A gloomy silence descended; people shifted uneasily in their chairs. Mrs. Henry wondered if the workers could give some explanation for their difficulties in fulfilling their obligations. This resulted in a few defensive explanations of emergency visits and of demanding clients.

Mrs. Clancy became aggravated with the whole affair and quickly and efficiently pointed out to the workers that if they did follow their schedule they would not find themselves with everything to do at once. Then when an emergency arose they would be able to cope with it without having everyone else running around in a panic.

The workers remained silent; a few of the clerical staff brought up complaints that had previously been revealed only to their own department. They seemed hostile and vindictive. These exposed feelings left everyone uncomfortable and many of the clerical staff felt somewhat embarrassed. They allied themselves with the workers saying that they really did not mind helping them out.

In an attempt to clear the atmosphere, Mrs. Henry told a story of an experience she had as a caseworker. During her day in the field, she decided to take the afternoon and go to the movies. Unfortunately the theatre caught fire and as she was rushing out she was stopped by a newspaper man for a statement regarding her feelings about being caught in this blaze. Without thinking, she cooperatively responded, and her name appeared in print in the evening paper. The next day her supervisor greeted her with, "Did you enjoy the movie?"

This amusing story relaxed the atmosphere. Mrs. Henry did not seem so far removed as she did before. There followed a brief discussion of how the two departments could work together more effectively, with the workers recognizing that they did do thoughtless things at times and needed to be more considerate. At the same time the clerical department became more aware of the fact that they too would have to help meet emergency situations. Most of the ideas came from the supervisory staff and discussion remained on a superficial plane.

A concentrated effort on the part of both groups followed the meeting. For several months they appeared to be more congenial. Within a relatively short time, however, they lapsed back into their old patterns of working and the complaints appeared again.

QUESTIONS

1. What would seem to be the chief responsibility of administrative leadership in this situation?
2. Discuss the concept of role as it relates to this problem.
3. Comment on the relationship between the problem and organizational structure, both formal and informal.
4. Evaluate the staff meeting from the standpoint of planning and participation.
5. How might this problem have been solved by administration more skilled in the group process?
6. What fundamental principles of human behavior are overlooked in this situation?
7. Why is there so often conflict between professional workers and clerical workers in social welfare agencies?
8. In analyzing this situation, what do you suppose to be the basic factors in the conflict?
9. What do you think of the approach that was followed here?

Case 5

The Camp Arrowhead Staff Discusses a Problem

Camp Arrowhead is a small, private agency treatment camp for boys with behavior problems. Each summer about thirty boys, who have been having difficulties in getting along at home, school, and other group situations, come here to experience five weeks of active group life under the guidance of understanding and accepting adults. Out of the referrals made by social agencies of the city's metropolitan area, careful selection is made of a limited number of boys who can be accommodated at the camp. Only boys between nine and thirteen years of age, not too seriously disturbed nor physically handicapped, and who show potentialities of profiting from the camp group experiences, are selected. In turn, much care is taken in assigning the boys to five different cabin groups. Despite these calculated measures, errors in judgment may occur, and because of them some unexpected difficulties may arise after the camp season begins. This will be a discussion of such a situation and how the camp dealt with it.

Counselor Marty had three especially difficult boys in his cabin. One was Davy, a boy with a quick temper, who constantly bullied the other campers because of his superior strength and size, and who was often quite negativistic in his behavior towards his counselor and different staff members. The camp selection committee had had some doubts about accepting him at first, but had finally done so to replace another boy who had been unable to come to camp. Another boy was Johnnie, an obese boy with effeminate mannerisms, who turned out to be a "scapegoat and whipping boy" of the campers. His ways of almost deliberately provoking attacks and taunts upon himself caused frequent disturbance in the cabin. His behavior, which at times seemed to border on the psychotic, had not been expected by the selection committee. However, the most difficult of the three turned out to be ten-year-old Eddie, a seriously disturbed boy who seemed to find it almost impossible to establish relationships with his peers or with adults. His behavior was such as to cause much tension and disruption in the cabin, and he often severely tested the patience of his counselor and other adults.

General staff meetings at Arrowhead were held once a week through the camp season at night, after all the boys had retired. The end of the day was not an ideal time for these sessions since staff members were all usually tired, strained, and uninspired after a full day spent with thirty difficult and active boys. But it was the only time of day that the whole staff could assemble without interfering with the general course of the camp program. It was at one of the earlier meetings that the issue came up as to the advisability of changing Eddie to another cabin to relieve the particularly difficult situation existing in the cabin where he was assigned.

When the camp director, who presided over the meeting, brought this issue before the staff, there was a fairly general discussion for a while, but soon it narrowed into a spirited debate between two principals: Marty, the counselor, and Neal, the treatment director. Neal presented the following viewpoints. There was no doubt that Marty had the most difficult cabin to handle, and that Eddie was quite a problem for him. It was apparent that Eddie would continue to be difficult to deal with, and in order to relieve the present cabin situation, which was tough enough even without Eddie, the boy ought to be moved to another cabin.

Marty expressed his dissenting views. It was true that without Eddie his job would be a little easier. But what would the cabin change mean to Eddie? Would he not interpret it as a rejection of him by his counselor, one more of the number of rejections he must have experienced during his life? Also consider the group in the cabin to which he may move: would he be less disruptive in his behavior there? If he could believe that Eddie would make a better adjustment in another cabin, then he would not oppose the change, but he had doubts about that. At least, he and his cabin group were somewhat used to having Eddie among them, but how would another cabin group be able suddenly to adjust to having Eddie with them? Eddie had been assigned to his cabin and should remain there; and he, as his counselor, would continue to try to work with the boy and make the best of the existing situation.

Neal stated that what Marty had said was true for the most part. But, as Marty undoubtedly was aware, an especially difficult situation existed in his cabin. He had Johnnie who constantly provoked Eddie and whom Eddie could not tolerate. He had Davey, who competed with Eddie for cabin leadership, and by whom Eddie felt intimidated because of his superior strength. Although Eddie would be disruptive in any cabin, the situation would not be so difficult as it was in Marty's cabin. Marty had done a very good job under the circumstances he had to put up with, but why continue to burden himself needlessly? Also, it was possible that his and Eddie's personalities were such as to make smoother relationships between them difficult. This was not a reflection on Marty, but it was a factor to be considered. Maybe another counselor, due to different personality but not better ability, could do something with Eddie.

Marty spoke out that he wasn't sure what Neal had just said. He still could not agree with Neal's views, and he still deemed it inadvisable to move Eddie to another cabin; more harm than good would be done. In any case, he wanted to make it clear to the staff members that if they felt that there should be a cabin change for Eddie, he would go along with it, but under protest. Neal came back to say that he did not think the staff would want to make the change as long as Marty was opposed to it, but Marty should give it careful consideration for the benefit of all concerned.

While Neal and Marty debated back and forth, the rest of the staff sat back and listened, only occasionally interjecting a few comments, pro, con, or neutral to the issue. Finally, the camp director stated that since Marty felt that the change was not advisable and that he could continue to try to do something about the situation, perhaps it would be best to let matters stand. The rest of the staff seemed to concur. Thus the decision was made not to transfer Eddie to another cabin.

During the remaining days the cabin situation showed some improvement. Eddie's relationships with his counselor also made some progress, but his relationships with the other campers grew worse. During the last week of camp Eddie ran away three times, each time after a fight with different boys. The last time that he was retrieved, he became quite disturbed and kept crying to be sent home. Therefore he was sent home.

Making a cabin change of a boy during the camp season is an unwelcome task. For it brings disruption to intracabin relationships which have been developed, and what the boys at camp need is to experience steady group relationships. But, in certain cases it may be necessary to give the proposal for cabin change serious consideration. It is not an easy decision to make. The camp director did not try to make it himself, instead he brought the issue before the staff to hear their viewpoints. And he did not try to put pressure on one side or the other. The decision which was finally made was a group decision, although Marty and Neal had taken up the major portion of the discussion. Any of the other staff members would have spoken up more if they had had anything more to add to the discussion. It was typical of the camp staff to make major decisions through group discussion.

It is not impossible that the differences in opinions between Neal and Marty could have led to ill feelings and staff dissension. But the friendly relationships and cooperative spirit which existed among the staff members throughout the camp season negated such an occurrence. There was free communication all along the staff line. The camp director and the head counselor were readily available to listen to complaints or suggestions, or to be consulted for advice. No one person or clique tried to run the camp; instead the staff worked together. Responsibilities were delegated to each staff member according to his function. The camp director, who had the general responsibility of the whole camp, put his faith on the capability of each person to do his task to the best of his ability and judgment.

Any administrative decision must give careful consideration to the feelings of people who will be affected by it. The issue of cabin change was not looked upon as mere manipulation in cabin organization, but took into account feelings of individuals and effects on human relationships.

QUESTIONS

1. What particular factors must be taken into account in the camp situation?
2. What is the purpose of the staff meeting in the camp setting?

3. Evaluate the procedure that was followed in this problem situation. What did you like about it? What would you question about it?
4. How would you define the role of the Camp Director in relation to the role of the Treatment Director?
5. Do you think it was appropriate to use staff meeting time to deal with this kind of problem?
6. What are the criteria of choice of items to put on the agenda for staff meetings?

CASE 6

An Agency Examines Its Health Education Policies

In order that clear lines of communication could be established among committees, this agency had established an over-all Program Committee. This brought together representatives from all major program committees plus representatives from the Board of Directors as well as from the Finance and Personnel Committees.

This committee structure had changed as the staff structure had also changed. Every staff member carried a major area of responsibility but might also carry minor responsibilities in other areas, thus allowing for flexible shifting of job loads when needed. Such a structure increased the possibility of good communication because each staff member did not or could not operate in her own little department by herself.

The major responsibility of the Program Committee was program co-ordination, evaluation, interpretation, and planning. This Committee brought or coordinated recommendations from all program areas to the Board of Directors for action. Such a structure was set up in order to help cut through problems in communication so that each person could be heard and, in turn, could hear what was happening throughout all areas of the agency, no matter on what level she participated.

The organization believed that in order to develop responsible, thinking members, regardless of their age, methods must be devised whereby each member had a chance to have some part in over-all planning and policy-making at the level of their readiness and ability to participate.

The Program Director, a top administrative leader, was assigned to work with this Committee. She was also staff supervisor for the program area responsible for coordinating the staff the work of committees.

Following is an example of how the Program Committee through the use of established lines of formal and informal communication investigated the possibility of required physical examinations for all members active in physical education programs.

February 11. Physical Education Committee Meeting.

In preparation for the triennial national convention of the agency, the Physical Education Committee was studying a draft of a national health examination policy which would be under discussion at the convention. This policy called for an annual health exam for all members before they participated in any physical activity.

The staff person working with this Committee and responsible for the physical education area questioned whether requiring exams only for those taking part in physical education classes was valid. To clarify this she said that no teenagers, unless they took classes, were covered, yet they roller-skated, swam, and played basketball as part of their group activities and as members of the agency. The leaders had no specific way of knowing if these people were physically able to participate.

As a vivid example of potential harm to a person because of the lack of knowledge, the staff person explained what happened the week previous to this meeting when she was supervising an afternoon session of roller-skating. By chance a leader responsible for a junior high coed group spotted a girl as she came in to skate. She told the staff that this girl had fainted at the dance last week. From this she learned the girl had a heart condition. Staff and leader immediately spoke to the girl. She was most convincing in her arguments that her mother had said roller-skating was all right. However, staff insisted on phoning the mother for confirmation. The parent was shocked and thanked the agency for stopping her daughter from this activity.

A member of the Committee, a doctor, immediately said each child should be examined. Other committee members saw this as a responsibility the agency had for its participants to protect them from physical harm. Others saw such an exam as a means of protection to the agency and to the leader of a group. The Committee was unanimous in its decision to recommend this as a policy for the agency to follow.

March 7. Program Committee Meeting.

The Physical Education Committee Chairman requested that the Program Committee in April discuss general health education practices and the question of extending requirements for health exams to club groups with sports programs.

March 8. Informal Communication.

The Program Director questioned the Teen-Age Staff on the Physical Education Committee action. She had not read anything about this in the Teen-Age Committee minutes. Staff said this was right because she was not aware of this action. The Program Director said the Physical Education Committee minutes had not come to her desk yet, so the Program Committee meeting was the first she knew of this discussion.

The same day staff had an opportunity to discuss this action informally with the person responsible for the physical education area. The latter felt the dramatic episode related at the committee meeting had moved the members to action without weighing some of the possible effects of such action on 300 teen-agers. It was agreed that a memo would be sent from the Physical Education Committee to the Teen-Age Committee Chairman requesting the Committee to discuss the recommended policy.

March 14. Conference with Committee Chairman.

Staff talked with the Teen-Age Committee Chairman on this matter. The latter felt timing was such that she should request deferment of discussion by the Program Committee until its May meeting. The chairman said she would send a note to the Program Committee Chairman and asked staff if she would notify the Program Director.

April 20. Teen-Age Committee Meeting.

The matter of physical exams was on the agenda but full committee meeting was spent choosing summer conference delegates, due to a much larger number of applicants. This had a higher priority due to summer conference deadlines. The chairman of the committee notified the Program Chairman of this by phone.

May 10. Teen-Age Committee Meeting.

The chairman presented the recommendation of the Physical Education Committee with background material. Much discussion pro and con followed. The Committee from the start was in complete agreement on one point. The policy would take much interpretation and they strongly recommended if such a policy was accepted by the agency that a year be allowed for education and interpretation before putting it into effect. In general, the Committee was in favor of the policy, recognizing the difficulties involved. One committee member, a club leader, felt the agency would run into parental objection and the cost of the exam might keep members away. She felt interpretation would be difficult, particularly to clubs who had little or no physical activity. Staff raised the question that the agency might be duplicating exams, since we were not sure how many girls had had exams within the last year. It was recommended that facts be obtained as to how many club members had exams during the program year. The Committee suggested a written report of its discussion be sent to the Physical

Education Committee and their opinion be voiced via the chairman at Program Committee. The Committee felt the agency had a responsibility to the girls to protect them from their own desire to participate with their group even though not physically capable of this. They also felt it would be advisable to ask the girls' opinion about this.

Staff was unable to obtain information on exams, since clubs were closing for the program year and were meeting at irregular times for special events.

June 13.   Program Committee Meeting.

The Physical Education Committee Chairman presented its policy for discussion with a summary of action to date. The Program Committee Chairman clarified that this was only a recommended policy not one in operation yet. The Teen-Age Committee Chairman presented the various sides of her Committee's discussion.

The Adult Committee Chairman felt that a quick and cursory exam did not accomplish much. The Executive Director stated that even a simple, brief exam of the heart, blood pressure, and other vital functions was a help and could show that a person was in a state of tension, overweight, or similar condition. The Physical Education Chairman added that the agency doctor was alert for danger signals and either questioned further or referred the member to another doctor for a more thorough examination. The type of exams given by this agency is essential for such an activity as swimming in a chlorinated pool because of its effect on certain ear and eye conditions.

Discussion was given to the kinds of activities requiring a health exam now as well as to kinds not covered but that the Physical Education Committee felt should be covered. The Adult Committee Chairman suggested the exam had meaning for everyone and should be discussed more than with the two committees already concerned.

The Program Director suggested that use of exams is one way for the agency to foster a positive health program. Much discussion followed on the broad area of health education. A recommendation was made that exams and the area of health education for members be discussed by all program committees, with the Physical Education Committee taking the lead. The Executive Director recommended that the Teen-Age Committee and Physical Education Committee meet together to work through their difference of opinion on approach to exams for teenagers before exploring this with teenagers. The Program Committee felt it should consider health education in its many aspects during the next program year.

Program Year.

Following is an account of how these recommendations were carried out. Emphasis will be on tracing the physical exam policy, since this precipitated the whole matter. There will be a summary of what happened elsewhere in the agency on health education. Committees do not meet in the summer in this agency.

September 17.   Teen-Age Committee Meeting.

Chairman of the Physical Education Committee joined the Teen-Age Committee briefly to set a time when both groups could meet together. February was the time selected, since the policy if adopted could not be put into effect during the present program year. This would allow time for both committees to pursue other matters as well as ample time for consideration by the Program Committee, teenagers, and the Board of Directors if a policy was recommended.

October–February.   Summary of Actions by Committees on Health Education.

Adult Committee. This Committee spent parts of several meetings discussing health exams for children attending nursery once a week during Mom's Day Out program. This matter was referred for discussion to the Mom's Day Out Council, made up of participants in that event. The mothers said most of the children saw a doctor approximately every six months. They suggested a checklist activity card to be filled out by each mother, thus giving staff some information on the health of each child. A tentative card was drawn up and recommendation made that it be put into action in the spring term, if feasible. This was done.

The same Council initiated and carried out a series of discussions on mental health during the lunch hour. For the spring term a series on the healthy family was set up. Community resource people were used.

Physical Education and Public Affairs Committees. The whole area of mental health was under much discussion in the city and by many of the members of the agency. The Physical Education Committee invited the Director of Community Organization for the State Division of Mental Health to their December meeting. The purpose was to discuss a possible program to acquaint some of the civic leaders with the possible need to educate the public about mental illness. The city had no lay-professional organization on mental health.

A luncheon meeting was set and held in January, at which time a film on mental illness was shown followed by small discussion groups with trained leaders. Invitations had been sent to key lay and professional groups in the community. The meeting was well-attended and participation was good. When it became apparent that these people were anxious for some kind of group to be formed, the agency relinquished its leadership to the state organization which was better equipped to aid in this procedure.

Public Affairs Committee. This Committee had planned a luncheon meeting with key community people to clarify specifically what was being done in this area in regard to mental health clinics. This meeting was taken over by the Community Council. The Committee then devoted its whole attention to a meeting for board, staff and committee members of the agency for discussion of this same specific topic.

From these meetings stemmed activities by members within the agency and in the larger community in the whole area of mental health.

Action was reported to the Program Committee.

February.

Staff discussed the matter of health exams with all club leaders to interpret the thinking of the committees and to obtain their feeling on the matter. With the exception of the leaders whose clubs did very little of an active nature, all reacted in a relieved fashion, saying immediately it would protect them and the child. Several cited relatively minor examples of where it would have been good to have such information.

*February 8.   Joint Meeting of Teen-Age and
Physical Education Committees.*

The National Association's statement on health policies and health exams was reviewed as well as background material on the topic, there being some new committee members present.

The staff member responsible for the teen-age area said that the club leaders had reported approximately 50 per cent of the girls had had physicals within the present program year. Of this 50 per cent approximately 10 per cent "thought they had but weren't sure." Also, all clubs had had active sports activities in the gym or pool which, if conducted under the class program, would have required a physical exam. This had changed over the last year because some of the clubs had not had such activities. Part of this was due to freeing of the gym at times when clubs were meeting.

The committee chairmen felt the committees needed to discuss why it was thought health exams were valuable or not valuable to club members. Discussion at this point showed almost complete agreement in the broad areas of: (1) need for people to have exams somewhere once a year, (2) need for a leader to know of any health limitations members of her group might have, (3) need for the agency to foster the idea of exams in an educational program if it is found that people are not having checkups, (4) need for teenagers to "belong" in a group, and because of this they may at times have difficulty saying no to an activity even if known to be detrimental to their health.

A member of the Teen-Age Committee questioned whether such a requirement would affect membership in club groups. Staff were asked an opinion because of their closeness to the feeling tone of groups. Both staff felt both committees would need to give considerable attention to interpretation to members and parents if such a policy went into effect. If a good job of preparation went before initiation of the policy, then staff did not feel members would be lost. It was stated that the first year is always the hardest in initiating any new policy.

Staff raised the question of whether teen-age club members should not have a voice in this proposed policy and explained the vehicles by which each club member would be able to have a voice in the matter.

The Committee spent much time on whether this was a matter for teen-age discussion or whether this was a matter where adults should make the decision. One of the Teen-Age Committee members voiced a strong opinion that teenagers must have a voice, citing an example of a policy on an area level being reversed by the Committee because clubs had been helped to discuss the pros and cons. This was one way of training responsible, thinking citizens. A few members feared teenagers would say no because it would cost more money to be a member. Most felt this objection was not valid because the exam was only fifty cents and a fund could be made available to pay for those not having money. The consensus was that teenagers should discuss the proposed policy and that staff be responsible for interpreting to them the thinking of the Committee on why such a policy was proposed.

Staff was asked by the Committee how long this process would take. She stated a report would be available by the two April meetings. Procedure for back-and-forth reporting between the Teen-Age Council and groups was set for a minimum of time so that a decision could be reached quickly before the issue became stale.

At this point the Physical Education Chairman suggested the alternative of a checklist for parents to fill out. A mother of a teenager questioned the number of parents who had this information about their child, if they had not had them have a medical checkup. Other members felt parents did know physical limitations of their child which would limit activities. Staff said that other agencies in the country were using this method of checking on club members instead of a physical exam.

The decision reached by the committee was that some check was strongly recommended for all club members, either by a physical exam or a checklist for parents to fill out. The former was preferred, but final decision would be made in April after the results of the discussion by teenagers were known.

March.

Staff discussed the recommendation of the joint committee with all club leaders, saying this would be discussed at the Council and they should be prepared to help their representative bring this up in club for opinions.

The procedure of how this might eventually become a policy was explained so that club leaders could interpret to their groups. Again, most expressed a desire for some method of checkup. Stress was laid on helping girls to think through their reasons for wanting or not wanting exams and/or checklists. Since this was a familiar procedure for club leaders, this did not present difficulties to them.

March 4.   Conference with Teen-Age Council Officers.

At the regular monthly meeting of officers to set up the agenda the item of health exams and/or checklists was discussed. The group was divided in its opinion over which was better, but were in agreement from the beginning that something was needed.

March 9.   Teen-Age Council Meeting.

Representatives from all teen-age clubs were present. The chairman of the Council presented the subject of medical exams or checklists for discussion. A series of questions followed, mainly of the type to clarify details such as who would give the exams, when, where, etc. A lot of joking passed about the agency doctor, since several had had exams from her. This was not aimed personally but at exams and doctors in general.

Gradually the discussion moved into the pros and cons of the exams. From the beginning, the tone was positive in favor of exams. The girls seemed to grasp the reason for them at once. The main objection raised was "feeling funny about being examined." No objection was raised as to price. The girls felt this was a "cheap" price. Most seemed to feel the activities their clubs did throughout the year warranted such a checkup. In this discussion every representative named at least one such activity and most named several. Some said they had just had an exam at school. Others said they had not. Staff explained that the schools gave a checkup every three years. Staff added that it would be possible to obtain this information from schools. Also, girls could be examined by their own doctor. One girl gave an example of the school doctor finding something wrong with her, so she "believed in medicals, gosh, you never know what is wrong with you."

The chairman interjected the possibility of using a checklist for parents to fill out. Most Council members thought this would be good if most had had medicals. Otherwise, "what good would it do?" In answer to this, some members said they felt most parents knew what was wrong with them. This became a rather involved discussion as to how parents could know what was wrong with their child unless the child had had an exam or had a permanent defect. Out of this discussion, with the help of the staff and chairman, evolved a summation of the Council's discussion. One member suggested they talk with clubs only about medical exams, not activity checklists. Several immediately objected, saying they had learned much from the discussion and now thought "everyone needed an exam every once in a while." Others thought it would be dishonest not to present both ideas. Thus, the Council agreed to present the two alternatives for discussion by clubs and report results back at the April meeting. Staff went over the procedure again of how this would or would not become a policy in the agency. The Council had been exposed to this procedure on other matters not involving policy this year, so that the procedure was not strange to them.

Memo by Staff to All Leaders.   March 9.

Immediately following the Teen-Age Council meeting, the staff sent a memo to all club leaders summing up the discussion and requesting a discussion take place before the April 7 Council meeting.

In this agency all leaders keep reports on each club meeting. From these reports staff had a fairly clear idea of the direction of the discussion and general feeling in each club. This helped her at the Council to help the club representatives bring out most of the points her club had discussed.

April 7.   Teen-Age Council Meeting.

The chairman called for reports from all members. The main objection seemed to be to the whole idea of "being examined." Although this had been the main objection by Council members, representatives had not expressed this feeling in club reports when presenting the recommendation. It seems they were expressing a fairly widespread feeling. All clubs seemed to see quite clearly the need for some sort of checkup. However, only two clubs had seemed able to get past their feeling about a doctor examining them to the point of agreeing that the need for an exam was the important factor. Consequently, the majority of the clubs recommended a checklist for parents to sign. There seemed to be no objection to this.

The Council members were not too happy to make a recommendation to the Committee that checklists were favored over exams. They thought the attitude of their clubs was "silly," forgetting many had had this attitude a month ago. Staff spent quite a bit of time helping the Council discuss why this recommendation was necessary at this point but no such decision is permanent and could be changed.

April 14. Joint Meeting of Teen-Age and Physical Education Committees.

The Teen Council recommendation was given by staff with a summation of the process by which it was arrived at. The committees found it interesting that they had overlooked the most obvious objection in line with this age group's physical, mental, and emotional growth, even though they themselves had stressed the need for interpretation. They felt this was probably why they had stressed this. They agreed with the Council that exams should not be recommended as a policy this year. The doctor felt this was a second best but felt in view of some of the changes of Council attitudes through education, this natural bloc might be overcome.

Three recommendations were made to the Program Committee:

1. A checklist for parents to sign be drawn up with an interpretive letter. This would be put into effect with the start of the program year. No child would be allowed to take part in club activities listed on the card unless her card was on file at the agency.

2. Another check be made of a more thorough nature as to the last time each teenager had had a physical exam.

3. Committees work hard on creative health education methods on the teenage level to help overcome the apparent stigma an exam has for them, recognizing that some of this is natural for this age group. More important, the Committee felt, was the apparent neglect of this whole area of health at a period when the child was very concerned with himself, physically. It was felt that this should be incorporated in the over-all goals for the coming program year.

The committees were impressed with the thoughtfulness with which most of the groups approached the subject and felt they had learned from this not to fear including teenagers in over-all planning when appropriate.

April 16.

A memo with the recommendations and a summary of the year-long process was sent to the program director. The chairman had recently resigned. The memo requested this item be put on the agenda of the Program Committee at the earliest possible moment.

May 15.

Recommendations were accepted by the Program Committee and incorporated into the over-all goals of the agency. These were to be presented to the Board of Directors' next meeting.

The whole process described brought to life the underlying philosophy of the agency—the belief that every member should have a voice in the over-all planning and policies of the agency at the level of their readiness and ability to participate. In order for such a belief to be put into action a flexible structure was necessary. Staff had to believe in the philosophy and constantly search for ways to make this come alive to people. The top administrative leaders had to set a climate in this agency to allow the foregoing to happen. This they did.

Staff often see a need about which they feel something should be done. It is their responsibility to bring this to the attention of the proper body for examination of its validity. The whole discussion and action on health education was precipitated because staff saw a need and started the process going. All of this points to the principle that every staff member, every committee member, is part of administration and must see his role in the agency in this light. The situation traced is a clear example of this principle. The two key administrative leaders, the Program Director and the Executive Director, were seen only a few times in the record but they appeared at very crucial points.

The Program Director picked up immediately on the question of medical exams as soon as she was aware of what was happening. The lag in the timing of her gaining this knowledge is a flaw in communication and could have had very negative results. From the knowledge of the committee action she saw at once how this policy would affect other parts of the organization and thus, the need for these parts to become involved in this process of policy making. The formal structure for this involvement to happen was part of the agency all the time, but in order for it to be used, people had to be helped to see how best to do this. The Program Director was active in this helping role. She knew her staff and that relationships were such that informal communication would help change the process already in motion.

Once the need for further involvement was pointed out, the Program Director withdrew active participation, placing confidence in her staff that they would carry through on the procedure bringing together the right people at the right time. Through committee minutes and staff reports and supervision she was kept posted on progress and did "behind the scenes" helping.

In the June 13 committee meeting, the Executive Director and Program Director, as administrative leaders, identified the problem of exams as only part of the total area of concern in the agency. They pointed out in specific ways how once one part of an agency program was touched, another part of the agency program was also affected. They helped the committee members see exams as only one part of the total need for health education. From this evolved program emphasis for the coming year to examine what was being done in this area throughout the whole association and determine if there was need for more work with members at this point.

After the administrative leaders had played this important role, they then assumed that staff and committees would work on this together to determine what the real needs were. The working climate was such that staff felt free to carry out this function, make decisions along the way, and involve individuals and groups as needed.

Work is shared and job loads shifted as the need arises in an agency. During the program year the major responsibility for reaching a decision on procedure for health exams or checklist for teen-agers shifted from the staff responsible for the physical education area to the staff responsible for the teen-age area. The former shifted her attention to the broader area of health education for all members, as this had become a function of the Physical Education Committee. This was a logical division of work and occurred with little formal notice; rather it occurred because it was natural and staff structure was flexible. The Program Director played a role in seeing that both jobs were being carried out and not slipping between two people.

Informal communications and formal communications operated with a minimum of blocks once the original block in formal communications was overcome by the Program Director. Committee chairmen knew and had respect for each other which facilitated their communication and willingness to cooperate. The same was true of staff plus the fact that formal structure was such that a minimum of red tape existed.

A time limit needs to be set so that assessment of progress can be made. This situation required a program year in which to work on the whole area of health education and specifically, exams for club participants. This time span was set to fit into the other priorities of committees and staff and to allow for the maximum needed involvement.

Agreement usually is possible in broad areas. There was common agreement almost from the beginning that something needed to be done about health education in general and exams in particular. There was disagreement as to what needed to be done and how to go about this. The ultimate goal of all was the best possible safeguards for the health of members and thus, the best possible service the agency could offer to people.

Those most closely affected by a policy need to have a part in formulating the policy. This was not stated as such by committee members in the February 18 meeting; however, it was implied by some as they advocated the inclusion of teenagers in the discussion of exams. The decision to do this was only a moment in the whole process, yet it was a decision that affected much of what followed.

If people are involved in policy-making, then their opinions must be considered carefully. Staff played a role in helping the committees realize that once the opinion of the teenagers was asked they would need to consider it carefully. This the committee did, arriving at a compromise situation to the one they desired.

A decision is only a moment in process. This was pointed out clearly in the final decision by the committees to try a checklist within the next program year. However, the process was already underway to work on education in the general health area, since need for this was pointed out clearly through the club discussions. The committees still felt that health exams were needed but would not impose this on club members.

Involved in the series of meetings on mental health was the principle that administration must conceive of an agency as part of, affected by, and affecting the larger community within which it exists. The need for such discussions was first seen in membership groups in the agency and then tied in with broader issues which were predominant in the community at the time.

As part of the larger community, an agency relinquishes a function to others who are better able to perform it and when the function no longer fits into the framework of the agency. This was clearly pointed out in two instances as groups came together to discuss—in general, mental health, and, in specific, the resources available in the community.

In the total process described, the involvement of people at the right moment and in the right combination was crucial to continued positive movement. An example of this was the Public Affairs and Physical Education Committees' involving community people in the discussion of mental illness at a time when the subject was being discussed widely in the city. A need was felt for some more formalized structure, and the key people to bring this about had been brought together.

Another example was the way various staff worked with various individual chairmen and leaders at the time when certain matters needed to be discussed or knowledge imparted. Also the committees were brought together when needed.

In this involvement no one group was able to decide something without affecting some other group. The decision of the Mom's Day Out Council to have a checklist for nursery children aided the development of the final compromise on health exams.

Discussion of health exams led members in the adult area to discussion of mental health. Exams had served as a stimulus to aid in bringing out a real interest and concern that a group had about a subject.

All of this involvement was not primarily to get a job done, although this was important. It was a way of helping people grow and develop in responsible ways. This was done in many ways. Committee members learned to understand teenagers a little better. Some teenagers looked at physical exams in a broader perspective. Some members became involved in the larger community through interest in mental health clinics. Some members simply learned to give a little and make a little in a group. Behind all of the examples were relationships between people. All that was done throughout the process described, affected these relationships in some way.

QUESTIONS

1. Make a list of the individuals and groups who were involved in this examination of health education policy.
2. Evaluate the way the Program Director carried forward the process and coordinated the work of these various individuals and groups.
3. What is your opinion of the quality of interaction and flow as the work proceeds?
4. Do you think it was appropriate to involve group members in this decision?
5. To what extent do you agree with the analysis as presented by the writer of the record?

CASE 7

A Community Center Develops a Summer Program

This situation took place in a Community Center in a large eastern city. This agency had recognized the need for a well planned year-'round approach to programming for the Junior High age member (twelve through fourteen years, seventh through ninth grades in school) as a sound step in the development of the socially mature teenager. Their approach to the problem of anti-social teen-age behavior was one of prevention rather than one of cure. In accordance with this, the agency was in the process of developing a Junior High Department which would be a department in its own right within the over-all Youth Department. During the year, the agency had hired a new graduate from a school of social work, Mrs. Janine, whose assignment was the development of such a Junior High Department. One of Mrs. Janine's assignments, in connection with the entire Junior High program, was the development of a summer program for the Junior High-age member.

During the previous summer, there had been a very successful trip program open to Junior Highers. This program was directed by a full-time Center staff member. However, at that time it was just an isolated program within the Youth Department open to members of Junior High School age. There was no separate department devoted to Junior High programming and needs. This summer program took place for two and one-half days a week over a six-week period during July and August. It was based upon the desires of this group to see new places and try new things, and yet not to be tied down to a lengthy week-long program. Enrollment in this program still allowed much individual freedom during the remainder of the week.

Mrs. Janine received the assignment to develop the summer program based upon the previous summer's experience. She spoke with Mr. Harkness, the Youth Activities Director of the Center. Mr. Harkness reviewed the recommendations concerning the summer program. These recommendations were from the Youth Activities Committee, the lay committee that concerned itself with all programs for youth. It was the general feeling that the Junior High Summer Program should be continued.

At this point, Mr. Harkness and Mrs. Janine called together a group of women, some of whom were Youth Activities members but all of whom had children in this age group and all of whom had expressed interest in a summer program for children. Those present included: Mrs. Janine; Mr. Harkness; Mrs. Sharon, Chairman of the Youth Activities Committee; Mrs. Wilson; Mrs. Kent; Mrs. Safros; Mrs. Menken; and Mrs. Gordon.

Mr. Harkness introduced Mrs. Janine to the women, and Mrs. Janine together with Mr. Harkness discussed the need for a summer program for the Junior High members. This discussion had not proceeded very far when Mrs. Wilson interrupted. She said that she saw a definite need for such a well-run program in the community and wanted to know specifically what the previous summer's experience has been. Mr. Harkness answered this, and then Mrs. Kent spoke up. Mrs. Kent wanted to know what type of program was to be planned for this year based upon the recommendations of last year. Mrs. Sharon, Chairman of the Youth Activities Committee, discussed the recommendations. It had been recommended by the Y.A. Committee that the program be increased by one day, and that it be continued on a six-week basis.

Mrs. Janine presented a possible program for the extra day. It was her feeling that the Junior High schoolers in the summer program might enjoy doing some type of volunteer work at one of the hospitals in town. This could be an excellent learning experience for them. Mrs. Safros was delighted with this idea, and expressed it. Mrs. Gordon, however, wondered if these youngsters would really enjoy doing something like this. Mrs. Sharon answered her quite vehemently. She stated that the children had been protected for too long, and it was about time that they thought of someone else besides themselves, and that this type of volunteer work would be an excellent opportunity for learning this. Mrs. Menken backed her up, saying that perhaps this would be for a short period once a week, and that she would like to see time devoted to the learning of some type of skill. She said that she realized that youngsters of this group did not want to devote any long time to skills, but she felt that they could greatly benefit by some attention being paid to this area. The hour was getting late, and some of the women had to leave to pick their children up at school. Mr. Harkness thanked them for coming, and stated that Mrs. Janine would be working up an outline for the program, and that their suggestions would be quite helpful to her.

After the meeting, Mrs. Janine went over the expenses in the buget for the previous summer's program and was able to come up with an approximate cost of the program for the summer. The figures included the cost per child for forty in the program and the cost per child for eighty in the program. She had these figures for both a two-and-one-half-day program and for a three-and-one-half-day program. In a conference with Mr. Jackowitz, the Executive Director of the Center and Mrs. Janine's supervisors, Mr. Jackowitz suggested to Mrs. Janine the possibility of including a week-long trip to some place such as the Center in Montreal, Canada, or the Center in Williamsburg, Virginia. He cautioned that such a trip might double the cost of the program, and that it might be best to make it an optional trip for those who wished to register for it. He suggested that Mrs. Janine look into the possibility and cost of such a trip.

After the budget and tentative program ideas were worked up by Mrs. Janine, she presented it at one of the weekly staff meetings to get the reactions of the staff. The staff liked the program as Mrs. Janine presented it, and were quite excited at the prospect of a trip to Montreal. Mr. Charf, the physical education director of the Center, began talking about making this trip a real camping trip, and the types of equipment that would have to be purchased. Mrs. Janine explained that this was not the purpose of the trip, and if the program had been planned as a camping-out program for the entire summer, such a week long camping-out trip might be workable, but under such a program, she did not think it would be possible. Mr. Charf agreed that this was probably so.

Other than this, the program as presented was approved by the staff, and the next step was to present it before the Youth Activities Committee for approval. Mr. Harkness spoke to Mrs. Sharon about this, and it was put on the agenda for the next Youth Activities Committee meeting.

Mrs. Sharon introduced Mrs. Janine to the committee and explained the purpose of the program presentation. The committee was to decide whether or not the program would be feasible, and they were also to decide the number of days which the program would cover, as well as the number of youngsters which should be admitted to the program. To give the committee a frame of reference for their decisions, Mrs. Sharon reviewed the program of the previous summer, and the recommendations which the committee had made for the program, based upon this experience. After Mrs. Janine presented her approach to the summer program, the committee gave very positive reactions to it. After much discussion, they felt that the program should be continued as Mrs. Janine had presented it, on a three-and-one-half-day-a-week basis for six weeks during July and August. The committee felt very positively about the so-called Service and Skill Day. The morning of this day was to be devoted to a volunteer service project, and the afternoon was to be devoted to the learning of a skill, such as life-saving, swimming, tennis, golf. The committee further felt that there was enough of a need in the community for such a program to warrant opening the program to eighty youngsters. The idea of having a week-long trip to Canada on an optional basis, with an alternate program being run here, was also strengthened. After the approval given by the committee, Mrs. Janine worked on the program to finalize the trips which would be taken, the bus company which would be used, the cost of the program (the committee had stated that they did not think that the cost for the six weeks should exceed the projected $60). After weeks of correspondence, Mrs. Janine was able to work out a pamphlet which would go out to the members who had children within this age category, along with a registration blank for the program. The most difficult part of the development of the new program was over. Now it was up to the community to accept or to reject it through registration.

This case illustrates the way an agency was able to work with a need in the community and to develop a service to fulfill this need. In order for the agency to consider planning such a program, the need for such a program within the community which the agency served must be thoroughly understood. In addition to this, the role which the agency must play in providing this service, as well as the purpose for such a service must be clearly defined. This situation also called for a knowledge of the people involved, and how they viewed this need which the agency defined.

This case also serves to illustrate the different levels of administration involved, and different administrative functions. The executive, as part of his supervisory and educational functions, worked with Mrs. Janine, and pointed out areas that needed clarification. His role as executive of the agency enabled him to give the assignment to Mrs. Janine to develop the Junior High Summer Program.

Coordination between several people and departments was quite necessary. Mrs. Janine worked closely with Mr. Harkness, who had had indirect responsibility for the program the preceding summer. The administrative use of recording can be seen. Mrs. Janine made extensive use of the records of the previous summer's experience in order to prepare a preliminary budget and program for this year's approach to the program.

Mrs. Janine's chief responsibility for the development of this program seemed to be budgeting. In program preparation, the cost of each of the events and trips had to be considered. It was Mrs. Janine's responsibility to give out the bus contract for this program, and she therefore had to accept bids from several bus companies and select the one which best fulfilled her list of criteria and necessary qualifications.

Once the tentative program was set up, Mrs. Janine had the responsibility of interpreting it to the Youth Activities Committee. Based upon their recommendations to allow eighty youngsters into the program, Mrs. Janine had to decide upon the staff needs and qualifications for staff personnel. Along with this was the development of an application form for staff, and the development of a contract form. Interviewing prospective applicants for positions and the hiring of staff was the next step in the completion of the program.

During this entire process of planning, Mrs. Janine was able to discuss problems and seek advice from Mr. Jackowitz during their weekly supervisory conferences. In the presentation of the tentative program to the staff at a staff meeting, the process of circular supervision within the administrative process was involved.

Throughout the entire development of the program, the constituency was kept in mind. The program was developed to answer an expressed need in the community and could only succeed as long as it fulfilled this need. Therefore, the desires of the people who were going to make use of the program had to be kept in mind as the program was developed.

Once this process of organization and development was finished, the publicity was sent out to the constituency and registration in the program was opened. Mrs. Janine's task now changed. She now had the job of interpreting the program to the community. One of her major jobs, the direction of the program, would only begin with the start of the program early in July.

QUESTIONS

1. List the tasks performed by Mrs. Janine.
2. List the individuals and groups involved in the process.
3. Was any group left out of the planning?
4. Contrast the roles carried by Mrs. Janine, Mr. Harkness, and Mr. Jackowitz.
5. What was the role of the Youth Activities Committee?

CASE 8

Social Work in a Crowded Public School

The situation described in this record occurred at Barnes School when an already crowded school increased its staff but not its office space. Thus resulted the "space problem," necessitating several changes in the school and at the Board of Education.

The persons involved in this situation were:

Mr. Howard—Principal of Barnes School
Miss Page—Social Worker and Supervisor
Miss Anderson—New Social Worker

Miss Blake—Director of Speech Department of Board of Education
Miss Mulville—Reading Consultant
Mr. Henderson—School Psychologist
Mr. Mason—Director of Social Work Department
Mr. Chapman—Social Worker at Lincoln School

Barnes School is a large elementary school serving 1,100 children from kindergarten through sixth grade. The building, of contemporary architecture, is attractively situated on a half city block, leaving much room for grass and trees. Although the school was built only seven years ago, the growing school population and added special services have literally occupied every nook and corner. The children attending Barnes School live in a housing project for low-income families. People from the project are known to almost every social agency in the city, and some families would well typify the "hard core" families spoken of so often. These families do present a great many problems, both of a financial and emotional nature. Children reflect some of these family disturbances in their school adjustment, and every effort is made to help children with problems to make the most of their educational opportunities.

Barnes School has a full-time school social worker who works with teachers, children and parents around the child's school problem. There also has been a full-time speech therapist, since many of the children have had speech difficulties. It is the only school in the city having these two specialists on a full-time basis. A school psychologist serves the school on Thursdays, and a reading consultant comes every Wednesday.

In August a decision was made to hire another social worker because office space was available. The speech therapist would not return at the beginning of the academic year, and the Board of Education had not been able to replace her. Thus the arrangement was made that the new worker occupy the "speech room," sharing it with the psychologist and/or reading consultant when necessary. The social work supervisor, Miss Page, had her own office.

It should be added that the new worker's in-school days were Wednesday, Thursday, and Friday, and with the other specialists there on Wednesday and Thursday, these were full days. The year progressed quite smoothly, causing only minor changes in the schedules of all persons involved. On Wednesday the reading consultant used the supervisor's or social worker's office, hoping that one of them might plan a home visit. Thursday morning the psychologist used the supervisor's office because she, at this time, was dictating at the Board of Education. In the afternoon he was free to use the worker's office because this was her dictation time.

In January on the first day after vacation, Mr. Howard, principal at Barnes School, and Miss Blake, director of the speech department, met Miss Page and Miss Anderson in the hall and told them that a full-time speech therapist had been hired and would begin work in three weeks. Miss Anderson was asked to take her things out of her office as soon as possible. Miss Blake said she herself would use the office for the interim period to set up a speech program for the new worker. Mr. Howard thought that Miss Page and Miss Anderson could arrange some other plan for their work, and said he would speak to them again about the matter later in the week.

Miss Page and Miss Anderson discussed the change briefly; what it meant to Miss Anderson, being new, and how she might be able to rearrange her schedule to find another place to work, at least temporarily. Miss Anderson did express some surprise at the quick decision made by Mr. Howard, saying she thought he was rather abrupt. She also said he could have chosen a more appropriate time and place to discuss the change. However, Miss Page helped her to recognize that the principal was also under pressure, especially from Miss Blake who was quite fearful of losing the "speech room" and did not approve of its use by other specialists.

The following day Miss Page again spoke with Mr. Howard about the "space problem," at which time some solutions were discussed. Mr. Howard said it would be all right with him to have either social worker use his conference room when interviewing a parent, and also suggested the use of the library office when the school librarian was not there. Miss Page thought she and Miss Anderson would try to share her office, at least for interviewing children. This was the end of the week, and after telling Miss Anderson about these ideas, they decided to wait until the following week to see how things worked out.

The next Wednesday was hectic! Miss Blake arrived and occupied the speech room, followed by Miss Page and Miss Anderson in their office, and finally Miss Mulville, the reading consultant, who was scheduled to test several children that morning. She had not known of the office changes, and, as a result, used the nurse's office and the teachers' room for her work. She was quite dissatisfied with this arrangement, and told this—but in her usual good-natured way—to Miss Page and Mr. Howard.

On Thursday, the psychologist, Mr. Henderson, made his visit to the school, and was duly surprised when he walked into Miss Page's office— which he always used—and found Miss Anderson interviewing a child. In the afternoon he spoke with Mr. Howard about the problem, reminding him of the agreement between Barnes School and the psychology department, that an office would be free for his use on Thursdays. Mr. Howard promised to have the room available the following week.

On Friday, Miss Page, in speaking with Miss Anderson, said she believed she was arranging a more satisfactory plan for the following week. She had changed Miss Anderson's dictation time from Thursday afternoon to Wednesday afternoon. In doing this, several important steps were involved. She first talked with Mr. Mason, head social worker for all the schools, to see who was already scheduled for Wednesday afternoons. Then she spoke with Mr. Chapman, explaining the situation at Barnes School, and asked if he would be willing to change his dictation time. After he had cleared with his principal as to the feasibility of this, he replied to Miss Page that he would gladly change. The purpose of this was to lessen the demands for rooms on Wednesdays. This seemed to be the worst day, since Miss Page was already at the Board on Thursday mornings.

Shortly after, Mr. Howard spoke to Miss Anderson to tell her of Mr. Henderson's need of the social worker's office. Miss Anderson agreed to use the teachers' room or librarian's office during this time. Mr. Howard offered another suggestion, that she try to arrange one or two home visits on Thursday mornings. Both thought this was a plan well worth her attempts.

The succeeding weeks were not so pressured, although Miss Mulville sometimes did her reading consulting in such unusual settings as the combination sewing-room-library, doctor's office, or gymnasium. Miss Anderson did have weekly home visits on Thursday mornings, and she and Miss Page shared the latter's office. Each usually took a half morning or afternoon for their interviews. Both kept a flexible schedule that could be changed, as indeed it often was. Mr. Henderson was satisfied to have an office back. Mr. Howard seldom mentioned the "space problem" again although his awareness of the situation was revealed whenever he asked, "How is everything?"

One of the positives in this case, and one that helped to ease the tension, was that focus remained most of the time on the problem and not on personalities. The reality factors were always brought to the foreground. This could be seen at the beginning when Miss Anderson voiced disapproval of Mr. Howard's quick decision. Miss Page pointed out the pressure he was subject to, and his realization that the school did need a speech therapist, but he also made a commitment to other specialists and a new social worker. A real "solution" was never found in this case. However, the various people were able to work well together, joke about their "space problem," and view the situation quite objectively.

Miss Page played an important problem solving role in this process. The social work supervisor can be seen to have both a teaching and an administrative responsibility. It was she who assumed major responsibility in changing Miss Anderson's dictation time. She also had the most contact with Mr. Howard concerning all the persons involved. She was able to break the problem into parts, providing a basis for cooperative effort. In talking early with Miss Anderson about the office change, she was putting into use the principle that what happens to individuals as the result of an experience is more important than "getting the job done."

Some of the various groups with whom the administrator of a school works are seen in this record. There is the staff, both instructional and specialist, pupils, parents, the larger community, top administrators, and the Board of Education. Within each of these groups there are both formal and informal subgroups. Mr. Henderson and Miss Blake functioned somewhat like a pressure group. They wanted to keep the status quo, and tried to influence Mr. Howard to this end. Miss Blake did not return to the school after the initial three weeks. Mr. Henderson did return almost weekly, and his relationship with other staff members was one of friendliness and cooperation after he was able to see that people were working on this problem.

The principal in this case, Mr. Howard, like all administrators, is faced with a variety of major and minor problem-solving tasks each day. As in a social work agency, he must plan, organize, guide, coordinate, decide, delegate, and motivate. Because the teacher, psychologist, or social worker, is likely to see only his own segment, the administrator must see the enterprise as a whole. Mr. Howard is very proud of his "community," as he prefers to call his school. Although most of the time it operates smoothly, dissension is occasionally found in the informal staff groups. The "gripes" may be about the change in coffee break schedule, the transfer of students from one room to another, or a change in staff meetings. These instances and this record seem to illustrate a general lack of group process. The decisions, to a large extent, are made by Mr. Howard, and announced to the staff. Two-way communication, a vital link in the administrative process, is not always found. In this case, if he had taken into consideration that the real focus of administration is relationships with and between people, the changes might have been made with less effort and more understanding between the people involved. If Miss Mulville and Mr. Henderson had been forewarned of the office changes before they arrived at the school, or this had been discussed with them as soon as they arrived, before looking for a place to work, it might have been easier to understand the problem. After the initial contact, Mr. Howard had several good suggestions to offer Miss Page and Miss Anderson. Both appreciated his offering his conference room for interviews, because they knew how seldom he did this.

This problem could never be said to be the "fault" of any one individual or group. It was a very realistic situation that doubtlessly occurs in many schools during the course of a year. It illustrates that more serious crises can be avoided by the prompt handling of one. Miss Page's spirit of "flexibility" seemed to have been contagious, even to the point of Mr. Henderson's saying to Miss Anderson at the end of the year, "Why don't you use the office for half the morning. I'm not too busy."

QUESTIONS

1. What are some of the administrative factors that must be taken into account by the school social worker?
2. What were some of the reasons that there was such a problem about space?

3. Why are adequate facilities for professional staff so important?
4. Evaluate the way the Principal, Mr. Barnes, handled this situation.

CASE 9

The Establishment of a Social Service Department within a Medical Setting

Michael DeVita had returned to his home town, in which Murray Hospital was located, to take over the job of setting up the hospital's first Social Service Department. Social service was not only new to the hospital but to the community as well.

Many of the inhabitants of the river valley town were first- or second-generation immigrants, mostly Italian, but also Polish and Portuguese. It was a close-knit community; the men worked hard in its factories. Their recreation and entertainment was largely within ethnic and fraternal organizations; there was no "Y" or Community Center; they knew little of social work as such. The town had a Welfare Office where you could go if you couldn't make it on your own. There was also the Catholic Social Service—most of the people were Catholic—where you could get baby clothes and food when you were hard-pressed. People did know that there had been some talk about hiring a health commissioner to work for all of the valley towns. They were also aware that Murray Hospital had been trying for some time to become accredited.

Mr. Ardito, the Administrator, felt that Murray Hospital needed a social worker. He knew that city hospitals had Social Service Departments; he also knew that they counted toward accreditation. It was after talking with Mr. Ardito that Michael DeVita agreed to become the hospital's first social worker. He understood that it would be a pioneering effort and that he would have to interpret social work not only to the hospital staff and patients but to the community as a whole. In this he would be without the support of other agencies or kindred disciplines as the town had no psychiatrist or psychologist. He saw this as a measure of their need and felt that social service could do something to help the people of his town.

The Social Service Department Begins at Murray Hospital

When Michael DeVita set up his Social Service Department at Murray Hospital, the staff consisted of himself and a part-time secretary. In the fall, two new social workers arrived. Space was at a premium, and they were given a room in the nurses' quarters to use as an office. Not only were the new workers physically separate from the main hospital but they were newcomers to the hospital and the valley. Further, the fact that a room in the nurses' quarters had been turned over to them had particular significance for the nurses. They were a closely-knit, loyal group; it was difficult for them accept two strangers suddenly set down in their midst. Lacking an understanding of social work, they wondered what encroachments other than physical ones the social workers might make. Would they attempt to assume more or some part of the nurses' role? What about their status? The nurses had yet to see them as a resource or to recognize the mutuality of their goals.

The social workers sensed a certain distance between themselves and many of the nurses, but they were too concerned with their own adjustment problems to focus upon their relationships within the hospital. Occasionally they would air grievances between themselves, fuming when bedside interviews were interrupted by having a thermometer placed in the patient's mouth. They felt such intrusions were detrimental to the casework interview and to the patient's image of the worker, but they were too insecure to handle such situations.

An Incident Points Up the Need for Interpretation

One morning when Michael DeVita was absent from the hospital and the workers were left in charge of the department, they received a call from a nurse in Ward 3. They were having a little trouble with Miss Bull and a problem had arisen around her discharge from the hospital. The workers explained that Mr. DeVita was not available, whereupon the nurse retorted that this was a fine state of affairs, as the doctor had said this was a job for Social Service and then ducked out. The workers thought it over; if this were a job for Social Service, perhaps they should attempt to step into the breach. They realized that Miss Bull was an elderly patient who had been fretting in the hospital for several months with a broken hip. They did not relish the prospect of taking her on single-handed, so they decided to go together to look into the situation.

When they arrived on Ward 3 they found Miss Bull packed and determined to leave the hospital. The difficulty was that she had not permitted anyone to unlock her house so that the gas and electricity might be turned on and the furnace started. There was no food in the house and the telephone was disconnected; Miss Bull lived alone and had no relatives or close friends. She was still a sick woman and could navigate only clumsily in her walker. However, having been discharged by her doctor, she was set on leaving the hospital, and became frantic at the prospect of interference with her wishes. The workers attempted to talk with her but she became increasingly adamant, stating that Mr. DeVita had accepted her decision to make no arrangements about the house until she returned to it. The workers felt helpless and confused; they did not know what their supervisor had said to Miss Bull. Recalling their newly learned social work principles of self-determination, while at the same time feeling that Miss Bull needed help in managing, they stood in conflict. At this point a young nurse hurried by and, in passing, told them to go away and stop bothering Miss Bull. Accepting Miss Bull's decision, the workers retreated without saying a word to the nurse.

Upon reaching their office and shutting the door they angrily discussed what had happened. One thought that they had been insulted; she planned to seek out the nurse privately and tell her so. The other thought it might be best just to ignore the nurse, henceforth. Neither of them realized the extent to which their own feelings played into the situation—feelings of separateness and lack of communication with the nurses, and uncertainty and inadequacy in the situation with Miss Bull.

A Conference Is Arranged Between Social Service and Nursing

When Mr. DeVita returned that afternoon, one of the workers began to describe the incident during her supervisory conference. He suggested that it was something the Social Service Department as a whole might want to consider, and the other worker was invited to join them. They told their story together and from the immediate incident gradually led back to other instances with the nurses that had been upsetting to them. He listened to their story, recognizing their desire to help Miss Bull as one of the positives in the situation. He further relieved their feelings of failure and inadequacy by stating that had communication been better between himself, the doctor, and the nurses, the situation with Miss Bull might never have arisen. He thought there was a need for greater policy clarification within the department and suggested it as an area for future discussion. He also thought that the nurse's reaction was indicative of general lack of understanding and acceptance of social work, not only within the hospital but in the total community. The workers were encouraged to view the incident as a step that could lead to better understanding and feeling. He wondered if it were not up to the Department to make its services meaningful to others. The workers accepted this and were eager to begin the process of interpretation: they even had some ideas as to how it might be initiated. Mr. DeVita said that he would like to take the problem and their ideas to Mr. Ardito, the Hospital Administrator; this the workers readily accepted.

Mr. DeVita telephoned Mr. Ardito the following day and made an appointment to discuss a problem of concern both to him and his staff. The workers were kept informed of all arrangements.

As Mr. DeVita and Mr. Ardito discussed the situation, the problem was identified as one of lack of understanding and acceptance between the Department of Social Service and Nursing. Mr. Ardito recognized its importance for the hospital as a whole and hoped that a mutual solution could be worked out. Mr. DeVita mentioned that a conference between the two Departments might be helpful. Mr. Ardito endorsed it and placed the responsibility of handling the situation with the Social Service Department.

It was his feeling that problems of understanding and relationship could not be solved by administrative pronouncement but rather by a mutual coming together of those concerned.

Later in the day, Mr. DeVita dropped into the head nurse's office and spoke with Miss May, the Director. Her first reaction was defensive. However, as she sensed his friendliness and sincere desire that Social Service be helpful to the nurses, she began to talk about it. Mr. DeVita suggested the possibility of having a conference. Miss May could think about the problem further and let him know if she wished to discuss the matter with him and his workers.

Five days later Miss Day dropped by the Social Service office and indicated to Mr. DeVita that they could have a conference between the two Departments in the Library the following day. She would like for her Supervisor of Nurses to be present. The conference was scheduled and Mr. Ardito was notified to that effect.

The Conference

As the conference between Social Service and the Nursing Department began, there was a renewed feeling of tenseness in the air. Each group was uncertain as to what might be expected of the other. The social workers began to anticipate the nurses' reaction to their story and along with their growing anxiety, some of their former anger and need to vindicate themselves returned. The nurses too felt that they might have placed themselves in a vulnerable position where they could be attacked. Miss May and Mrs. Williams sat at one end of the table together and Mr. DeVita and his workers chose the opposite end.

Mr. DeVita was quick to sense the barrier between the groups and the atmosphere of tension. With ease and humor he recognized what they were all feeling. He wondered if the positions they had chosen at the table were not in part symbolic of the very problem they had come to discuss. After this friendly gesture on his part, the group relaxed a bit, all except Mrs. Williams. She was the supervisor of the nurses; she was accustomed to working closely with them, to ironing out their personal difficulties, and to insuring their effective performance. In a sense, any failure on the part of her nurses was a failure on her part as well; she was prepared to defend her girls from outside attack.

Sensing Mrs. Williams' continuing defensiveness, Mr. DeVita began to define the problem they had come together to discuss. He said that social work was something new to the valley and the town. How could the nurses be expected to understand when the community did not? He thought that possibly Social Service was at fault for not interpreting the ways in which it might be of real use to the nurses without in any sense replacing them. These remarks again helped the situation by relieving Mrs. Williams of her feelings that she and her nurses were personally lacking and at fault in the situation. They were thus freed of the burden of error and guilt so that they could participate in the conference.

Miss May asked the social workers to tell their story. They described the "Miss Bull Incident" and the thermometer and bedpan intrusions as well. They spoke of their uncertainty about approaching the nurses for information about the patients which they sometimes needed.

Miss May and Mrs. Williams were able to recognize the social workers' real difficulties. The nurses could understand their feelings of insecurity and uncertainty in a new situation as they attempted to learn and practice their new social work skills. No longer defensive, the nurses accepted the problems as real and indicated their desire to work together toward mutually satisfying solutions.

Mr. DeVita wondered what might be done to help matters. The two social workers, feeling accepted by the nurses and desiring to help, volunteered to ask the floor nurse each time they went on the ward to speak with a given patient. Miss May and Mrs. Williams revised a part of this idea, saying that they should not ask permission of the nurses to do their job; they should simply tell the nurse in charge that they would be talking with Mr. XX. The nurse could then tell them about the patient's condition. The nurses were able to suggest times such as early morning and meal periods when it would be best to avoid interviewing patients. They were able to assure the social workers that there would be no more thermometers or bedpans.

The conference ended with good feeling on both sides; they all realized that should other questions arise, they could again talk together. Mr. Ardito was notified that the conference had taken place and its results were explained to him by Mr. DeVita and Miss May.

Results

Following the conference with the nurses, Mr. DeVita and his staff felt that a process of interpretation of social work had begun. He pointed out that social work functions through a subtle system of warm relationships and that the nurses would accept and use Social Service as they came to see it as a helping process. Whereas the social workers had been accustomed to sitting alone in the hospital cafeteria, Mr. DeVita wondered what would happen should they begin to sit with the nurses and other hospital employees. In supervisory conferences Mr. DeVita helped one worker to handle some of her own specific feelings of insecurity and hesitancy about moving out to the staff.

At first, change was merely informal—that is, the social workers spoke to the nurses when they went on the wards. Gradually, however, relationships and understanding began to grow and with these acceptances of the workers and their social work skills. By the end of the year the social workers and nurses had begun to realize that through mutual efforts on the part of both disciplines, patients could be helped. Social work at Murray Hospital had made a happy beginning toward integration within its setting.

QUESTIONS

1. What is the focus of the process of social work administration as described in this study?
2. Discuss Mr. DeVita's role as supervisor, as administrator.
3. Comment on administrative skill involved in the development of group participation and interaction.
4. Discuss the importance of communication as illustrated in this situation.
5. What administrative skills made possible the creative use of an apparently negative incident like the "Bull Incident?"
6. Discuss the general principles of social work exemplified in this case.
7. Comment on administrative process of organization, coordination and integration relative to this situation.
8. Why was a knowledge of hospital organization structure important?
9. Why was community relationship an important part of this pioneering venture in establishing a social service department?

CASE 10

A Social Service Department Reviews Its Role within a Hospital Setting

A state mental hospital had recently initiated a program involving the transfer of certain categories of older patients to a convalescent home. The Social Service Department, which had not been closely drawn in on departure or transfer planning and procedure in the past, was now presented with almost total responsibility for the rapid transfer of these older patients.

The Social Service Department was understaffed; the transfer meant that existing caseloads were further increased. Part of the procedure involved the time-consuming job of writing letters to the family or nearest of kin; it also involved considerable telephone communication. Interpretation to the patients was necessary; some of them had spent many years in the hospital and were fearful of and resistant to change. Some of the workers saw the transfer itself as controversial from a therapeutic standpoint. Because of the time involved in this activity, it was necessary for them to shorten or skip their regularly scheduled interviews. This caused ill feeling between workers and patients.

At a staff meeting, shortly after the inception of the new program, the Director of Social Service asked how things were going in relation to the aged transfers. There were a few guarded replies, then a number of less cautious remarks. It soon became evident that there was a good deal of feeling about the situation. The Director, who had raised the issue just prior to the closing of the staff meeting, suggested that time be allotted at future meetings for the purpose of talking about the problem and reviewing the role of the Department within the total hospital setting. There was mutual agreement that this be added to the agenda.

Staff Meeting, March 4

The following week the staff took up the discussion of their role within the hospital environment. While their original concern was around the transfer of aged patients to another facility, it soon became evident that their feelings were not confined to any one area.

Mrs. B. said that much of her time was spent in rendering nonprofessional services such as telephone and letter correspondence. Mr. V. felt that he was losing valuable time in chauffeuring patients on shopping excursions. He wondered if volunteers could not perform this service equally well. The Director had heard that Case Aides were used in some hospitals and said he would look into the matter. Miss W. felt that the hospital administrators were not familiar with the educational requirements for social workers and, therefore, were unaware of many of their areas of competency. Two workers from the Out Patient Clinic said that their roles were to be a part of an over-all team approach toward helping the patients. Most of the other workers did not feel this way. Miss W. felt that the Social Service Department was regarded as a group of environmental manipulators—never consulted about changes in administrative policy and told about new programs only after they had been instituted. One of the workers mentioned that after all it was a large hospital which made communication difficult.

At this point, Mr. Z., the Director of Social Service, mentioned that he had conferred with the administration on matters such as the interstate compact, admissions, and other procedures. He had not always received clear interpretation or the support needed. Upon occasions he had taken the initiative in policy formation but it sometimes led to the countermanding of the position he took. However Mr. Z. did indicate that progress had been made and that administrative cooperation was essentially good. Many nonprofessional functions formerly executed by the Social Service Department were not handled by volunteers or channeled back to the wards. Mr. Z. suggested that it might be well if the next meeting were focused on how the workers themselves saw their role, their present function, and methods of implementation.

Staff Meeting, March 11

At this meeting, Mr. V. presented a report of the role of social workers in hospital settings. It pointed out several areas where the staff might be more actively engaged, such as doctor's conferences or administrative staff meetings. Discussion following the report revealed that the workers had many divergent views of their roles. There was agreement that their specialized area was primarily in the field of interpersonal relationships. The report did indicate that the clinic workers functioned pretty much as workers did in the most advanced clinics, which they had previously indicated was in a team relationship.

Mr. S. said that the Social Service Department seemed to have the role of expeditors. Other workers thought that their heavy caseloads served to emphasize the quantitative rather than qualitative aspects of social work.

The Director wondered how the staff felt they might improve their position within this setting. Many of the social workers indicated that they felt the Department should have a voice in administrative decisions regarding functions and practices of the Social Service Department.

Staff Meeting, March 18

This meeting was largely a review of the three previous meetings. There was less discussion, which may have been due to the decreased rate of transfers and also to the fact that individuals had talked out their problems. The consensus was that workers had been called on by the hospital to perform many activities not directly related to professional social work. Hospital administrators did not seem to be aware of the role and function of the Social Service Department. There was need for interpretation of the professional role, training, scholastic preparation. There was a need for close team harmony with other departments and with the administration.

At the close of the meeting Mr. Z. asked if the workers wished to continue the discussions. They did not feel that it was necessary but did indicate that a similar procedure might be hopeful in clarifying future issues.

QUESTIONS

1. What is the role of a social service department in a hospital setting?
2. What is the role of the director of a department in relation to total hospital administration?
3. Comment on the administrative responsibility for interdisciplinary integration.
4. How might the incident of the transfer of aged patients have been used to interpret social work concepts to the hospital administrator?
5. What was the result administratively of the staff discussions?
6. What are the purposes of staff meetings?
7. What principles of administration are illustrated in this situation?
8. Do you feel that the attitudes of the workers were changed as a result of the staff meetings?
9. What principles of leadership are or are not illustrated in this situation?

CASE 11

Administrative Leadership and the Urban Crisis *

A key group of professional and volunteer leaders of Jewish Community Centers and YM-YWHAs has reaffirmed the determination of their agencies to continue to participate in Jewish communal efforts to contribute to the solution of the urban crisis despite anti-Semitic utterances of black extremists.

This was the position taken by the participants in a two-day conference convened by the National Jewish Welfare Board at its headquarters in New York City. The conference was designed to arrive at guidelines for relevant and effective Center functioning in dealing with the issues generated by the urban crisis.

General agreement was expressed on the reassertion that a principled approach is called for in which there is full recognition that the conditions contributing to the urban crisis affect all elements in American society and that therefore every group must endeavor to effect changes necessary to eliminate poverty, sub-standard housing and unequal educational opportunities.

A series of 12 guidelines to help Centers and YM-YWHAs to be more effective in coping with the problems and issues they confront in their involvement in the urban crisis was outlined by Sanford Solender, JWB executive vice-president, in summarizing the conference.

Attended by some 50 Center and Y leaders from communities across the nation, the conference was convened by JWB upon the recommendation of its Public Affairs Committee. Sheldon S. Cohen of Washington, D.C., former Commissioner of the U.S. Internal Revenue Service, was chairman of the Conference. Morris Reisen, Maplewood, N.J., is chairman of JWB's Public Affairs Committee, and Mr. Cohen is co-chairman. JWB is the National Association of Jewish Community Centers and YM and YWHAs.

William Kahn, executive director, St. Louis Jewish Community Centers Association, analyzed some of the problems encountered by Jewish Community Centers and YM and YWHAs in acting on the urban crisis. Arnold Aronson, director of program planning and evaluation, National Community Relations Advisory Council, and Dr. John Morsell, associate director, National Association for the Advancement of Colored People, presented their viewpoints. Howard Adelstein, executive director, Jewish Ys and Centers of Greater Philadelphia, highlighted the implications of the analysis and discussion for the Centers.

The guidelines offered by Mr. Solender flowed from the thinking, ex-

* "Twelve Guidelines for Centers in Action on Urban Crisis Outlined at Parley." Reprinted with permission from *The JWB Circle*, issued by The National Jewish Welfare Board, Volume XXIV, No. 3, April 1969, p. 1 and p. 7.

change of experience and feedback that highlighted the conference, and were intended to identify action approaches to dealing with problems of Center practice, program and policy related to Center participation in urban crisis projects.

The 12 guidelines are:

1. Clarification of the Center's role in the urban crisis as integral to its basic Jewish purposes and the assertion by the Center board of directors of a clear policy for the Center on its urban crisis program.
2. The board of the Center has a crucial part in implementing the Center's role in the urban crisis through leadership, exercise of initiative, understanding of the community's needs and problems, intelligent shaping of policy and appropriate support of staff workers in implementing urban crisis activities.
3. An accurate assessment of the interests and concerns of members of the Jewish community will reveal a greater interest in urban crisis action than is generally recognized among teenagers, college youth and adults which can be captured through effective programming. The failure of Jewish institutions to be identified with such action contributes to their alienation from organized Jewish life.
4. A wise balance must be maintained between emphasis by the Center on attacking the urban crisis through social action that influences change through legislation and on activity to deal with inter-group prejudices and conflicts through affecting changes in attitudes and relationships.
5. Stimulating, guiding and enabling study and action on urban crisis issues by Center members is basic to urban crisis action by the Center.
6. In its outreach for contact and association with those particularly affected by the urban crisis the Center should be concerned with relating to deprived whites as well as blacks and with non-militants as well as militants.
7. Programming in the area of black-white relationships must be knowledgeable and sophisticated in regard to the dynamics of such relationships, including the nature of anti-black attitudes within the Jewish community and the reality components of black anti-Semitism.
8. Effective programming with teens in urban crisis projects requires close communication with parents and the total family base.
9. Clear understanding is required of the multi-faceted role of the Center's professional staff in urban crisis programming.
10. There must be recognition of the potential impact of the Center as a social institution and a community force in influencing change in social policy and action for social progress.
11. The Center needs to take advantage of and to use effectively the wide variety of community resources such as urban coalitions, community relations agencies and universities that can aid the Center in its urban crisis role.
12. The Center needs to build understanding and acceptance of its relevant role in the urban crisis in the Jewish and general communities.

Mr. Kahn called for "confrontation and engagement" so that "we can deal with attitudes and attitudinal change." He said that Jews could and should get "sustenance and support" for their involvement in the urban crisis from their Jewish sources, which call for "justice and compassion, concern for others, decency, humility, and help for the oppressed."

Mr. Kahn said that "black anti-Semitism has been blown up out of all proportions." He said that in his opinion, only a minority of Negroes are affected. In the relationships between blacks and whites, however, Mr. Kahn painted a bleak picture. He noted an increased interest in weaponry, a polarization between the races and a breakdown in communications.

The speaker called for a "decent humanism above resolutions." We have to deal honestly with what we feel and what we think," Mr. Kahn said. "We have to bring ourselves and those with whom we work to live the citizenship concept. Boards, staffs, and members of Jewish Community Centers and YM & YWHAs must be engaged. The Centers and Ys have a noble heritage, and they must be encouraged to participate in public life today. JWB has to be of real help to us in providing us with guidelines and other resources."

Mr. Aronson said that he believed that it would be more productive to attempt to change conditions and institutions. "The urban crisis is more than race," Mr. Aronson said. "It is conditions—pollution, taxes, housing, poverty and all the rest. Society is in crisis, and this is what we must understand and interpret."

Mr. Aronson said that there is a "complete contradiction in national priorities. The reality is that we are moving toward a society which is between anarchy and massive repression. At stake is a free, plural, democratic society. This is what is threatened. This is how you can mobilize people. We must deal in the broadest framework and it is going to be costly."

Dr. Morsell expressed a viewpoint between that of Mr. Aronson and that of Mr. Kahn.

"Legislation is essential," Dr. Morsell said. "There must be pressures from local citizens. Attitudes are too complex; they have to change."

The NAACP official criticized what he called "the white 'caving in' to black demands, just because they are black demands." He called for "racial justice, based on knowledge." Dr. Morsell noted that "sometimes encounters have exacerbated relationships rather than improved them."

Mr. Adelstein said that one of the Jewish Community Center's main tasks is the "development of a concerned community." He asserted that the urban crisis is much broader than black-white or black-Jewish relationships and includes such "gut" issues as "unemployment, education, health and welfare services, pollution, housing, crime and security and big government." The Centers should deal with the urban crisis in this broader sense, Mr. Adelstein said, and they ought to use a wide range of differential approaches, based on the purposes of the Center as stated by the agency and as seen by board members, staff personnel, and Center members.

Mr. Adelstein called on Centers and Ys to give their members greater opportunities for "involvement and decision-making." He said that board members should be encouraged to take positions and that they have the contacts and the ability to influence legislation. He saw an important role for staff personnel to develop a "base of action."

In his summary of the conference, Mr. Solender emphasized that significant involvement of Center members and Center professional staff and of the Center itself in urban crisis activities can represent an authentic and relevant expression of Jewish values in modern life that will attract young Jews who have become alienated from the Jewish community. He said further that the contribution of the Center to urban crisis projects can be both in terms of developing social action to help remedy the serious social evils which are at the root of the crisis as well as through building sounder relationships between blacks and Jews.

Conference discussants made repeated references to the recent JWB study entitled, "The Jewish Community Center and the Urban Crisis," by Irving Brodsky, executive vice-president of the Associated YM-YWHAs of Greater New York. This was a report on what Centers and YM-YWHAs are now doing in programs related to the urban crisis consistent with the primary Jewish purposes of Centers and Ys and with the skills and knowledge of their professional personnel and board members.

Nathan Loshak, director of JWB program services, and Moe Hoffman, director of JWB's Washington office, were the staff coordinators for the conference.

QUESTIONS

1. What is the responsibility of the administrator in helping his agency volunteer leaders to think through their role in a crisis situation?
2. What goes into the planning and conducting of a conference such as this one?
3. Discuss the twelve guidelines in terms of their implications for administration.

CASE 12

Conflict in a Hospital Setting

Healthy Hospital is a long-term care facility for older persons who are chronically ill. This is a story of a change decreed by administrative order and the conflict which arose from it.

The conflict in this incident was primarily between the Patients' Council and the Hospital Administrator, Mr. Derby. Mr. Derby was a strong-willed man with an excellent background of experience. He considered his appointment as administrator at Healthy Hospital a step up the ladder from his most recent position as the administrator of the Harbor Hospital and Clinic.

I make this point to show with what high regard Healthy Hospital was held nationally. Mr. Derby lived by the philosophy that he would do the most good for the whole hospital within the limitations placed on him by the Board. He would cater to no one group to preference to another. He was constantly praised by the Board for the wonderful job he was doing to bring the budget into balance. Two things disturbed him. One was the increasing interference by the Board in the performance of his job. Second was the constant criticism leveled against him by the Patients' Council for failing to fulfill their demands. This led him openly, and at times actively, to question the reason for the existence of the Council. This attitude, in turn, caused the Council to watch him even more closely. They often criticized his noncooperative spirit to the ladies' auxiliary, the Welfare Committee of the Board, and the Medical Director.

March 16.

On this date the trouble started. Mr. Derby made no announcement, but when the patients came to breakfast that morning they found a new form of butter at their places. Only a few recognized the possibility that they were eating oleomargarine; the others ate and liked what they thought was butter. Among these was a very vocal patient who did not like Mr. Derby. He began spreading the word among the patients that they were eating oleo. He got the patients riled up because they were not informed by Mr. Derby before the change was made in order to get their feelings about the change. Many of the patients who had been eating the oleo, thinking it butter, suddenly stopped using it. A number went out and had the store man buy them butter, which they kept in the ward refrigerator. A number of other patients stopped eating any kind of spread, especially those who could not afford to buy their own butter. As butter consumption or its substitute, oleo, was an essential food in the patients' high-protein diet, the situation began to grow serious. Furthermore, as the hospital had always prided itself on the fact that it served the highest quality of foods and in as much quantity as the individual patients could eat, the patients' attitude seemed to be a reflection of a change in basic policy.

The matter eventually came to the attention of the Patients' Council at their meeting the following week. The Council unanimously authorized the Liaison Committee to take the matter up with Mr. Derby. The President of the Council, Mr. George, was on excellent terms with Mr. Derby. He had influenced the Council in the past to approach Mr. Derby not only with constructive criticism, but also with praise for deeds well done. This paid off as the Council received more cooperation from him than any previous Council. However, some of the patients feared that Mr. George would be too soft in pressing the patients' demand for a change back to butter. Therefore the motion to see Mr. Derby was tabled until after the coming Council election the following week.

The principal issue during the election was which candidate of the two would be better able to get Mr. Derby to change his policy of serving oleo. Mr. George's opponent had always been the most vocal critic of Mr. Derby. Having served some four terms as Council President in the past and having been a mayor of a small town before his illness, this was his chance to really give Mr. Derby "the business." The patients knew this, as Mr. George knew it. Mr. George campaigned on the idea of cooperation with the administrator, but to press the patients' case in the spirit of what was best for the hospital as a whole. His opponent wanted to run immediately to the Welfare Committee of the Board to blast him without first discussing it with Mr. Derby. In a close election, Mr. George won.

April 3.

The Liaison Committee, consisting of the Council President, Vice-president, and Secretary, arranged for a meeting with Mr. Derby this day. As the Committee had a number of things to discuss with him, they held off the issue of butter, about which they knew Mr. Derby had deep feelings, until they could feel out his present attitude toward the Council. He was very friendly and cooperative in discussing the other matters. Therefore, it was hoped to get a fair hearing from him regarding the reason for the sudden switch to oleo.

In a continuing calm voice he presented his case. Oleo was cheaper than butter. He showed figures of how the hospital could save almost $2,000 a month on this item alone. He explained the Board's economy program and how great pressure had been put on him to operate as efficiently as possible without sacrificing any essential service to the patients. He then did something he never did to any Council before. He showed the committee the hospital budget and how deep in the red it was before his coming and how the budget was almost balanced because of his efforts. He spoke of this with a great deal of pride. The committee expressed its thanks for a job well done. Going further, he said this change had been discussed with the Board and Medical Director and approved by both. Another reason for the change was its nutritional superiority to butter. When he finished, the committee could sense a feeling of triumph in him. His arguments were strong and well-stated.

In presenting the patients' case, the committee acknowledged that all he said made a great deal of sense, but the Council was present to tell the patients' side of the story, regardless of the individual Council member's own personal feelings in the use of oleo. Mr. Derby listened quietly as the committee said a number of patients were not using the oleo, but buying their own butter. Secondly, this attitude on the part of the patients would reflect badly on the Board, especially if the patients started to write to them about the matter. Mr. Derby was acquainted with their power so that this implied threat carried some weight. When the committee stated its third point, that they had not been informed about the coming change, Mr. Derby lost his temper and wanted to know who was running the hospital, he or the patients. In anger, he told the committee to go to the Board if they didn't like the way he ran the hospital. The committee left shortly thereafter, saying they would probably end up there.

In looking back at this situation, it seemed that Mr. Derby had taken the patients' coming to him as a personal affront and a questioning of his ability to run the hospital. For the first time, Mr. George became angry at Mr. Derby for not being sympathetic in even letting the committee talk to him about the patients' side in a rational, calm manner similar to the way the committee had listened to him. He too felt affronted. The result was that battle lines had become drawn and the matter would probably now be aired before the Welfare Committee of the Board. Lines of communication between the Council and Mr. Derby were suddenly cut down. A tense, uneasy atmosphere pervaded the patient body.

April 4.

An appointment was arranged between the Liaison Committee and the Medical Director to talk the matter over. The Medical Director was a much-beloved doctor because of his liberal policies in treating the "whole person" and not just a patient. Insofar as was medically feasible he would "okay" any patient activity. When he said no, the patients knew they had gone too far in their suggestions and made no complaints. His attitude on the subject of oleo went something like this. He agreed with Mr. Derby that oleo was in every respect preferable to butter. He used oleo in his own home. However, he was sympathetic with the patients. Because butter or oleo was a necessary ingredient in the patient's daily diet, he would be concerned if they used neither. Therefore he suggested that the Council make a survey of the patient body and their attitude toward the use of butter and oleo so that the Council would have facts to present to the Welfare Committee rather than just scattered opinions from a few vocal patients. As far as he was concerned, economy was not the main reason for the change to oleo, but its superior nutritional value. Whatever the patients wanted was all right with him. The Medical Director's opinion was a decidedly neutral one because it was he who had nursed the Patients' Council to its present stature and vitality when it was on the verge of dying, yet he had a good relationship with Mr. Derby, which he wanted to preserve.

April 5–7.

The survey of the patient body was taken by the Council. Four questions were asked: 1. Do you like and use butter? 2. Do you like and use oleo? 3. Do you like and use either? 4. Do you buy your own butter now? "Yes" or "no" spaces were allowed for the marking of the patient's choice. Frankly, it was no time to take a survey because the matter had lost any semblance of rationality for the majority of the patient body. In this issue they saw their golden opportunity to vent their bitterness and spite against Mr. Derby, whom they did not like. Regardless of their true feelings in the use of oleo, one patient after the other marked the ballot to register their preference for butter. A number of other "fence-sitting" patients were forced to succumb to the persuasion of their neighbors to mark the "right space." The result of this decidedly loaded and weighted survey certainly registered the patients' long suppressed grievances against Mr. Derby. What would disturb the Board and Mr. Derby most about the survey was the fact that 10 per cent of the patient body said they were buying their own butter. Because of this survey, the Council felt they had won a victory over Mr. Derby even before the meeting with the Board took place.

One other important influence was operating in this situation. The local ladies' auxiliary had a tradition of visiting all the patients every week to see if they not only could do some personal task for them but also to find out how things were going with them, in general. Many of the patients looked forward to these weekly meetings and came to trust the women. Several of them had husbands who were prominent men on the Board. In this manner, the Board members usually knew how the patients felt about everything that took place in the hospital. This is the informal way the Board and patients communicated with each other, and it proved highly effective in fostering good relationships and gaining cooperation from the patients. The Board then knew how the patients felt about the matter even before the official meeting took place.

April 9.

In this full meeting of the hospital staff, the Welfare Committee of the Board, and the Patients' Council, the matter came to its head. The meeting started off in a fairly calm matter as the agenda, prepared by the President of the Patients' Council, got the less emotional matters out of the way first. Where Mr. Derby's opinion was asked, he was polite in rendering it in his usual forceful and rational manner.

Then the matter of the use of butter or oleo was brought up. The Patients' Council President chaired the meeting. The survey was then brought up and its results announced to the gathering. The same Council arguments that Mr. Derby had heard before were stated again. It was here that Mr. Derby broke in to challenge the validity of the survey, calling it "loaded" with leading questions. In a calm manner, Mr. George defended its validity with other Council members getting into the act.

Everything was still in order. However, when a Council member challenged Mr. Derby's integrity in the making up of the hospital menus, the meeting disintegrated into a verbal brawl. Mr. Derby vented his full anger against the Council, and again expressed his feelings that it had no place in the hospital setup. "Who do they think they are? Are they running the hospital or am I?" In his angry manner, he defended the use of oleo with the same arguments that were heard before. A Council member baited him into a more hostile attitude, and Mr. Derby got up to leave but he was called to a sudden halt by the Chairman of the Board's Welfare Committee. Mr. Derby was reminded that patients have the right to express their opinion about hospital matters that personally concern them. Hospital officials should listen to them with courtesy. And they had no right talking about the Patients' Council the way Mr. Derby did. Shortly thereafter, Mr. Derby excused himself from the meeting, a bitter man.

When they got back to the matter of the use of butter, all those present, the Board Members, Medical Director, Social Service Director, and Head of Nurses gave their views. The result was that the Welfare Committee Chairman recommended that the matter be tabled for one month to see whether the patient attitude in the use of oleo continued. It should be noted that the Chairman had been a patient of Harbor Hospital many years ago. Both he and his wife had been among the most active members in giving of time and money to see that the patients were kept happy. They represented the attitude of the hospital officialdom in that they believed the hospital existed primarily for making the patients well. It was for this reason also that the patient body was so free to speak up when they had anything to say regarding the hospital and how it affected them. The Council President thanked the members for giving of their time and consideration to this problem, after which the meeting adjourned.

After the official adjournment of the meeting, the Board members called the Council into a private huddle when the other hospital officials had left. They were warned against making any personal attacks in the future against any hospital official in a public session. From then on, an unofficial meeting was to be held to let the Council members say anything to the Board that they could not say publicly for whatever reason.

April 9 to May 15.

During the cooling-off period, just as the wise Chairman of the Welfare Committee had anticipated, the patients themselves began to lose interest in their complaint about the use of oleo. The patient body as a whole was well satisfied with the presentation of their case by the Council to the Board. They particularly delighted in hearing about Mr. Derby's being "told off." The few outspoken, non-Council patients lost interest in their cause and took up other things. The net result was that when the Council met with the Welfare Committee on May 15, there was no mention of the butter-oleo matter on the agenda. And the agenda was prepared by the Council!

July 7.

The hospital was given a huge shipment of surplus butter by the Federal Government. Butter again was in general use in the hospital. The "butter affair" was unofficially closed.

QUESTIONS

1. What is the major issue in this case?
2. What factors must the administrator keep in mind when instituting a change such as this?
3. Which individuals and groups should be involved in the change process?
4. What steps should an administrator take in seeking to inaugurate a change such as this?
5. Evaluate the way the administrator handled himself when confronted by the Patients' Council.
6. What are some of the principles of planned institutional change?

CASE 13

Crisis at Nevins—How Center and Clients Learned to Work Together *

This case focuses analytically on the processes by which the Nevins Social Services Center, Brooklyn, arrived at a positive working agreement with its client system. The Center is located in downtown Brooklyn but serves the Ocean Hill–Brownsville area.

There were many components involved in shaping this working agreement. However, for the purpose of better understanding, let me cite here three major important components and how they were interrelated and affected each other in the process that led to change:

Administration—Nevins Director, the Community Consultant and the Nevins cabinet.

Staff—Supervisors 1, Caseworkers, Consultants, Clerical and other staff.

Client System—Client Advisory Committee, community action groups composed of clients and non-clients, unaffiliated clients, and non-client pressure groups.

* By James A. Malone in *Welfarer,* January 1969. The City of New York, Department of Social Services. Reprinted by permission.

The administration component and staff component will only be separated in terms of decision-making. Otherwise, they may be looked upon as a total component.

One of the roles of a Community Consultant is to observe and assess the operation and mechanics of a particular situation involving the client systems, community groups, and individual clients. In social work practice, we usually look at crisis from the viewpoint of clients and their problems. We rarely think in terms of crisis existing in the Social Service Center's operational working relationship of staff, which inhibits the delivery of services to the client system.

A Series of Problems

At the outset of my assignment as Community Consultant to the Nevins Social Services Center, I found many problems confronting the Center. It was being bombarded daily by client groups. Requests for special grants were being submitted in mass. The volume of these special grant requests, in addition to the normal intake problems, had created a backlog in service to clients.

Staff reaction to the excessive workload created by the clients' group drive was negative. While staff agreed to the principle of clients being brought up to standard, the implementation fell ultimately on their shoulders and many felt that the Central Administration should work out a better system for delivery of services.

At the height of the Nevins crisis situation, many of the problems from client group pressure resulted from:

Lack of understanding of the nature of client groups.

Fear generated by militant group leaders, such as Brooklyn CORE, the Citywide Coordinating Committee of Welfare Groups, CJUSA (Christians and Jews United for Social Action), and other client groups located in the territory.

Lack of communication, resulting in the breakdown of client-worker relations.

Negative attitudes displayed by administrative staff in the Center against client groups, who acted in behalf of clients.

Mrs. Rose Stern, the new director, and the Community Consultant decided that in order to effect a better delivery of service and to improve communication between the center staff and the client system:

a. An initial understanding of the working relationship between the Director, cabinet and casework staff had to be worked out.

b. Communication had to be established between the center and the client system.

Establishing New Directions

The Director first had a series of separate and combined meetings with her cabinet and social service staff to establish a new direction in relating to the present crisis and the community, and to pull together staff into a viable working component in the social service system.

It also decided to hold a series of meetings between community group leaders and top administrative staff to examine the areas of conflict and to effect change which would expedite service.

On May 21, 1968, Mrs. Stern as Nevins Director called in the leaders of all of the community action groups operating in the Nevins territory. Six groups responded. This meeting focused on a more viable way through which the group leaders could best represent their clients and which would allow the best delivery of service by the Center.

Thus the first part of a working agreement evolved. Out of this meeting, the community group leaders accepted an agreement to stop badgering the caseworkers in Intake and in the field, and to direct their complaints and grievances to a liaison person of departmental expertise, who would follow up the complaints and make the groups aware that the problems were resolved. Minimum standard forms could also be left by the groups and caseworkers sent out to assess their validity.

The community group leaders stated at this time, that since the Director had invited them in for a meeting, this was a step toward positive change in the Center's attitude, and a moratorium would be called on this kind of activity in Intake and the field. The Director also advised the group leaders that she would be accessible to them for future meetings.

The material from this meeting was also shared with the total staff at the Nevins staff meeting of May 22, 1968. This gave the staff a feeling that they were not operating in a vacuum. The fact that a moratorium was called on hostile action towards staff showed that the Director was negotiating with the staff in mind.

A Nevins Tour

On May 24, the Consultant took the Director on a tour through the Nevins territory and observed the physical blight, the garbage-strewn streets and alleys, and the abandoned yards and buildings that fester pestilence and make the worst conceivable kind of playgrounds for children. We stopped in at several of the community action group headquarters for informal chats. This helped give the Director more insight into the need to work closely with other city agencies that affected the total milieu of the clients' living condition. It also made the Director aware of the kind of problems that faced the Nevins staff.

What the Consultant is saying here is that there must be some "feel" of role and responsibility between each major component to bring them closer together. This "reaching out" process supported the positive feelings that the client system and Nevins Center could work together.

A Client Advisory Committee

To further enhance communication between the Center and the community, the Community Consultant helped the Director establish a Client Advisory Committee. Client Advisory Committees are established for each individual center under certain guidelines. Caseworkers are asked to scan their caseloads for clients who they feel would like to participate in the CAC. The criteria for selection were that clients be vocal, articulate and able to disseminate information from the meetings of their respective neighborhood. Three prime reasons prevented utilization of this method.

1. Staff was new and could not realistically make this assessment.
2. There was a moratorium on field visits which prevented any genuine knowledge of the clients.
3. Time did not permit us to wait for such ideal conditions, in view of the crisis situation at the Center.

It was realized also that clients had an established basis of operations covering a large portion of the geographical area, where information was already being disseminated. The clients had a vested interest in service to their respective community groups. Therefore, the Director and the Consultant felt that since contact had already been established with client groups in the territory, each group was asked to submit the names of two client representatives.

One of the major reasons for selecting members for the CAC from community action groups was to insure that members not be co-opted by the Center of "establishment," thus stopping the flow of real issues the Center and the Department should be facing. The reason for the community or client-based facility to hold the meetings was to insure uninhibited interaction between the client system and the social service center.

The First CAC Meeting

The first CAC meeting took place June 4 at the CJUSA Marion Community Center (Christians and Jews United for Social Action), on Fulton St., Brooklyn. It was decided at this meeting that in view of changing policies and procedures, the Center would schedule two CAC meetings a month and even more if necessary. It was also agreed that the CAC meeting would move from one community action group facility to another to show impartiality and dispel any notion that the Center was favoring any particular community group. The Director and Consultant also decided that staff members at each level of staff would rotate in attendance at the CAC meetings to get a "feel" of the community and the client system.

The Director also scheduled a Nevins staff meeting for once a month on a permanent basis and indicated that staff meetings would be held as often as necessary for important policy and procedure feedback and information to be shared by staff regarding the Center's active involvement with community groups. This type of staff meeting for feedback would eliminate the amount of misinterpretation by total staff and would bring clearly to staff the Director's feelings on the policies and procedures and the community. In the past, policy and procedure were discussed at three different meetings—cabinet, supervisory and caseworker. In these separate meetings the material discussed somehow changed as it filtered down. The open staff meeting is a safeguard against this type of misinformation.

The Director and Consultant also felt that staff should be more knowledgeable and understanding about the concepts and purpose of Client Advisory Committees, community action groups and other existing pressure groups.

Small Group Seminars

The Director authorized the Community Consultant to develop small group seminars focusing on such subjects. Staff was quite receptive to this kind of training. This has great benefit for trainees who come to the Department with no conception of how communities operate and lends vision to their roles in the community.

The Director, utilizing staff to the fullest, also authorized small rotating group sessions of staff and a group worker focusing on attitudes and feelings regarding working with people of different racial, ethnic, and religious backgrounds.

An Open House

On September 13 the Director held an Open House at the Nevins Satellite Center (The Kingsboro Neighborhood Social Services Center). Upon the advice of the Consultant, she invited community action group leaders, CAC members, HRA representatives, local public school administration and other social service agencies operating in the Nevins territory. The purpose of this Open House was to create community interaction and communication and to bring about an exchange of ideas on how all involved might be helpful to each other in the delivery of services to the client system.

On October 4 the Director invited Mrs. Minnie Fraser, the chairman of the Nevins CAC, to the Nevins Center staff meeting. This, in the Consultant's estimation, was a forward step in public relations. This made everyone recognize that the CAC is a vital link of the Social Services Department's structure and fostered the ultimate in trust between the staff and the client system. It also strongly emphasized the need for continued client-staff meetings of this kind, displaying a good communication system vital to the operation of the working agreement between the Center and the community.

In summary, I have tried to show the distance between the local Social Services Center and the client system, and the steps taken to bring them together.

The modification of staff attitudes toward administration, the client system and their role that came about in the socialization process was most important. Establishment of an adequate communication system between staff and the community, which had to be implemented simultaneously, was equally as important. The sharing of feedback at the same time with total staff served to inhibit misconceptions and enhanced the working operation of the Center.

The education component (training sessions) that enables staff to understand what they have to deal with in total, as they work with the client system, proved to be quite positive.

In short, Nevins has developed a harmonious working arrangement in which all components have become deeply involved.

QUESTIONS

1. Discuss the role of the Community Consultant as a part of administration.
2. What are some of the potential contributions of Client Advisory Committees?
3. Make a chronology of the steps taken in this situation.
4. Consider the concept of "The Client System." What does it mean? What are the implications for administration?
5. What are some principles of social work administration as illustrated by this case?

Bibliography of Selected Readings

Administration of Organization and Methods Services. Department of Economic and Social Affairs, United Nations, New York, 1969.

ALBERS, HENRY. *Organized Executive Action*. New York: John Wiley and Sons, 1961.

————. *Principles of Management*. 3rd ed. New York: John Wiley and Sons, 1969.

ALLEN, LOUIS A. *The Management Profession*. New York: McGraw-Hill Book Company, 1964.

ANDERSON, THEODORE, and MARKOV, SEYMOUR. "Organizational Size and Functional Complexity: A Study of Administration in Hospitals," *American Sociological Review*. February 1961.

APPLEY, LAWRENCE A. *Management in Action*. New York: American Management Association, 1956.

ARGYRIS, CHRIS. *Diagnosing Human Relations in Organizations—A Case Study of a Hospital*. Studies in Organizational Behavior No. 2—Labor Management Center. New Haven: Yale University, 1956.

————. *Executive Leadership*. New York: Harper and Row, 1953.

————. *Interpersonal Competence and Organizational Effectiveness*. Homewood, Ill.: The Dorsey Press, 1962.

————. *Integrating the Individual and the Organization*. New York: John Wiley and Sons, 1964.

————. *Personality and Organization*. New York: Harper, 1957.

————. "The Organization—What Makes It Healthy?" *Harvard Business Review*. November–December 1958.

————. *Social Science Approaches to Business Behavior*. Homewood, Ill.: The Dorsey Press, 1962.

————. *Understanding Organizational Behavior*. Homewood, Ill.: The Dorsey Press, 1960.

ARONSON, ALBERT H. "Emerging Problems of Personnel Administration," *Personnel Administration*, May–June 1962.

AUERBACH, ARNOLD J. "Aspirations of Power People and Agency Goals," *Social Work*. January 1961.

271

BALDWIN, J. E. "Applying Management Principles to Public Welfare Administration," *Social Service Review*. March 1957.

BARNARD, CHESTER L. *The Functions of the Executive*. Thirtieth Anniversary Edition. Cambridge: Harvard University Press, 1968.

————. *Organization and Management*. Cambridge: Harvard University Press, 1948.

BARON, GEORGE and WILLIAM TAYLOR. *Educational Administration and the Social Sciences*. The Athalone Press, University of London, 1969.

BARKER, ROBERT L., and BRIGGS, THOMAS L. *Differential Use of Social Work Manpower*. New York: National Association of Social Workers, 1968.

BASS, BERNARD M. *Leadership Psychology and Organizational Behavior*. New York: Harper, 1960.

BECK, WALTER E. "Agency Structure Related to the Use of Staff." *Social Casework*, June 1969.

BECKER, SELWYN W. "Personality and Effective Communication in the Organization," *Personnel Administration*. July–August 1964.

BELLOWS, ROGER, et al. *Executive Skills—Their Dynamics and Development*. Englewood Cliffs, N. J.: Prentice-Hall, 1962.

BENNIS, WARREN G. "Leadership Theory and Administrative Behavior," *Administrative Science Quarterly*. December 1959.

————. "Revisionist Theory of Leadership," *Harvard Business Review*. January–February 1961.

————. *The Planning of Change*. New York: Henry Holt, 1961.

BERNARD, SYDNEY E., and ISHIYAMA, TOARU. "Authority Conflicts in the Structure of Psychiatric Teams," *Social Work*. July 1960.

BERNTHAL, WILMAR F. "Leadership Among Professional People," *Hospital Administration*. Winter 1965.

BIDWELL, CHARLES E. "Some Effects of Administrative Behavior: A Study of Role Theory," *Administrative Science Quarterly*. September 1957.

BILLINGSLEY, ANDREW. "Bureaucratic and Professional Orientation Patterns in Social Casework," *Social Service Review*. December 1964.

BLAKE, ROBERT R. "Three Strategies for Exercising Authority," *Personnel Administration*. July–August 1964.

BLAU, PETER M. *Bureaucracy in Modern Society*. New York: Random House, 1956.

————. "Orientation Toward Clients in a Public Welfare Agency," *Administrative Science Quarterly*. December 1960.

————. *The Dynamics of Bureaucracy*. Chicago: University of Chicago Press, 1955.

————. "The Structure of Small Bureaucracies," *American Sociological Review*. April 1966.

———— and SCOTT, RICHARD W. *Formal Organizations: A Comparative Approach*. San Francisco: Chandler Publishing Company, 1962.

BLUM, HENRIK L., and LEONARD, ALVIN P. *Public Administration—A Public Health Viewpoint*. New York: Prentice-Hall, Inc., 1951.

BOULDING, KENNETH E. "The Boundaries of Social Policy," *Social Work*. January 1967.

BOYER, WILLIAM W. *Bureaucracy on Trial: Policy Making by Government Agencies*. New York: Bobbs-Merrill, 1964.

BRODSKY, IRVING. *The Jewish Community Center and the Urban Crisis*. New York: National Jewish Welfare Board, 1968.

BURKE, EDMUND M. "The Road to Planning: An Organizational Analysis," *Social Service Review*. September 1965.

BURNS, TOM, and STALKER, G. M. *The Management of Innovation*. London: Tavistock Publications, 1961.

CAMPBELL, ROALD F., and GREGG, RUSSELL T. *Administrative Behavior in Education*. New York: Harper, 1957.

CAPLOW, THEODORE. *Principles of Organization*. New York: Harcourt, Brace & World, Inc., 1964.

CAUDILL, WILLIAM A. *The Psychiatric Hospital as a Small Society*. Cambridge: Harvard University Press, 1958.

CHAPPLE, ELIOT D. and SAYLES, LEONARD R. *The Measure of Management*. New York: The Macmillan Company, 1961.

Changing Services for Changing Clients. National Association of Social Workers, New York: Columbia University Press, 1969.

CLEGG, REED K. *The Administrator in Public Welfare*. Springfield, Ill.: Charles C. Thomas, Publisher, 1966.

COHEN, NATHAN E., ed. *The Citizen Volunteer*. New York: Harper, 1960.

COHEN, WILBUR J. "What Every Social Worker Should Know About Political Action," *Social Work*. July 1966.

COLLIER, ABRAM. *Management, Men, and Values*. New York: Harper and Row, 1962.

COLLINS, BARRY E., and GUETZKOW, HAROLD. *A Social Psychology of Group Processes for Decision Making*. New York: John Wiley & Sons, 1964.

CORSON, JOHN J. "Innovation Challenges Conformity," *Harvard Business Review*. May–June 1962.

COSER, ROSE L. "Authority and Decision Making in a Hospital: A Comparative Analysis," *American Sociological Review*. February 1958.

COSTELLO, TIMOTHY, and ZALKIND, SHELDON. *Psychology in Administration*. Englewood Cliffs, N. J.: Prentice-Hall, 1963.

CROZIER, MICHEL. *The Bureaucratic Phenomenon*. Chicago: University of Chicago Press, 1964.

CULBERTSON, JACK A. *Administrative Relationships—A Casebook*. Englewood Cliffs, N. J.: Prentice-Hall, 1960.

DALTON, GENE W., BARNES, LOUIS B. and ZALEZNIK, ABRAHAM. *The Distribution of Authority in Formal Organizations*. Boston: Harvard University, Division of Research, Graduate School of Business, 1968.

DALTON, MELVILLE. "Explicit and Implicit Administration," *Hospital Administration*. Winter 1962.

DAVIS, KEITH. "The Organization That's Not on the Chart," *Supervisory Management*. July 1961.

———— and SCOTT, WILLIAM G. *Readings in Human Relations*. 2nd ed. New York: McGraw-Hill Book Company, 1964.

DIMOCK, MARSHALL E. *Administrative Vitality—The Conflict With Bureaucracy*. New York: Harper, 1958.

————. *A Philosophy of Administration—Towards Creative Growth*. New York: Harper, 1958.

DOWNS, ANTHONY. *Inside Bureaucracy*. Boston: Little, Brown and Company, 1967.

DREW, E. B. "HEW Grapples With PPBS," *The Public Interest*. Summer 1967.

DRUCKER, PETER F. *Managing for Results*. New York: Harper and Row, 1964.

————. "The Effective Decision," *Harvard Business Review*. January–February 1967.

————. *The Practice of Management*. New York: Harper, 1954.

DUCE, LEONARD. "A Philosophical Dimension of Administration," *Hospital Administration*. Summer 1966.

EATON, JOSEPH. "Role Expectations: The Social Worker Looks in the Mirror," *Public Administration Review.* September 1963.

ETZIONI, AMITAI. *Complex Organizations.* New York: Holt, Rinehart, and Winston, Inc., 1962.

————. *Modern Organizations.* Englewood Cliffs, N. J.: Prentice-Hall, 1964.

EPSTEIN, LAURA. "Differential Use of Staff: A Method to Expand Social Services," *Social Work.* October 1962.

EWING, JOHN D. "Patterns of Delegation," *Harvard Business Review.* July–August 1961.

FANSHEL, DAVID, ed. *Research in Social Welfare Administration.* New York: National Association of Social Workers, 1962.

FISK, GEORGE, ed. *The Frontier of Management Psychology.* New York: Harper and Row, 1964.

FOLSOM, MARION B. *Executive Decision Making—In Business and Government.* New York: McGraw-Hill Book Company, 1962.

FREEMAN, RUTH B., and HOLMES, EDWARD M., JR. *Administration of Public Health Services.* Philadelphia: W. B. Saunders, 1960.

FRENCH, DAVID G., ed. *Planning Responsibilities of State Departments of Public Welfare.* Chicago: American Public Welfare Association, 1967.

FRIEDRICH, CARL J., ed. *Authority.* Cambridge: Harvard University Press, 1958.

FRITSCHLER, LEE. "Bureaucracy and Democracy: The Unanswered Question," *Public Administration Review.* March 1966.

GARDNER, JOHN W. *Self-Renewal—The Individual and the Innovative Society.* New York: Harper and Row, 1964.

GILBERT, NEIL. *Clients or Constituents.* San Francisco: Jossey-Bass, Inc., 1970.

GINSBERG, ELI and REILLEY, EWING W. *Effecting Change in Large Organizations.* New York: Columbia University Press, 1957.

GLASER, WILLIAM, and SILLS, DAVID L. *The Government of Associations: Selections from the Behavioral Sciences.* Bedminster Press, Inc., N. J., 1967.

GLOVER, E. E. "Social Welfare Administration: A Social Work Method," *Child Welfare.* August 1965.

GLOVER, JOHN D., and HOWER, RALPH M. *The Administrator—Cases on Human Relations in Business.* Homewood, Ill.: Richard D. Irwin, 1963.

GOLDMAN, SAMUEL. *The School Principal.* New York: The Center for Applied Research in Education, Inc., 1966.

GOLDMAN, THOMAS A. *Cost Effectiveness Analysis—New Approaches in Decision Making.* New York: F. A. Praeger, Publishers, 1967.

GOLEMBIEWSKI, ROBERT T. and GIBSON, FRANK. *Managerial Behavior and Organizational Demands.* Chicago: Rand McNally & Company, 1967.

GORE, WILLIAM J. *Administrative Decision-Making.* New York: John Wiley and Sons, 1964.

GOULDNER, HELEN P. "Dimensions of Organizational Commitment," *Administrative Science Quarterly.* March 1960.

GREEN, A. D. "The Professional Social Worker in the Bureaucracy," *Social Service Review.* March 1966.

GREINER, LARRY E. "Patterns of Organization Change," *Harvard Business Review.* May–June 1967.

GROSS, BERTRAM M. *The Management of Organizations, The Administrative Struggle.* 2 Vols. Glen Cove, N. Y.: The Free Press of Glencoe, 1964.

GUEST, ROBERT H. *Organizational Change—The Effect of Successful Leadership.* Homewood, Ill.: The Dorsey Press, Richard D. Irwin, Inc., 1962.

HAIRE, MASON, ed. *Modern Organization Theory—A* Symposium of the Foundation for Research on Human Behavior. New York: John Wiley & Sons, 1959.

HALPIN, ANDREW W., ed. *Administrative Theory in Education*. Chicago: Midwest Administration Center, University of Chicago, 1958.

HAMILTON, JAMES A. *Decision-Making in Hospital Administration and Medical Care—A Casebook*. Minneapolis: University of Minnesota Press, 1960.

HANCHETTE, HELEN, et al. *Some Dynamics of Social Agency Administration*. New York: Family Service Association, 1960.

HANDLIN, N. "The Organization of a Client's Advisory Committee." *Public Welfare*. October 1967.

HARDY, OWEN. "Voluntary Cooperation and Coordination—Requisites for Effective Hospital Administration," *Hospital Administration*. Fall 1966.

HARDWICK, CLYDE T., and LANDUYT, BERNARD F. *Administrative Strategy*. New York: Simmons-Boardman Publishing Company, 1961.

HARRISON, ETHEL G., and HOFFMAN, ISAAC L. *The Management of Time, Case Assignment, and Communication in the Team Approach*. St. Paul: Amherst H. Wilder Foundation, January 1960.

HAWKES, ROBERT W. "The Role of the Psychiatric Administrator," *Administrative Science Quarterly*. June 1961.

HELD, VIRGINIA. "PPBS Comes to Washington," *Public Interest*. September 1966.

HENDRY, CHARLES E., and ROSS, MURRAY. *New Understandings of Leadership*. New York: Association Press, 1957.

HENNESSEY, JOHN. "The Administrator and Policy Processes," *Hospital Administration*. Winter 1965.

HOULE, CYRIL O. *The Effective Board*. New York: Association Press, 1960.

HUNGATE, JOSEPH. *A Guide for Training Social Welfare Administrators*. Washington, D. C.: U. S. Department of Health, Education and Welfare, Welfare Administration, Bureau of Family Services, 1964.

HUSH, HOWARD. "Collective Bargaining in Voluntary Agencies." *Social Casework*, April 1969.

JENSON, THEODORE J. and CLARK, DAVID L. *Educational Administration*. New York: The Center for Applied Research in Education, Inc., 1964.

JOHNS, RAY. *Confronting Organizational Change*. New York: Association Press, 1963.

———. *Executive Responsibility*. New York: Association Press, 1954.

JOHNSON, ARLIEN. "Social Policy Goals of Voluntary Agencies," *NASW News*. National Association of Social Workers, February 1967.

JOHNSON, RICHARD A., et al. *The Theory and Management of Systems*. New York: McGraw-Hill Book Company, 1963.

KAHN, ROBERT L., and KATZ, DANIEL. "Social Work and Organizational Change," *Social Welfare Forum 1965*. Published for the National Conference on Social Welfare by Columbia University Press, New York, 1965.

KAST, FREMONT E., and ROSENZWEIG, JAMES E. "Hospital Administration and Systems Concepts," *Hospital Administration*. Fall 1966.

KATZ, ROBERT L. "Skills of an Effective Administrator," *Harvard Business Review*. January–February 1955.

KAUFMAN, HERBERT. "The Administrative Function" in David L. Sills, ed. *International Encyclopedia of Social Sciences*. New York: The Macmillan Company and the Free Press, 1968. Vol. I, p. 61.

KIDNEIGH, JOHN C. "Simplification in Administration—A Point of View," *Social Service Review*. June 1954.

————. "Social Work Administration—An Area of Social Work Practice?" *Social Work Journal*. April 1950.

KEPNER, CHARLES H., and TREGOE, BENJAMIN B. *The Rational Manager: A Systematic Approach to Problem Solving and Decision Making*. New York: McGraw-Hill Book Company, 1965.

KNUDSEN, HARRY R. *Human Elements in Administration*. New York: Holt, Rinehart, and Winston, Inc., 1963.

KOONTZ, HAROLD. *Toward A Unified Theory of Management*. New York: McGraw-Hill Book Company, 1964.

———— and O'DONNELL, CYRIL. *Principles of Management—An Analysis of Management Functions*. 3rd ed. New York: McGraw-Hill Book Company, 1964.

KRAMER, RALPH M. *Participation of the Poor—Comparative Community Case Studies in the War on Poverty*. Englewood Cliffs, N. J.: Prentice-Hall, Inc., 1969.

KYLE, JOHN D. "Informal Relationships in the Hospital," *Hospital Administration*. Fall 1961.

LAWRENCE, PAUL R. *The Changing of Organizational Behavior Patterns*. Boston: Harvard University, Graduate School of Business, 1958.

LEAVITT, HAROLD. *Managerial Psychology*. Chicago: University of Chicago Press, 1958.

————. *The Social Science of Organizations*. Englewood Cliffs, N. J.: Prentice-Hall, 1963.

LEBRETON, PRESTON P. *Comparative Administrative Theory*. Seattle: University of Washington Press, 1968.

LEFTON, MARK and ROSENGREN, WILLIAM R. "Organizations and Clients: Lateral and Longitudinal Dimensions," *American Sociological Review*. December 1966.

LEVINE, A. S. "Cost-Benefit Analysis and Social Welfare Program Evaluation," *Social Service Review*. July 1968.

LEVINE, HAROLD and CAROL. *Effective Public Relations for Community Groups*. New York: Association Press, 1969.

LEVINSON, HARRY, et al. *Men, Management and Mental Health*. Cambridge: Harvard University Press, 1963.

LIKERT, RENSIS. *New Patterns of Management*. New York: McGraw-Hill Book Company, 1961.

————. *The Human Organization—Its Management and Value*. New York: McGraw-Hill Book Company, 1967.

LIPPINCOTT, EARLE, and AANNESTAD, ELLING. "Management of Voluntary Welfare Agencies," *Harvard Business Review*. November–December 1964.

LUNDSTEDT, SVEN. "Administrative Leadership and Use of Social Power," *Public Administration Review*. June 1965.

McGREGOR, DOUGLAS. *The Human Side of Enterprise*. New York: McGraw-Hill Book Company, 1960.

McLEAN, ALAN, ed. *To Work is Human—Mental Health and the Business Community*. New York: The Macmillan Company, 1967.

MAIER, NORMAN R. F. *Creative Management*. New York: John Wiley & Sons, 1962.

Managing Major Changes in Organizations. The Foundation for Research in Human Behavior. Ann Arbor, Mich.: 1961.

MARTONA, S.V. *College Boards of Trustees*. New York: The Center for Applied Research in Education, Inc., 1963.

MASSIE, JOSEPH L. *Essentials of Management*. Englewood Cliffs, N. J.: Prentice-Hall, 1964.

METCALF, HENRY C., and URWICK, L. *Dynamic Administration—The Collected Papers of Mary Parker Follett*. New York: Harper, 1942.

MILLER, DELBERT, and SHULL, FREMONT. "Administrative Role Conflict Resolutions," *Administrative Science Quarterly*. September 1962.

MILLETT, JOHN D. *Organization for the Public Service*. Princeton: D. Van Nostrand, Inc., 1966.

MOGULOF, M. B. "Involving Low-Income Neighborhoods in Anti-Delinquency Programs," *Social Work*. October 1965.

MOMENT, DAVID and ZALEZNIK, ABRAHAM. *Role Development and Interpersonal Competence*. Boston: Harvard University, Graduate School of Business, Division of Research, 1963.

MONTGOMERY, HELEN B. "Practice of Administration: Role of the Executive," *Child Welfare*. February 1962.

MOORE, HAROLD E. *The Administration of Public School Personnel*. New York: The Center for Applied Research in Education, Inc., 1966.

MORELL, R. W. *Managerial Decision-Making*. Milwaukee: The Bruce Publishing Company, 1960.

MORRIS, WILLIAM T. *Decentralization in Management*. Columbus: Ohio State University Press, 1968.

MOSS, CELIA R. *Administration of a Hospital Social Service Department*. Washington, D. C.: American Association of Medical Social Workers, 1955.

NEBO, JOHN E., ed. *Administration of School Social Work*. New York: National Association of Social Workers, 1960.

NEWLAND, CHESTER A. "Current Concepts and Characteristics of Administration," *Child Welfare*. June 1963.

NEWMAN, WILLIAM H. and SUMMER, CHARLES E., JR. *The Process of Management*. Englewood Cliffs, N. J.: Prentice-Hall, 1961.

NIGRO, FELIX A. *Modern Public Administration*. New York: Harper and Row, 1965.

ORCHARD, BERNICE. "The Use of Authority in Supervision," *Public Welfare*. January 1965.

OSBORN, PHYLLIS. "Meeting the Needs of People: An Administrative Responsibility," *Social Work*. July 1958.

PAULL, J. E. "Recipients Aroused: The New Welfare Rights Movement," *Social Work*. April 1967.

PEABODY, ROBERT L. "Authority Relations in Three Organizations," *Public Administration Review*. June 1963.

————. *Organizational Authority*. New York: Atherton Press, 1964.

————. "Perceptions of Organizational Authority," *Administrative Science Quarterly*. March 1962.

PENCHANSKY, ROY. *Health Services Administration Policy Cases and the Case Method*. Cambridge: Harvard University Press, 1968.

PERLMUTTER, FELICE. "A Theoretical Model of Social Agency Development." *Social Casework,* October 1969.

PFIFFNER, JOHN and SHERWOOD, FRANK P. *Administrative Organization*. Englewood Cliffs, N. J.: Prentice-Hall, 1960.

PHILLIPS, BEATRICE. "A Director Examines the Director's Role," *Social Work*. October 1964.

PIGORS, PAUL and MYERS, CHARLES A. *Personnel Administration*. New York: McGraw-Hill Book Company, 1961.

PIGORS, PAUL, et al. *Management of Human Resources—Readings in Personnel Administration*. New York: McGraw-Hill Book Company, 1964.

PIVEN, FRANCES. "Participation of Residents in Neighborhood Community Action Programs," *Social Work*. January 1966.

POMEROY, RICHARD. *Studies in Public Welfare: Reactions of Welfare Clients to Social Services*. The Center for the Study of Urban Problems, Graduate Division, Bernard M. Baruch College, The City University of New York, 1969.

PRESTHUS, ROBERT. *Behavioral Approaches to Public Administration*. University of Alabama Press, 1965.

PRICE, JAMES L. "The Impact of Governing Boards on Organizational Effectiveness," *Administrative Science Quarterly*. December 1963.

PUGH, D. S., et al. "A Scheme for Organizational Analysis," *Administrative Science Quarterly*. December 1963.

REED, ELLA W., ed. *Social Welfare Administration*. National Conference on Social Welfare. New York: Columbia University Press, 1961.

RONKEN, HARRIET O., and LAWRENCE, PAUL R. *Administering Changes—A Case Study of Human Relations in a Factory*. Boston: Harvard University, Graduate School of Business Administration, Division of Research, 1952.

ROY, ROBERT H. *The Administrative Process*. Baltimore: Johns Hopkins Press, 1965.

RYAN, JOHN J. "Social Work Executive: Generalist or Specialist," *Social Work*. April 1963.

SAYLES, LEONARD R., and STRAUSS, GEORGE. *Human Behavior in Organizations*. Englewood Cliffs, N. J.: Prentice-Hall, 1966.

SCHATZ, HARRY A., ed. *Social Work Administration—a Resource Book*. New York: Council on Social Work Education, 1970.

———, ed. *Social Work Administration—a Casebook*. New York: Council on Social Work Education, 1970.

SCHMIDT, WILLIAM D. *The Executive and the Board in Social Welfare*. Cleveland: Howard Allen, Inc., 1959.

SCHWARTZ, JEROME, and CHERNIN, MILTON. "Participation of Recipients in Public Welfare Planning and Administration," *Social Service Review*. March 1967.

SELZNICK, PHILIP. *Leadership in Administration—A Sociological Interpretation*. Evanston, Ill.: Row, Peterson, 1957.

SHAFFER, A. "Welfare Rights Organizations: Friend or Foe?" *Social Work Practice 1967*. Selected Papers from the National Conference on Social Welfare. New York: Columbia University Press.

SIGEL, ROBERTA S. "Citizens Committees—Advice vs. Consent," *Transaction*. May 1967.

SIMON, HERBERT A. *Administrative Behavior—A Study of Decision-Making in Administrative Organizations*. 2nd ed. New York: The Macmillan Company, 1957.

———. "Administrative Decision-Making," *Public Administration Review*. March 1965.

———. *The New Science of Management Decision*. New York: Harper, 1960.

SINGER, HENRY A. "The Changing Role of the Administrators in the 1970's," *Hospital Administration*. Summer 1966.

SMITH, HOWARD R. "The Management Function: A Socio-Dynamic Overview," *Hospital Administration*. Spring 1966.

Social Work Administration. Pamphlet. New York: National Association of Social Workers, March 1968.

SORENSON, ROY. *The Art of Board Membership*. New York: Association Press, 1950.

SPENCER, SUE W. *The Administration Method in Social Work*. Curriculum Study on Social Work Education. Vol. III. New York: Council on Social Work Education, 1959.

STEIN, HERMAN D. "Administration," *Encyclopedia of Social Work 1965*. New York: National Association of Social Workers, 1965.

———. "Administrative Implications of Bureaucratic Theory," *Social Work*. July 1961.

———. "Board, Executive, and Staff," *Social Welfare Forum 1962*. Published in 1962 for the National Conference on Social Welfare by Columbia University Press, New York.

———. "The Study of Organizational Effectiveness," in David Fanshel, ed. *Research in Social Welfare Administration—Its Contributions and Problems*. New York: National Association of Social Workers, 1962.

STUDT, ELIOT. "Worker-Client Authority Relationships in Social Work," *Social Work*. January 1959.

SUMMER, CHARLES E., and O'CONNELL, JEREMIAH J. *The Managerial Mind— Science and Theory in Policy Decisions*. Rev. ed. Homewood, Ill.: Richard D. Irwin, Inc., 1968.

TANNENBAUM, ROBERT and SCHMIDT, WARREN H. "How to Choose a Leadership Pattern," *Harvard Business Review*. March–April 1958.

TANNENBAUM, ROBERT, WESCHLER, IRVING R., and MASSARIK, FRED. *Leadership and Organization—A Behavioral Approach*. New York: McGraw-Hill Book Company, 1961.

TEAD, ORDWAY. *Administration: Its Purpose and Performance*. New York: Harper, 1959.

———. "Reflections on the Art of Administration," *Hospital Administration*. Winter 1959.

———. *The Art of Administration*. New York: McGraw-Hill Book Company, 1951.

THOMPSON, JAMES D. "Common and Uncommon Elements in Administration," *Social Welfare Forum, 1962*. National Conference on Social Welfare. New York: Columbia University Press, 1962.

———. *Organizations in Action: Social Sciences Bases of Administrative Theory*. New York: McGraw-Hill Book Company, 1967.

———, et al. *Comparative Studies in Administration*. Pittsburgh: University of Pittsburgh Press, 1959.

TITMUSS, RICHARD M. *Commitment to Welfare*. New York: Pantheon Books— A Division of Random House, 1968.

TRAXLER, RALPH N. "The Qualities of an Administrator," *Hospital Administration*. Fall 1961.

TRECKER, HARLEIGH B. *Citizen Boards at Work—New Challenges to Effective Action*. New York: Association Press, 1970.

———. *Group Process in Administration*. New York: Association Press, 1950.

———. *New Understandings of Administration*. New York: Association Press, 1961.

URWICK, L. F. *Leadership in the 20th Century*. New York: Pitman, 1957.

———. *The Pattern of Management*. Minneapolis: University of Minnesota Press, 1956.

UTZ, CORNELIUS. "The Responsibility of Administration for Maximizing the Contribution of the Casework Staff," *Social Casework*. March 1964.

VASEY, WAYNE. *Government and Social Welfare*. New York: Holt, Rinehart, and Winston, Inc., 1958.

————. "Partnership Between Administrator and Staff in Developing Social Welfare Programs," *Social Casework*. April 1952.

WALTON, JOHN. *Administration and Policy-Making in Education*. Baltimore: Johns Hopkins Press, 1959.

WARHAM, JOYCE. *An Introduction to Administration for Social Workers*. New York: The Humanities Press, 1967.

WEIL, THOMAS P. "Some Guidelines for Evaluating the Performance of an Administrator," *Hospital Administration*. Spring 1967.

WILDAVSKY, AARON. *The Politics of the Budgetary Process*. Boston: Little, Brown and Company, 1964.

WORTHY, JAMES C. "Ethical and Moral Responsibilities of the Executive," *Hospital Administration*. Summer 1962.

YOUNG, VIRGINIA C. *The Library Trustee—A Practical Guidebook*. New York: R. R. Bowker, 1969.

ZALEZNIK, ABRAHAM. *Human Dilemmas of Leadership*. New York: Harper and Row, 1966.

ZELTER, ROBERT C. "The Newcomer's Acceptance in Open and Closed Groups," *Personnel Administration*. September–October 1962.

Index